IN HOSTILE
TERRITORY

IN HOSTILE TERRITORY

BUSINESS SECRETS OF A MOSSAD COMBATANT

GERALD WESTERBY

📖 HarperBusiness
A Division of HarperCollins*Publishers*

To protect the innocent and the author from the guilty, some names have been changed and some events relocated.

A portion of this book's proceeds shall be donated to the Center for Special Studies at the Memorial for the Israeli Intelligence Community and to the Palestinian Fund for Human Rights.

HarperCollins books may be purchased for educational, business, or sales promotional use. For information please write: Special Markets Department, HarperCollins Publishers, Inc., 10 East 53rd Street, New York, NY 10022.

FIRST EDITION

Designed by Helene Wald Berinsky

Library of Congress Cataloging-in-Publication Data

Westerby, Gerald.
    In hostile territory : business secrets of a Mossad combatant / Gerald Westerby. — 1st ed.
        p.   cm.
    ISBN 0-88730-901-1
    1. Management.   2. Israel. Mosad le-modiʿ in ve-tafḳidim meyuḥadim.   I. Title.
    HD31.W468   1998
    658—dc2   98-2652

98 99 00 01 02 ❖/ RRD 10 9 8 7 6 5 4 3 2 1

To Daniko and Yariv,
Who Made Every Mountain a Molehill

To My Wife,
Who Made Returning Better Than Leaving

And to My Children,
Who Make Every Day an Adventure

Before my first mission, I approached General Amit, the legendary creator of the modern Mossad, and asked his advice on undercover work. "Patience, preparation and persistence," the general advised. "All the rest, young man, is detail."

CONTENTS

▰▰ PERSISTENCE

FOREWORD

Israel's storied Mossad, or "Institute" ("The Institute for Intelligence and Special Operations"), is recognized around the world as the most effective clandestine special operations organization of its kind. Yet few recognize that the Mossad derives most of its glory from its anonymous workhorses, the Mossad Combatants.

A Combatant is a "special operations" agent assigned to perform military tasks under the cover of an assumed civilian identity. Published reports on the exploits of these Combatants range from the kidnapping of Adolf Eichmann, the Nazi architect of the Jewish genocide, to the assassination of the perpetrators of the Munich Olympics massacre.

The Combatants who performed these daredevil operations did so while managing substantial business enterprises in order to provide themselves with the requisite cover for their clandestine activities. Operating alone, without ready access to outside support, without the support of business advisors and management consultants, the Combatants have nowhere to turn but inward. It is within themselves that they must find the answers, tactics, and strategies to carry their businesses forward.

I was a Combatant.

I cannot tell you my real name, but can only reveal that my "nom de guerre" ("war name," a code name given to each Combatant) was "Schoolboy." I have adopted the pen name Gerald Westerby for the purpose of writing this book.

This book contains part of the accumulated wisdom and experience of those who preceded me. These business rules were an essential part of my long training. It is an essential part of each Combatant's training. This collected wisdom and experience is the core of our management handbook, *The Combatant's Management Handbook,* and, as such, it is the ultimate management handbook.

The book is structured as we Combatants were taught its lessons: Each chapter begins with a biblical quotation. In training, before embarking upon an exercise or a lesson, we were provided with this quotation and instructed to consider the context within which it appears.

Each quotation is followed with a discussion by the ancient Sages. These wise men address each quotation in its biblical, spiritual context while seeking the inner message of the passage. We, too, in the best spirit of the Talmud (the Jewish Law) were encouraged to debate the meaning of these passages and their relevance to our clandestine existence.

Lastly, the discussion of the Sages is reduced to "hard-boiled" business guidance: The Mossad Rules of the Business Road, as taught by those who have been there before—the "Fortunate 500," if you will—Combatants who have run successful business enterprises and successful clandestine operations.

I have woven real experiences into the book for purposes of illustrating these principles and their day-to-day impact on a Combatant's thinking. I hope they serve that purpose. I also hope they entertain. For the truth is this: You cannot be a good Combatant unless you thoroughly enjoy the work. And I was a good Combatant. To me it was the best kind of fun: adventure in the service of a good cause.

The Combatant's handbook is divided into three parts: Patience, Preparation, and Persistence, the trinity of success.

We are taught that with patience, most problems fade away and many others can be caused to disappear. With preparation, most "surprises" are discovered in ample time and are revealed to be not surprises at all. With persistence, most obstacles can be removed or conquered. The Mossad teaches that businessmen and -women who embrace these directives shall succeed. My experience—both undercover and above—suggests that the Mossad is right. Scores of successful businesses worldwide prove it.

Only an organization as clever, innovative, and effective as Israel's Mossad could forge Combatants who are James Bond at night and Sam Walton by day. Only a Combatant could have compiled this book.

Here then is that book: The guide for that executive to whom business is not a metaphor for war but war itself.

PART 1

PATIENCE

Rescue in Yemen

HOW TO SET A GOAL AND ACCOMPLISH IT

▌GOAL

> "*VeSamta Oto KeMatara LeNeged Eynekha.*"
> "And You Placed It As a Target Against Your Eyes."

VeSamta Oto KeMatara . . . The Sages of Israel brook no doubt: Keep your goal as a target against your eyes. Not in your mind. Not in your heart. But "against your eyes." In constant sight. In continuous sight. Against your eyes.

Total, undivided attention and focus. On the goal.

Stay focused.

I was knee deep in mud, my gear was waterlogged, and both my Jeeps had sunk so far into the ground that I could no longer see their windows. Worst of all, the rain continued to pound me as though the skies were a goddamn waterfall.

Yemen does that; with one single cloudburst, its dry, parched mountainous land metamorphosed before your very eyes into a primeval mud hole of slime.

Define

You cannot focus without an object to focus upon. You cannot arrive somewhere unless there is a "somewhere" to arrive at. You cannot achieve a goal unless there *is* a goal. And you cannot have a goal unless a goal has been defined. Therefore, to achieve your goal—define your goal.

Obvious? Perhaps. But most people do not define their goal before they begin its pursuit.

For most people, action precedes thought. Action then equals, and often substitutes for, progress and therefore becomes the target. When you cannot define a goal, you consequently cannot define the path toward that goal. Thus, without a goal, you expend a great deal of energy in pursuing multiple "fuzzy" goals.

Most people will pursue a vague, fuzzy notion of a goal. They will look for a "job," "happiness," a "spouse." What they do not do is to pursue that job which bears specific job responsibilities with known advancement opportunities yielding a specific annual return. They do not determine what makes them happy before pursuing "happiness." They do not determine what they want in a spouse or why they even want a spouse before getting married.

They have pursued the abstract goal whose attainment can never be measured.

In business, your colleagues may pursue a "deal" rather than the goal to which the deal, any deal, is merely a way station. If your goal is to increase your company's revenue, then an acquisition of another, revenue-generating company may make sense. What will never make sense will be the acquisition of another company for the sake of "expansion" or "growth." What will never make sense is an acquisition without a clear understanding of the goal that warrants such acquisition.

Consider your plight in choosing a supplier of goods. One supplier offers a low-cost product. The second offers high quality. The third, speedy delivery. When you choose one of the suppliers, the other two will go on to find other, perhaps exclusive, buyers. You can't make a decision. You are paralyzed.

But is your goal the choice of supplier? Absolutely not. Your goal may be to make the lowest-cost product that you can. Or it may be to sell the best-quality product that you can. Or it may be to rush your product to a young market. It may be all of the above. But no matter what your goal, choosing a supplier is merely a step toward achieving your goal. There will always be more elements in achieving any of the aforementioned goals than choosing a supplier. Stay focused on your goal and the choice of supplier will revert to what it should be: simply one decision along the path of many decisions to be made in pursuit of your goal.

Defining your goal is not an easy task. It requires you to pin down your desire from an abstract notion to a very real commitment. And in so doing, defining your goal appears to close doors of opportunity.

How so? Well once you define your goal as A, you come to realize that by choosing A, you are not choosing B, C, and D. Yet many individuals are unwilling to "lose" the Bs and Cs at so early a stage of their vision. Of course, what such individuals fail to see is that they are extremely unlikely to get *any* of A, B, or C unless they firmly set their sights and aspirations on only *one* of A, B, or C.

Look at it this way. If you constantly shop, you never buy. If you never buy, you never own. And if you never own, you can never accumulate and build wealth. Nor can you move on to the next item on your shopping list.

So while it remains true that defining your goal reduces your options, it is also true that defining your goal allows you to achieve a goal.

Defining your goal also forces you to consider where you will be *after* you have accomplished that goal. On occasion this recognition can be disconcerting and discouraging. For example, defining your goal as a business merger will cause you to consider your business after it is merged into another. Will it still be "your" business? Defining your goal as the sale of your business will force you to consider what you shall do after you have sold your business.

Yet, if you are unwilling to engage these thoughts and facts, if you are unwilling to define a goal and consider your life and actions after the attainment of that goal, then your goal is ephemeral; it is one that you do not truly seek and one that you will therefore certainly never achieve.

I wasn't a tourist and I wasn't battling North Yemen's weather for pleasure. I was there because hundreds of Yemenite Jews were isolated and trapped in faraway ancestral mountain villages. I was there because this was the very reason I had become a Combatant: to protect the lives of innocents. To add my small contribution to the post-Holocaust phrase of "Never Again."

The Yemenite Jews, descendants of Israel's earliest Diaspora (the exile of Israel after the destruction of its First Temple in the year 422 B.C.), were being held as human ransom to malevolent political will. Unless rescued they would die off without the world noticing. We were there to see that that did not happen.

The government of North Yemen, a weak and poor state, was an Islamic military dictatorship. It was determined, however, to show its "tough" anti-Israel (and, therefore, anti-Jew) stance to its Arab brethren. The easiest and least expensive way for it to do so was to keep these Jews, their honest, loyal, and law-abiding citizens, under house arrest, cordoned off from the rest of the world. No foreigner was allowed into the Jews' villages, and the Jews in turn were not allowed out of their villages. Ironically, even when the occasional journalist made it in to their remote mountain villages, few newspapers were particularly interested in the story.

But today, one of those families was going to make a break for it. One of those families was going to risk their life and attempt an escape from Yemen. Our job was to boost their odds.

Early in its existence, Israel determined that one of its sacred national missions would be to prevent new Jewish holocausts. The state would undertake any mission, no matter how difficult or costly, to rescue Jews wherever they may be. The captains of Israel's ship of state shared the belief that unless Israel acted on behalf of Jews everywhere it would lose its moral authority to act on behalf of Jews anywhere.

Richer in history than in natural resources, there was little that attracted commerce to North Yemen. It was virtually entirely dependent upon imports for all of its essential needs. Most of its hard currency came in from its ex-patriots working in the Gulf States and from foreign aid. In the not-too-distant past, North Yemen was self-sufficient in food, but today it was a major food importer.

The cultivation of qat, that mild narcotic leaf chewed by virtually the entire population all day long, commandeered fields that were once used to grow other, edible agricultural products. Unfortunately, perhaps, for Yemen qat was not cocaine; it had virtually no export market at all. So instead of exporting its drug problem and raking in the hard currency, à la Colombia, Yemenites simply grew more and more lethargic as they grew more and more qat. Even Yemen's startling and domineering sand and mud cities, its unique marketplaces, and its not completely unfounded claim that San'a, its marvelous capital city, was founded by Shem, Noah's son, was not enough to overcome the country's slide into the internecine politics of the Middle East. The tourists stayed away, as did their dollars. And the hostile and suspicious regime made foreigners unwelcome.

The Yemenites also suffered from the general disdain of the "High Arabs," those social-climbing princelings of the Gulf States. The Arab oil barons (AOB) looked down upon the Yemenites because even though Yemen had some very modest oil deposits, it had no refineries to speak of. Therefore, its oil revenues could not begin to place it in the league of the AOBs. Moreover, tribally and ethnically the Yemenites were just different enough from the rest of Arabia for them to be considered "lesser" or "not-authentic" Arabs. And as if that wasn't enough, the Yemeni nation was in chaos: It was divided, it had been through several civil wars and a border war with Oman, and it always came up wanting.

All of this may have been at the base of Yemen's irrational behavior toward these helpless and harmless remnants of a tribe long gone. The Yemenite authorities hoped to compensate for their failure to gain respect through industry by earning respect through belligerency. Yemen would be a part of the Arab holy wars against Israel by taking their fight to the poor Yemeni Jews, a people who had been an integral part of Yemen for nearly three thousand years.

In a way, it made perfect sense. Why take on a distant, powerful regional power when you can accomplish the same result by fighting a local weak image of that power?

So when a Yemenite Jew was willing to assume the risk of escaping what had become the Yemeni hell, we were there to make sure that he, she, or they had a fighting chance at success. And since over the course of the last several weeks, through an obliging journalist, a Jewish Yemenite family had made its willingness to do just that known to the Office, I was tasked to meet this family, this ancient link in Israel's five-thousand-year-old chain, and deliver them to their biblical homeland of Israel.

Albert, my deputy, and I entered Yemen several days before the arrival of the rest of my "Pod" (a team of Combatants). We entered through Yemen's Red Sea port of Al-Hudaydah. We were trying to fit the profile of those Spartan and intrepid tourists who brave the elements to undertake that ultimate quest: the much-ballyhooed "undiscovered" tourist site; the tourist destination not yet visited by the Carnival Cruise Lines and not yet listed in Condé Nast's "Ten Best Summer Vacations."

Al-Hudaydah sits conveniently at the landfall of a long and narrow peninsula that parallels the Yemeni coast. On the land side of Hudaydah Bay, the narrow and long inlet that the peninsula forms, are the cities of As-Salif, an ancient port town, and As-Zaydiya, an old traders' city where among other things, traditional Yemeni daggers are made and illicit rhino-horn saber handles can be found. As tourists, we had every reason to be there. So it was quite unremarkable when we rented two Jeeps to traverse the sandy and rocky terrain to see the sights. After all, if we were willing to reach Yemen all the way from Europe, surely we would avail ourselves of the full "tourist experience."

Getting north of Hudaydah on the land side of the peninsula was essential, because it was there that we would rendezvous with the rest of our Pod. They had to enter Yemen clandestinely because Albert and I would have been unable to smuggle all of our electronics gear and weapons past the Yemeni customs. At least Illusions (the Mossad department responsible for camouflaging Combatant equipment) didn't think that we could.

Our Pod was placed on an Israeli naval missile ship, called a Satil, in the Israeli Red Sea port city of Elat and endured what must have been a rather unpleasant cruise down the Red Sea, against the winds and into the waves, to Yemen. Upon approaching the Yemeni shore, the Satil would come to a dead stop. Too big to risk a sandbar and too large to evade radar, the Satil's utility to this operation was at an end. My Pod members would make the balance of their trip on naval commando ("SEALs") Zodiacs: rubber boats powered by oversized, muffled outboard motors.

Under cover of darkness, the SEALs ferried the sea-sick Combatants and our precious equipment down the bay to the coast of As-Safir, where Albert and I were waiting.

We drove our Jeeps to the landing site. We placed infrared filters over our flashlights and aimed them out to sea. Albert kneeled several feet closer to the water than me. To the SEALs wearing infrared eye goggles, our beam would appear as a vertical. So long as they kept our lights in a straight line to their boats, the SEALs would land in the clear beachfront that we had checked prior to their arrival. If they missed, or if Albert and I were not aligned correctly, then the SEALs, their Zodiacs, my Combatants, and all our secret equipment would hit the rocks and be scattered on a hostile shoreline thousands of miles from home.

Albert and I tried to stay calm even though we were both tense. We dealt with our tension through silence. There simply was nothing more to say until we were able to hear the muffled engines of the incoming Zodiacs.

In the dark night, on a hostile coast, the mind plays games. In my imagination I heard the Zodiacs arrive several times. As it happened, I saw the Zodiacs before I heard them. My Combatants jumped ashore and pulled the Zodiacs up behind them. The SEALs, as a human chain, moved our equipment from the boats to the Jeeps. The entire Pod was in the cars minutes later. The Zodiacs were gone before we could even wave good-bye.

The Pod's cover story was that we were commodity traders seeking out new sources of cotton and hides. We hoped this would prove useful in the event we were stopped along our long route for a routine police check or in the event we were split up, tortured, and interrogated. Even though we had rehearsed this story hundreds of times and we knew one another's cover story better than we knew our true life stories, as a mantra, as a therapeutic exercise, we went over it once again, in the cars. Practice makes perfect.

We left the coast for the country's highland interior, toward the Jewish Yemenite villages. We were expecting to meet our passengers below the city of Shihara, which is located atop an 8,500-foot mountain range. To get there we would first have to traverse the Yemen highlands, a plateau of some 4,500 feet and home to much of Yemen's agricultural produce. It fit our cover story well. What did not fit us at all were the horrendous rains we found ourselves trapped in.

Driving recklessly, trying desperately to battle both the rain and the clock, we made our way on and off road toward the rendezvous. But despite our four-wheel-drive training or perhaps because of the overconfidence it bred, we quickly found ourselves and our vehicles sinking into the heavy Yemeni ground.

Deep in the mud, my colleagues were thinking aloud, analyzing the situation. Avi wanted to abandon the Jeeps, burn their contents, and get away from the scene as quickly as possible. Omri suggested that we sit tight, throw yet more mud on the vehicles to avoid detection, and wait through the night. By then, he correctly argued, the ground would dry up to the hard earth it was and usually is.

The goal.

The issue before me was the goal. Again, as always in this line of work, nothing would be accomplished before we determined what it is that we sought to accomplish. We could have argued whether to abandon the Jeeps or to camouflage them all day and all night. In fact, if we had brought Gray Cell (Mossad Special Operations planners) into the picture, that is precisely what they would have done. But for us that, after all, wasn't the point. The point was, why abandon the Jeeps? Why camouflage the Jeeps? Only to advance toward our goal. And today my colleagues were not focused on the goal.

A goal establishes both a subjective and an objective criterion for success. Subjective because, after all, you define the goal. Objective because no matter how you define the goal, once it is defined it exists independently of its creator; its accomplishment can be measured in a context that is detached from its creator's mind.

A goal defined alters an abstract existence. It changes soggy into crunchy, fuzzy into firm, blurry into focus. A goal pursued demands planning and forethought. Thus, the effect of a goal and the impact of a pursued goal are to radically regiment even the most lackadaisical existence. Once you have defined a goal, every moment of your being is measured against the attainment of that goal.

First you define the goal and then it defines you.

> **As team commander of this Pod, I had to get these Jeeps to the staging point by nightfall. Some of the Pod objected. They were older, from a time past, when the Office was less hierarchical, less formal, less businesslike. These guys preferred the collegial "European Model" that prevailed in the Office's early days. Nowadays, the prevailing view among the old-timers was that the Office had adopted the "American Model": efficiency, individualism, accountability. The older guys did not want to be bound by rigid goals and objectives. They sought to "stay loose," to allow room for imagination and creative responses. They sought to improvise even when planning would eliminate the need for improvisation.**
>
> **They sought to leave too much to chance, and that meant leaving everything to chance.**
>
> **"You can't plan every damn detail in this line of work," Yoav exhorted. "This isn't a bloody science. This is art, bloody perfect art."**
>
> **But Yoav was wrong. You can plan every damn detail, you must plan every damn detail, and you had better plan every damn detail. Then you had better perform every damn detail. Otherwise, you wouldn't make the Office's team and you sure as hell were not going to make mine. As far as I was concerned, the only thing you didn't plan for was the unexpected. And since in this line of work the unexpected is expected, you plan for it, too.**

Defining a goal compels you to know that which you wish to accomplish. In business as in war this rule does not vary. Define your goal. Know your goal. Absent such knowledge, enter neither battle nor business.

In failed war after failed war, the losing side loses because it has no defined goal. Vietnam and Lebanon are banal examples of the same unremarkable proposition. Corporate dinosaurs, behemoths seemingly invincible, disappear into oblivion, proving the business side of this same equation.

Who today can recall the names of now defunct or deflated industry titans? McLaughlin Steel, International Harvester, Pan American Airlines, are but a few of the once-proud names to be humbled. Who can explain the nightmare that has been made of the once-perfect Apple dream? Who can explain how Range Rover, the four-wheel drive that beat the Germans in two world wars, finds itself owned by the very Germans it trounced?

The explanation is this: failure to define the goal, failure to pursue the goal.

Yet despite compelling evidence and in the face of striking examples, all too often you will charge into a business negotiation without a clear, firm, unshakable notion of what it is that you wish to accomplish. There is no better recipe for failure than that.

There is a persistent school of thought that argues that defining your goal rigidly precludes you from taking advantage of various opportunities as they arise. That, however, is not the argument being advanced.

Of course you should be open to opportunities as they arise. You should not, however, be waiting for such opportunities. You should have a clear view of your goal, a view that can be clearly articulated, so that you do not get set off course with each sighting of opportunity, however far away and however vague. You can't get to where you wish to go unless you have decided where that place is. If you set out on the road without that objective in mind, you will no doubt be attracted and diverted by every interesting twist or fork in the road. You will be easily overwhelmed because, like a ship adrift without an anchor, you are not moored to an idea, to a goal. You have not decided ahead of time what you want. You have not made a commitment to your goal.

Say you are walking along a highway and a car drives up and offers you a ride to your destination. Should you take it? Of course you should. But the car is going to *your* destination, not the other way around. That is the difference between setting a goal but being open to opportunities as opposed to simply remaining open to opportunity.

Now transfer that to the business world. Do you want to buy

Company A or Company B? Are you going to wait until an investment banker approaches you with an acquisition target or are you going to tell the investment banker which company it is that *you* wish to acquire? The deal is in that difference.

And what of the criticism about lost opportunities?

Accept it. It is true. When you choose one goal you forsake other options. You marry or you do not. You expand your business or you do not. You succeed or you do not.

My goal was getting the Jeeps to the staging point. No doubt I would. But first, I had to achieve a "pathway goal," an essential task—a milestone—on the way to my goal. I had to realign my objective. I had to get the damn Jeeps out of the mud.

I had no time to lose. We were already surrounded by curious natives. It wouldn't take long for a wandering patrol of the Yemeni police to stumble across us, the biggest prize they could imagine: a Pod of Combatants, lock, stock, and gun barrel.

"Yoav, find a tractor, a truck, anything with four wheels and a winch. Take an hour and a half . . . no, make that seventy-five minutes, then you're back. No exceptions, no excuses, no prisoners. Buy it, steal it, I don't give a shit. . . . Avi, you take some of these natives and unload the Jeeps."

"Everything?" Avi asked, somewhat incredulously.

"Every bloody thing," I countered. "Strip these babies down until they look like the day they came off the General bloody Motors assembly line. Cargo, panels, doors. If it's not welded to the chassis take it off. If its not a goddamn engine part, screw it off."

I needed the Jeeps and I needed them light. I would dig the Jeeps out of the mud. I would get the Jeeps to the staging point before dawn. I would achieve my goal.

Prepare

If defining your goal is the first step in attaining your goal, then preparing for it is your second. Doing that often requires spending time on something you believe you already know: your business, your deal, your human interaction skills. Most individuals, however, believe that preparation is not required for something they already know.

Nothing could be further from the truth.

You walk every day of your life. But if you are to engage in *competitive* walking, you had best be out there learning how to walk competitively. If you don't, you might as well be sitting down. You may talk every day of your life but unless you have talked in public, you had best prepare for it. If you don't, you will be in for a very rude, very humbling awakening.

So even though you have thought about the "deal" with yourself off and on hundreds of times before, until you do so in a concentrated, businesslike manner and businesslike setting, you have really not yet thought about it all. It is the context in which you will now be performing these acts that matters as much as the acts themselves.

Prepare a detailed presentation of your plan. Open it to criticism. Invite questions. Defend what you can and cede what you must. Consider its survivability in light of the unanswered attacks. Live it. Revise it. That is preparation.

Forty-five minutes into the effort, getting rid of the jeep's "ballast" was making a demonstrable difference on our vehicles' "waterline." We began to see the top of the Jeeps' tires, and mud had started to drop off of their springs. Off on one side was a pile of "hardware," large metal panels that were dismantled from the jeeps, and "software," all of our operational gear, which, itself, could sink a small ship. In the distance I could see Yoav astride a small John Deere coming my way.

Some of my guys could find a jellyfish in the desert.

The natives, who assembled around our mudbound Jeeps, were waiting to see if we were capable of getting the Jeeps out of the mess we got them in. As the John Deere

**approached, the natives scattered to one side. It was hard
to believe that all of this was taking place in the heart of
what is more often than not a dry mountainous region in
the middle of nowhere. The closest town, Shihara, was
over thirty miles and four thousand vertical feet away.**

Keep your efforts focused and concentrated. Be like a mighty
river, not its weak tributaries. If you do, you will sweep all that
stands before you. By concentrating your thoughts, energy, and
efforts on one goal and one goal only, you shall be able to compete
and beat those competitors of divided attention and focus. You shall
also eliminate any possibility of excuse based upon the tired refrain
of "too much to do." If there is too much to do, don't do it.

Better a job not done than a job not finished.

**The guys were getting tired. It was hot, it was muggy, we
were covered in slime and mud from head to toe. We
were hungry and we were thirsty. Most of us were suffering from diarrhea that would have dried up lesser men
like a drought. Albert had tapeworms the size of king
cobras. But there were to be no breaks, no lunch, no
water, and no shitting, goddamn it, even if it meant
adding another brown layer to our already soiled pants.
Not until the Jeeps were out of the mud.**

    **Some of the guys weren't happy. Neither was I. But
happiness wasn't today's goal. Liberating the Jeeps was.**

Achieve

The facts are these: Most individuals do not define a goal. Of those
who do, most won't prepare for it. And among those who both
define their goal and prepare for it, most will fail to reach it. They
will fail because of an inability to work single-mindedly in a completely focused fashion toward that goal.

If your goal is to meet the president of BigCo, do not work
toward meeting the vice president of BigCo. If you do so, you will
wind up meeting the vice president and not the president. More-

over, you shall be wasting the precious time and resources which you shall require in order to meet the president.

Similarly, if while you are trying to get to BigCo's president, the president's secretary is rude, forget it. Do not show your anger and do not reciprocate. Do not succumb to the petty pleasure of a biting response. Do not sulk. Do not act offended. Spare her the good-manners lecture. Otherwise, if you succumb to the temptation, you shall veer wildly off course. You shall be closing a critical path toward your goal. And, worst of all, you shall be allowing yourself to divert from your goal, thus failing to single-mindedly pursue it.

If your goal is to complete a task in two days, and you indeed mean to complete the task in two days, do not socialize during those two days. Do not try to appear sociable in those two days. Do not spend time with your friends and family. Do not try to maintain a "well-balanced life" during those two days. Rather, devote all of your time and your energy to the pursuit of that goal.

If your goal is to sell your product, stay on the phone until you have done so. Do not stop for lunch. Do not stop to reassess your career. Do not stop, in fact, until you have completed selling as much product as you have determined to sell.

After you have achieved your goal, if you have to apologize, there will be plenty of time to apologize. You may derive some comfort in the knowledge that successful people spend much less time apologizing than others.

Many individuals fail to achieve their goal because they change it while they are working toward it. Why do they do so? Because working toward a goal with single-minded determination is difficult. It is easier to modify your goal or to do away with it altogether than it is to achieve it.

At first you modify a small, seemingly inconsequential component of your goal: a deadline moved back an hour, a product component simplified from its blueprint. Then you change another item and another until soon you find yourself changing and modifying your plan wholesale. "Din Pruta KeDin Me'ah." (The verdict for a penny is the verdict for a hundred pennies.) Treat a minor change with the same gravity and thoughtfulness that you would a major one.

A small retreat is not always a "small" retreat. A small compromise is not always an inconsequential one. Therefore, no matter how reasonable a change seems to be, no matter how warranted a modification appears to be, and no matter how attractive a new goal now beckons, do not change your goal until you have achieved it. Doing anything less will habituate you to surrender and failure.

Of course, there are stories about those who have worked toward a goal, fulfilled it, and then regretted it all of their lives. Most of those stories are false. Most of those stories are told by individuals who have failed to achieve their own goal. They are told by individuals seeking to rationalize and live with their own failure.

The fact is, fairy tales aside, there are more people who gave up on achieving their goal and have lived all of their lives in regret for it than there are people who have achieved their goals and lived to regret it. Far more. Most of us, in fact, are surrounded by those failed lives every day. Most of us could become one.

Do not fail.

I *would* get these Jeeps out of the mud, I *would* get rid of these natives, and I *would* make it to the staging point on time. I had not left my business career, spent years in training, and risked life and bloody limb to miss this appointment. I had places to go and people to meet and no bloody cloudburst would keep me from my appointed rounds.

With the brute force of the tractor supported by our angry force of frustration, we unlodged the Jeeps from the gluelike grip the earth had had them in. We were free. The natives were not.

In swift action upon a given cue, several Pod members pulled a large thick rope out of one of the Jeeps and in motion worthy of an Olympic synchronized swim team pulled it around the qat-chewing, partially stoned Yemenites. The rest of us pushed them inwards toward the center of an imaginary circle and threatened them with big pieces of the Jeeps' chrome strips to assure their lack of resistance. We didn't really fear them and none of them were likely to raise a ruckus about our presence anyway. But one couldn't leave these things to chance. We bound and gagged them and left them in a valley below us. No one would hear them or see them for quite a while. In fact, so long as their qat held out, they probably wouldn't even mind.

I had refrained from splitting the Pod up until we were out of the mud. But Yaniv was now long overdue at the landing site. While I could hardly spare him or his Jeep until we dislodged ourselves from the quicksand, things were different now. He was late and he'd have to make up for lost time.

Yaniv had to cover the long and treacherous distance between where we would later rendezvous. Sixty deadly miles, thirty of which were off road. He would then have to navigate the last ten or so miles with only one eye on the path and one hand on the wheel because with the other eye and the other hand he would be looking through his starlight vision enhancer seeking the three small infrared (IR) lights that we had left at the site last night. These IR lights marked the small strip of land that we had chosen as a landing site for the IAF rescue helicopter.

Under cover of darkness, the crew of the Satil, cruising deep off the Saudi Arabian peninsula, would carefully unwrap and unpeel the protective shrink-wrap material off of a Bell naval helicopter, the workhorse of the Israeli navy, which until then had been resting on the ship's open deck. The pilots would be roused from their hibernation to fly this fragile device over the Red Sea and deep into Yemen's interior. It would then circle the landing site until we cued it to land. If all went well, we would load the escaping family onto it and send it home.

Assuming Yaniv found the landing site as planned, he would retest the soil compaction to see whether it too came under the cloudburst and, if so, how likely it was to suck the Bell aircraft into its grip. He would also have to make sure that no one else, like the Yemeni army or police, had stumbled across the marked site or made camp on it while we were gone. And then he would send two short radio bursts to the Hole (Israel's Military Command and Control Operation Center, named so because it was situated deep below ground in a Tel Aviv highrise) to let them know we were ready.

Yaniv had a little over two hours in which to get this done. Fortunately, the truth was that if anyone could do it, Yaniv could. After all, there were not many people who survived Sayeret Matkal (the premier and preeminent Israeli "Ranger" team, comparable to Britain's SAS).

Yaniv could. That is what made him Combatant material. Training and experience made him a Combatant.

Once Yaniv's message was received, the Hole would send a coded message to the Israeli air force (IAF) alerting them that it was now "NoR" for "No Return." With that message, the Bell aircraft, now circling over the Red Sea, would begin its final leg: the dangerous flight inland over Yemen.

Define. Prepare. Achieve.

Was I confident that Yaniv could do it? Without a doubt. Was I confident that he would do it? At this point it didn't matter. He would try to do what he had to do and he would try his best. My job was to do what I had to do. If I did that, we might succeed. If I didn't, whether he made it or not would have no consequence to me or to this operation.

As Yaniv drove off, we climbed back into our vehicles and hit the road. We were only ten or fifteen miles from the family meeting site. Over narrow mountain roads,

roads held together by their pebbles' sheer willpower and nothing else, we drove full throttle to our destination. (Whenever possible and time allowing, the first thing we did upon renting vehicles we were going to use in an operation was to jerry-rig a throttle to the gas pedal. We found that the throttle offered more immediate and responsive control over acceleration. To this day I wonder why car manufacturers have not made it an option on their vehicles.)

We approached the Shihara meeting site just a few minutes before the prearranged time. I was tired and nervous and jumpy. I was alert to the tremendous responsibility I bore: responsibility to my Pod and its safety, responsibility to the chopper and its crew, responsibility to this poor Yemeni family, and responsibility to the state of Israel, my dispatcher. This weighed heavily upon me as I counted away the seconds to the scheduled meeting. There were so many variables in an operation of this sort that prepare as one may, there was always room for surprise.

It didn't take long to arrive.

A few moments after our arrival, up from under the road's bend, a family of six appeared: parents, a grandfather, and three small children, just as we expected. They were followed by a small herd of goats. We intuitively knew that these were our kindred. There was no need to exchange code words or signals. We had that unique sensation one has when meeting for the first time a much-revered and spoken-of family member.

Zion, our Yemenite interpreter, gave us the bad news.

"They want to take the goats."

"You're joking," I said.

"No. I'm afraid not. They want to take the goats. Without the goats, they fear that they will not be able to support themselves."

"Listen, you've got to talk them out of this. And we don't have a lot of time. I mean, I understand their concerns, but tell them that they will be taken care of. They will not need their goats."

"I've tried. But they are not going to go without the goats."

These were the uncontrollable variables. These were the things that could not be planned for.

Zion and I pleaded with the family to no avail. They would not go without the goats and we could not take the goats. I contemplated abducting them but couldn't bring myself to do so. First of all, it would have been a major change of plans and could have ramifications far beyond this one operation. If somehow it were to become known that we forcibly kidnapped Yemenites from Yemen, we would have lost trust throughout the Arab-Jewish Diaspora. Second, and equally important, I could not bring myself to force these good people to abandon their security blanket, their goats, even if it was unneeded.

After lengthy and frustrating discussions, the family agreed that the grandfather would accompany us to the holy land. If, in fact, it turned out that goats were not required, he would get a letter to the family and they would then join him without their goats.

The family embraced, the old man kissed the goats, and we were off to our meeting with Yaniv and the Israeli air force.

A Box for Baghdad

HOW TO CHOOSE YOUR TIMING

▮TIMING

> *"LaKal Zman VeEt LeKal Hefetz . . ."*
>
> "To Everything There Is a Season; a Time for Every
> Purpose . . ."

LaKal Zman . . . Life presents many ironies. One of the greatest is the
paradox of time, patience, and action.

Youth has all the time in the world but no patience. Age has much
patience but very little time. Youth prefers action to inaction, while age
opts for inaction over action.

Impatient action is doomed to failure. Yet, patience which leads to inaction is failure itself.

On June 7, 1980, after a massive attack by the Israeli
air force, the Iraqi nuclear reactor at Osirak lay in
ruins. Buried amid the Osirak ruins were also Saddam
Hussein's plans for a nuclear bomb.

The world's newspapers reported that the air attack
was a masterful and impressive operation. News reports
spoke of the Israeli F-15 jet fighters flying over Jordan,
Saudi Arabia, and Iraq, all enemy countries, in order to

attack the Iraqi reactor. But even more impressive than that feat, according to the papers, was the pinpoint accuracy with which the bombs penetrated the reactor and hit directly at the reactor's core.

"It was as though each and every bomb was hand-guided to the target by its very own homing device," said one.

Sometimes the media get it right.

Opportunities, Like Fruit, Should Be Picked When Ripe

The patient businessman is the wise businessman. Rather than jump into a business opportunity, you should circle it, observe it, sense it, provoke it, and perhaps even tease it. But you should not seize it until you have acquired a sense of perspective on it.

Patience

Patience provides the perspective, otherwise known as "maturity," which allows one to see the field of opportunity with somewhat more of an objective eye than he who acts precipitously. More important, perhaps, it provides the observer with the perspective essential for identifying times of unique opportunity. For one who has never experienced a depression, a down cycle, or a real estate crash, the risks of liquidity remain an academic concept. For one who has never experienced a booming stock market, inflation, or spiraling gold prices, the accumulation and retention of cash may seem like a sensible policy.

Patience enables you to strike with apparent impatience at the ripe opportunity. In the absence of patience, one is prone to depth-of-field errors.

Depth of Field

Depth-of-field errors occur when one views an object from only one angle and acts upon that perception. A person on the ground has a very different view of the landscape than one who is in the air. Who between them is more apt to correctly map the terrain? Who between them is more apt to correctly judge heights and depths?

Do not judge a company by only one feature of a company. In other words, do not look only at the company's sales without also looking at the company's intellectual property estate. The company's sales, after all, could be based upon a patent that is soon going to expire. Or they could be based upon no patent at all so that the company's success will soon pull in larger companies: sharks who have been patiently biding their time to see whether the minnow, the company, will be successful in its sales. The latter example, a classic depth-of-field error, stands the value of strong sales to an emerging, cash-poor company on its head. Because such a company will not have the financial wherewithal to fend off the predator.

The value of accounting for depth-of-field errors is, therefore, quite substantial. Consider the case of "Exemplo," a company with substantial revenue, solid growth, and adequate cash reserves. On paper, Exemplo appears to be a winner. But "on paper" is just one way to view the company. Meet some of Exemplo's personnel, talk to them about its people—not its products. If Exemplo's sales force is unhappy, forget the analysts' projections. If Exemplo's CEO has a large severance package, start to consider how the company will fare under a successor. If Exemplo's outside advisors have recently changed, perhaps there are some unsavory goings-on that the original advisors were unwilling to countenance.

Always seek more than one perspective on an object and always more than one reality shall appear.

It was sometime in early 1974 when, at a carefully orchestrated London cocktail party, I was introduced to a visiting Iraqi physicist, Dr. Ali Ragoub. Several months before our seemingly chance encounter, Dr. Ragoub's father was brutally killed by the regime's Imperial Guards. The father was accused and summarily convicted by his accusers of cross-border "collaboration" (that is, smuggling) with Iran.

Curiously, for all of its internal spying, the Iraqi

regime was not aware that Dr. Ragoub was the son of the man they had killed because, years ago, when he first left Iraq to study abroad, Ragoub had adopted his mother's maiden name. He did so for two reasons: First, his mother's family (and family name) was Sunni, as was the Iraqi majority and the regime's leaders, whereas his father's name was a Shia one and the Shias were always in general disfavor with the regime. Second, his mother's family were "Takriti," a mere tribal distinction to some but in Saddam's Takriti Iraq, an all-important distinction. It would be inconceivable to deny a Takriti the right to study abroad.

Gray Cell instructed me to meet Ragoub because at the time I traveled relatively freely in and out of Baghdad. My cover as a financial analyst provided me with strong links to Iraq's growing financial community. If anyone were ever required to contact Dr. Ragoub in person in Baghdad on behalf of the Office, it could only be someone he had met before. Otherwise, Ragoub would have no way of knowing that the person he was meeting with was in fact a Combatant and not an Iraqi plant. Gray Cell decided that that someone would be me.

Dr. Ragoub and I engaged in typical cocktail-party banter, which was exactly as Gray Cell had instructed me to do. After one or two minutes of chatter about nothing, I moved on to the scripted portion of this meeting. I raised my wineglass toward him and seized his eyes with mine.

"Well, Dr. Ragoub, it was nice to make your acquaintance. Here's to our next meeting, to Iraq, and to Falawi." I waited for a response.

Dr. Ragoub turned a very dark red and ran a sweaty palm over his thinning hair. He then asked in a hushed and conspiratorial tone: "What did you say? What exactly did you say?"

"To Iraq," I said rather loudly, looking him straight in the eye and ignoring his question.

"To Iraq," he replied rather haphazardly. I took a sip of my wine and turned around to mingle with the other guests.

Ahmed Falawi was Dr. Ali Ragoub's disgraced and deceased father.

It was almost six years to the day on which I had met Ragoub for the first and last time. The intervening years had been good to Ragoub. He had attained a position of prominence in Baghdad with a very prestigious appointment to the Osirak reactor project, Iraq's nuclear bomb program. And while this appointment precluded him from leaving the country, it afforded him a measure of independence and prestige in Iraq that few rivaled.

"Dr. Ragoub, a pleasure. You may not remember me, but we met in London, quite a while ago. In fact, you may recall I toasted your father. . . ." I let the words register before I said anything else.

The Time Value of Relations

In any relationship, the passage of time itself creates intimacy. The mere fact that one has remained in touch with another over the years, regardless whether anything of substance occurred between them, creates a bond of intimacy. Therefore, cultivate all of your acquaintances. Call them or drop them a card, even if only once a year. For you shall never know when you shall wish to call them for advice, a suggestion, a business alliance, or for information. Staying in touch provides the greatest payback for the least amount of effort. And it is a payback you should not dismiss.

Several weeks before my second meeting with Ragoub, I was called to a London meeting with my European "Marionette," a Mossad case officer who "runs" a Combatant. We called the operators Marionettes because even though they were supposed to be pulling our strings and "running" us, it rarely turned out that way. Her name was Daphna.

Girl-boy meetings were favored by the Office because they invariably aroused less notice than boy-boy meetings and were less prone to interference than girl-girl meetings. So a male Combatant was usually combined with a female operator and vice versa.

Daphna's plans for me were Baghdad. Show time at last.

Daphna outlined my task: I was to fly to Baghdad, rent a car along with the services of a government-approved tourist guide who, in Baghdad, was automatically assumed to be a Mukhabarat (secret police) informer, and take a trip to the Shanidat Cave, a well-known tourist attraction where many years ago a mummy had been discovered. I could try and drive alone, but that would only increase the authorities' interest in me. Better to disarm them and lower their paranoia threshold by inviting them into the car with me.

The cave was situated along the Tigris River northeast of the capital. Walking amid the spectacle, I would coincidentally meet a fellow businessman tourist who would be carrying the *Financial Times*. (The *Financial Times*, a newspaper printed on pink paper, is identifiable from a distance. It is therefore the paper of choice for discriminating undercover agents around the globe.) Over a drink at the museum café, my new acquaintance would leave the newspaper behind and I would adopt it; not an uncommon phenomenon among business travelers seeking out news from the homeland. Hidden inside the *Financial Times*' pages would be a series of thin metallic strips.

The fellow tourist will not have been a tourist at all but rather a member of Israel's most elite and secretive Ranger unit, Sayeret Matkal. The Sayeret made it its business to make these types of deliveries to Combatants. No doubt a Sayeret team would be flown in by helicopter to the Iraqi desert somewhere, where this one soldier would discard his military fatigues to don a civilian outfit and then be sent on his way to meet me. Afterwards, he would vanish back into the desert, from where he would depart as he came. Without the Sayeret, it would be extremely difficult for Combatants, who assume huge risks as it is, to get their war implements into hostile countries. For me, at least, this was a much safer approach.

Daphna then handed me what looked like a standard international electricity converter kit and a can of Flying Dutchman pipe tobacco.

"Buy a pipe and start smoking," she said as she pushed the two boxes across the table.

"What's this for?" I asked, holding the tobacco can up to the light, trying to discern some clue through its blue-and-white metal lid.

Daphna took the can back, and with a quick and firm counterclockwise turn of the lid, it came off. Inside it was what looked like a standard gray electric box. The kind that houses switches and wires and stuff. The bottom part of the can had a thin strip of double-sided tape on it and two strips of black electrical isolation tape.

"Don't forget the converter," she continued. "Inside the converter, when the British plug configuration is in place, you will see that directly behind them are two electrical wires. They are hidden behind it now but they are attached to it. Pull them out and strip the plastic coating off their ends. Then twirl them tightly around the metallic strips from the newspaper. Take the black electrical tape and wrap it around the exposed ends. Then push the British plug configuration back into the converter and wrap the metallic strips around the converter itself."

"Then what?"

"Then make your call to Dr. Ragoub. Meet him. Give him the converter. Tell him that he is to open the converter to its Iraqi configuration. When he does so, he might hear a noise that sounds like the breaking of a seal, which is what it actually is. So tell him not to be worried that he broke something inside it because he did and he was supposed to. Ragoub should then put the converter into the recess inside of the gray electric box, take it with him to Osirak, and adhere it to any wall in the immediate vicinity of the reactor's core. He must do so, however, within twenty-four hours of receiving this from you and within ten hours of breaking that seal."

"And then what?"

"Then he should stay away from work until he hears from us again. Time your meeting with Ragoub so that you are out of the country no more than two hours after your meeting. *Alles klar*, Herr Kaiser?"

"Not quite. What's the device do?"

"It's a bird call."

"It's a what?"

"It's a bird call. It attracts big birds."

"Big birds?"

"Yes. Big birds. So that they can fly over Iraq and shit on Saddam's plans of glory."

I planned on meeting Ragoub as near to the Baghdad International Airport as possible. The risk we were taking was enormous. I know of no other instance in which a Combatant met with a Retailer in the Retailer's country, or any enemy country for that matter. After all, if the Retailer told the authorities my true identity, there was no way out. No Geneva Convention, certainly no Amnesty International. In fact, even an exchange of spies wasn't a sure thing. Yet, this was different. Nuclear fallout is a more weighty concern than an individual Combatant's safety.

I met Ragoub later that day at what was then the Sheraton Hotel. I preferred a hotel meeting because we would attract less attention there than in a seemingly more private place. It was an irony of totalitarian countries that one was always better off conducting business

under the nose of the authorities than away at some
seemingly remote location. The hotel would, of course,
have its usual secret service contingent keeping an eye
on the foreigners there, but for them, this was a routine
assignment. They were tired, bored, thinking about the
mortgage or Iraq's equivalent. They were not likely to
notice or even think to notice a meeting between a Combatant and a Retailer taking place beneath their very
noses.

I recognized Ragoub instantly even though he had put
on some weight since I had last seen him. I nodded
toward him and he approached my table. I made it quick
and he helped me. Neither one of us wanted to prolong
this meeting. I quickly told him what he had to do. He
understood. He also seemed relieved that his long wait
was over. He might have been happy that he was now to
exact his revenge on the regime that killed his father. Or
he might have been relieved that he wasn't being asked
to do something more risky.

"What is in the box? What does the device do? I am
an Iraqi, you understand."

The implicit message Ragoub was sending me, not
unexpectedly, at least to me if not to my Marionette,
was that he was anti the regime in Iraq, not, however,
anti-Iraq. A sentiment I could fully appreciate and
empathize with.

"It's a recorder. A sophisticated recorder. It's a scientific instrument really. It will enable us to decipher certain operational routines of the reactor. It's far safer than
meeting with you here, like this, and asking you the
entire bloody list of questions headquarters wants to
know about. So hold this tight." I squeezed his palm.
"I'll be back for it in a month or so. Allah is merciful."

Seeking the quickest way out of Iraq, I boarded a
plane to Kuwait. From there, I boarded a British Airways
flight to London. By the time I arrived in Israel on elec-
tion day, June 7, 1980, a mere four days after my depar-

ture from Baghdad, the Iraqi nuclear reactor at Osirak lay in ruins along with Saddam Hussein's plans for a nuclear bomb.

Israel's air force had done its job, and for all I know, Ragoub had done his.

Strategic Surrender

WHEN TO EXERCISE POWER

▌POWER

> *"Avi Yiser Etchem BeShotim VaAni Ayaser Etchem BeAkrabim."*
> "My Father Chastened You with Whips but I Will Chasten You with Scourges."

Avi Yiser Etchem . . . The great and wise King Solomon has died. His legacy to Israel is the monumental building projects in the tribal footholds of Judea and Benjamin. These projects, however, were costly. They saddled the kingdom with large debts. To pay these debts, the king levied heavy taxes on his subjects.

The outlying ten Tribes of Israel, those tribes that did not benefit directly from the construction frenzy in Jerusalem, were very unhappy with the tax burden. But King Solomon was a popular king and, during his lifetime, the ten tribes were complacent. Upon his death, however, they request a reprieve from Rehoboam, Solomon's son and successor to the throne.

Rehoboam, a brash and inexperienced youth, rejects a conciliatory approach to the Tribes of Israel. Instead, he decides to demonstrate his resolve through harsh measures. In his first public address, Rehoboam tells the gathered thousands to brace themselves: Under his reign they shall bear a burden far heavier than any imposed by his father.

The people listen in shock and sadness. Within days, ten of the twelve Tribes of Israel secede from the Kingdom of Israel. From that day forward, the people of Israel have never again been united under one government in one place.

The successful employment of power is more often in its restraint than in its exertion.

I had little time to prepare for this assignment. My predecessor, Jean Claude, was pulled off the job because his identity had been compromised. In contravention of all internal procedures, one of Jean Claude's field reports was attributed directly to his true name rather than to his customary nom de guerre. Worse yet, that report traveled somehow from the Mossad's intelligence analysts to the Israel Foreign Office, albeit as a "Read Only Document." From there, not surprisingly, it was leaked to the press.

Fortunately for the Office, the business cover Jean Claude created was unblemished. So while the previous boss of "Forte France" was out of business, the employment agency he helped create remained very much in business. And I was its new "Patron."

Power

Power is a device. It itself has no positive or negative value. Its utility can be measured only through its accomplishments. And its accomplishments are elusive: Power can be as much of a detriment as a complement. Therefore, you should deploy power only when you understand its reach.

The agency was a Mossad master stroke. It was one of those business covers that cry out to be created. What better way to infiltrate agents, Combatants, and other intelligence operatives in and out of target countries than through the good offices of a worldwide personnel agency?

Coming into the agency, as I did, with little knowledge of the personnel industry, I had my work cut out for me. I would have liked to learn more from Jean Claude, but he was being held incommunicado until the domestic furor regarding his affair was settled. I would also have liked to engage an outside consultant to assist me in figuring out which way was the proverbial "up," but unfortunately, given what we do, one does not have the luxury of calling up a Boston Consulting Group or a McKinsey for advice.

No, it would have to be me and me alone to digest and sort out all of the details of this operation.

Most of the agency's work was legitimate. None of our Parisian employees, save me, were Combatants. All were simply Frenchmen and -women seeking to be gainfully employed in a personnel agency. So it would have been rather awkward to have to turn to them to request their advice. After all, my cover story was that I had been specially sent in from some faraway headquarters to replace Jean Claude and further build the agency. Therefore, I had to get a grasp on things myself and I had to do so quickly.

I started with the books. As I learned in training and later in operations, the one constant in business—any business—is the numbers. Forget the "opportunities," the "upside," the "long term" or the "short range." Ask yourself simply this: How much money is in the company's bank account? How much does it earn? How much does it "burn"?

This is the essence of a company. Everything else is dressing.

The next several weeks did not resemble the spy movies that I had grown up on and that had propelled me in large measure to "spydom" in the first place. Instead of cavorting with the likes of Ursula Andress and Pussy Galore, I spent all of my evenings examining the company's books. I might as well have been an accountant. What I found, however, was encouraging: The company was actually cash-flow positive and was in no fear of going under. The bad news was that it had a fairly large number of outstanding invoices that were not paid.

One might think that the Office would not particularly care if the agency made money on its placement services. After all, it was placing its personnel where it wanted them. To be paid for that too seems like the very definition of "chutzpah."

Well, one would be mistaken.

The Office was very concerned about getting paid for its effort. First because chutzpah, or outlandish behavior, was, after all, its calling card and stock-in-trade. Second, because if the agency failed to insist on payment, it would not take long for its employees and its clients to become suspicious or for the French fiscal authorities to come sniffing around.

As I absorbed more information about the business, I admired it more and more. Here was a business cover that not only generated revenue, if not enormous profit, but also allowed us to place our operatives in target countries with ready-made cover. And best of all, all requests for our operatives came from the target countries themselves. Therefore, they would be, and indeed were, beyond suspicion.

A handful of clients approached the agency directly because of their past experience with it. But most others we sought out and actively lobbied for work. This "sales" job of the agency was just as important to our operation as was personnel placement because in selling the agency, I gained entry into a host of target countries with ease.

The agency's niche was engineers and technical personnel. We placed true, innocent engineers and true, not-so-innocent engineers with international employers. By far, most of our placements were legitimate. But those that were not were worth their weight in gold. We placed

**engineers at the Pakistani reactor. We placed welders in
Libya's chemical-warfare factories. And we placed
phone technicians with the ArabSat satellite consortium.
All in all, it was a great operation. My task was to keep it
alive.**

The Nature of Power

Power is always, always, less effective than its possessor estimates it
to be. Rehoboam thought he had power to compel his subjects to
accept his edict. But he did not. What he had was the power to
issue the edict, nothing more. With the deployment of power,
Rehoboam effectively destroyed his kingdom and himself. Yet it was
his power and the use of that power which accomplished this—not
the power of anyone else.

The exercise of power is also always irreversible. Once unleashed
and employed there is no turning back. The exercise of power
assumes a life of its own which cannot be ignored. A thought may
be banished. A harsh word may be explained. But power so changes
the dynamic of a relationship that post-use, things are never again,
and can never again be, the same.

The Rules of Power

The first rule of power is to know its limitations. How does one do
that? By careful and close analysis.

Prior to using power, ask yourself: What is the nature of the
power I intend to use? Is it physical power? Is it authoritative
power? Is it psychological power? Ask then: What are the inherent
limitations to that form of power? Physical power, for example, may
work to *conquer* a nation, but it is a woefully inadequate tool with
which to *rule* a nation. Power derived from authority, like that
wielded so pitifully by Rehoboam, has force only if the authority
from which it emanates has force. In the case of Rehoboam, since
his authority was untested, it was foolhardy of him to rely on power
that emanated from that authority.

The next rule of power is to know when to wield one's power.

You should use power only when persuasion is known to be ineffectual. You should use power only when the outcome for which it is being exercised is the only acceptable outcome to you.

Consider a situation in which you are seeking to have a retailer of your goods display your products more prominently than those of your competitor. Assume that your product is an important one to the retailer because it attracts many buyers to its outlets. These buyers then acquire other goods from the retailer. This fact gives you power. It is economic power; you have the apparent ability to better or worsen this retailer's economic well-being. Assume also that your entreaties to this retailer have gone unanswered. All of your arguments as to why your products should be more prominently displayed than those of your competitor's have been rebuffed.

It is decision time.

Persuasion has failed. You have economic power. You can pull your products from the retailer. If the only acceptable outcome to you is to be more prominently displayed than the competition, you must exercise your power by invoking that threat. But remember Rehoboam. Rather than yield to his power his subjects chose to simply ignore his power. People, and businesses, do not always follow the rational economic model. The retailer may decide to suffer the economic burden, risk the loss of income, yet not yield to your power.

Can there be another outcome you would accept? Would you be satisfied if the retailer allowed you to have special promotions or tie-ins for your products? Would you be satisfied if the retailer agreed to certain minimum sales of your product by his store, thus shifting the risk of prominence of display from you to him? Surely there are other ways to accomplish your objective.

Real power not deployed—even when it could be deployed— can yield more benefit to its holder than if it were deployed.

The last rule of power is to account for its aftermath. As a general principle, the exercise of power rarely yields exactly the result sought, yet it always changes the field from what it was pre-exercise. Therefore, in assessing the outcome of an exercise of power, consider the alternatives to the outcome which you believe it will bring about. For rest assured, it shall be one of the alternatives that come to pass—not the one you had initially envisioned.

> One of our larger clients, the Pakistani Power Agency (PPA), a front for the Pakistani, or "Islamic," bomb, as Pakistan's nuclear weapons program came to be known, was deep in arrears on its payments. The PPA, which had a strong European presence and several official Swiss bank accounts, was not a client that could easily ignore its debts. Moreover, our agency contracts, drafted by Europe's most prominent attorneys, were ironclad. We could therefore have simply handed these delinquent accounts over to our attorneys for action.
>
> I chose a different tack. After all, enforcing these contracts and getting payment was not the most important purpose I had here. Preserving and cultivating an important client was. Had I chosen to take legal action to enforce these agreements, I had little doubt of our success. But I also knew that in the exercise of legal power we would lose both a valuable customer and an important client. Better to ignore the power and take a different approach.
>
> I contacted PPA's chief financial officer in Lahore. Rather than challenge him on the unpaid bills, I expressed our concern for the PPA and inquired whether there was anything we might do to assist it. "Was there something wrong with the candidates we had sent you?" I asked. "Might there be anything you wish to discuss?" I offered.
>
> Rather than wield the power I had, I made it clear to my client that I was ignoring it: I was not referring to it or brandishing it. There was no threat implied or suggested. And by refusing to resort to power I exercised that power.
>
> After that conversation, I traveled to Lahore to meet with the PPA executives. I was polite and respectful. I explained that we viewed our relationship as an impor-

tant one. All the same, in order to do the job that they wished us to do, we had to be paid in a timely fashion. I acknowledged the difficulties they must have had in effecting payment outside of the country and explained that that was the very reason I had brought with me the documents for a Swiss escrow account into which they could make advances against our invoices. I paid homage to their political bosses and to their bureaucrats. And I returned to Paris with full payment of our outstanding invoices, a deposit into the shared escrow account to be applied against future invoices, and enough requests for additional engineers and technicians to keep us busy for the next twelve months.

Cool Under Cover

HOW TO MAKE SILENCE YOUR ALLY

▌SILENCE

> "*Siyag LeKhokhma Shtika.*"
> "Silence—a Sign of Intelligence."

Siyag LeKhokhma . . . The Sages of Israel, writing in the now-vanished language of Aramaic, used only three words to describe the value of silence. Indeed, how could it be otherwise? These three Aramaic words, *Siyag LeKhokhma Shtika,* enunciate a philosophy that transcends the Anglo-Saxon "Silence is golden." While the latter ascribes a positive value to silence itself, the Aramaic idiom ascribes a positive value—*wisdom*—to the silent individual.

W e had stopped the trucks and pulled over to the side of the road. It was late afternoon and the heat was beginning to break. If we were lucky, the sweltering desert furnace would shut down long enough so that the temperature could get back down to the high nineties. In the Saudi desert, every little bit helped.

Joni was driving the Land Rover while I was attempting to read the map in between bounces. We were orienteering in the worst sense of the word. That is to say, we were totally disoriented. We were looking for a potential crash-landing site for F-15 and F-16 Israeli air force (IAF) aircraft. Why? At the time we could only guess.

All we knew was that our mission was to enter Saudia, find the "X" in the desert that matched the "X" Gray Cell had marked on its Saudi topographical map, and leave the high-radio-frequency transmitters (HRFTs), some other electronic gizmos, AK-47 automatic rifles, and emergency rescue supplies (first aid, water, food) at the site.

Anyone carrying a "dog's whistle," an electronic device that triggered the HRFT's signal mode and identified it, would be able to find the hidden cache.

The Value of Silence

Silence is defined in the negative; it is defined by what it is not. It is not noise. It is not sound. It exists only in the absence of something else. That is why silence is an act of self-restraint. You can create it only by refraining from breaking it.

Silence is a void; a space to be filled, or not to be filled, at one's option. The value of silence is, therefore, determined solely and entirely by he who maintains the silence. And in its maintenance a person's wisdom is revealed.

Combatants were kept in the dark about their missions for good reason. First of all, knowing only what we needed to know allowed us to focus on our assigned tasks. It prevented our second-guessing Gray Cell as to whether the task we had been assigned was, in fact, the best way to achieve the overall goal. No one at Gray Cell wanted wiseguy Combatants with real-life field experience and hands-on expertise getting in the way of Gray Cell's spy-book theories. Second, keeping us in the dark reduced the likelihood of "spillage," that is, inadvertent comments to third parties, at home or abroad. And lastly, it protected all of us in the catastrophic event of a Combatant "flare" (the capture of a Combatant by enemy forces).

But being human, we always tried to guess the purpose of our mission, and being fairly smart, we usually guessed right. In this case, from the task (and material) at hand, we deduced that: (a) wherever the pilots and their jet aircraft were going, there was an abnormally high likelihood that they would not make it back safely to base; (b) the pilots would be instructed to abandon their planes, if they should have to do so, over Saudia's north-by-southwestern desert; (c) in the event of an unscheduled landing, the IAF would send helicopters to this Saudi site to try and get the pilots out; and (d) the mission was so secret that the military didn't trust even its own Rangers to perform the task to which we had been assigned. From a, b, c, and d, we deduced that the IAF mission would be far from Israel's borders, that the IAF's route would not take it over any friendly territory, that there was a substantial risk of failure, that the mission was to be clandestine, and that, in light of the above, the mission had to be of vital national interest.

In fact, it was. The mission for which we were risking our necks was to be a "viability test": the IAF's first and only "test run" on the Iraqi Osirak nuclear reactor. Less than one year later, the real attack would take place.

Several days before our drive in the desert, Joni and I had flown to Amman, Jordan, from London. Our cover was that of international resort developers on our way to inspect several hotel sites in Aqaba, Jordan's Red Sea port. Aqaba was conveniently located less than a mile from Elat, Israel's Red Sea port. So it was a relatively easy matter for Israel's naval commandos to deliver our operational gear to Aqaba on the night of our arrival.

Upon our arrival in Amman, we rented a Land Rover (a very popular vehicle in the rabidly Anglophile kingdom of Jordan) and drove to Aqaba. On our way we stopped to admire the ancient Nabatian city of Petra and the wonder of Wadi Ram's dark towering rock columns. We were, after all, in the tourist business. Later that evening, we arrived in Aqaba and checked into one of the nicer beachfront hotels, which was actually not too far from King Hussein's Winter Palace.

In the meantime, the naval commandos, using their mini-subs, advanced underwater from Elat toward Aqaba carrying with them all of our operational gear: maps, electronics, rescue kits, and weapons, in water-tight packaging. When they were about several hundred yards away from our hotel's coastline, they attached the gear to a dead weight and to a tightly wound rope. The rope itself was attached to both the dead weight on one end and to a red rubber buoy on the other. The commandos deposited the weight and with it the gear and the buoy on the sea's sand floor and returned to Elat.

Despite its natural tendency to shoot to the surface and float, the buoy stayed underwater because the rope to which it and the dead weight was attached was bunched and bound together by a small metal wire. Since the dead weight was now resting safely on the coral floor, the buoy could not possibly reach the surface. The buoy, save for some small yellow spots and the fact that it was about twenty or thirty feet underwater, looked like every other fisherman's buoy in Aqaba Bay.

Part of the wire that bound the rope that held the buoy was encapsulated in a small sodium pellet. Within the pellet was a very strong acid. When the divers left their package underwater, the sea began to erode and melt the sodium pellet. Twenty minutes later the sodium pellet melted and the acid was released onto the wire. Exactly eight hours and forty minutes after that, the acid severed the wire. Now, with the wire severed, the rope unfurled, and with the buoy's natural buoyancy, the buoy ascended rapidly to the surface, where Joni and I were waiting in our Bahaman bathing suits and diving gear; just two guys snorkeling the coral reef.

Easily spotting the well-marked buoy in Aqaba's clear blue waters, we harvested the gear and stuffed it into our diving bags. Later that day, back at our hotel, we stripped the watertight packaging from the gear and repacked it in specially made, padded, sandproof bags that we had brought with us from London. We then drove to the city market, where we stocked up on food and water that we stored in the car. We returned to the hotel to catch some sleep before our invasion of Saudi Arabia.

We awoke at 2:00 A.M. We left all of our clothes and fake personal belongings in our hotel room so as to ensure that it would be several days before someone would notice our absence. We made it clear to the male room attendant that we were in search of "action." We hoped that that would cause him to not take notice of our unmade beds for at least a day or so.

We checked the hotel lobby, and as we expected, it was empty save for one sleeping desk clerk. We walked past him quickly and out of the lobby into the dark night. We had taken the precaution of parking our Land Rover away from the hotel's parking lot and main entrance so as to not wake anyone up when we started its motor. We got into the car, released the emergency brake, placed the car in gear, and allowed it to roll down the modest incline it was parked on. When we were a fair distance from the hotel, I released the clutch and let the engine purr into action. We were off.

Now deep in the desert in Saudi territory, we stopped the Rover and got out to briefly stretch our legs and change the car's license plates. Sunrise was rapidly approaching. The air was still chilly and the sky's colors were changing from black and white to pale yellow. We pulled the Saudi license plates that our frogmen couriers delivered to us out of one of our bags and attached them on the Rover in place of its Jordanian ones. We then buried the Jordanian plates in the sand.

As the night turned to day and after we were well within Saudi territory, we took out our global positioning devices to try and orient ourselves on the map. The ter-

rain was flat, and whatever sand dunes did exist could not be relied upon to have been there for long. Orienteering would be a bitch.

It took us a good three hours until we got our bearings. By then the sun was at full blast and it was hot. We were a bit behind schedule and Samson (Mossad's director of Combatants) would be waiting to hear from us. As far as I could tell, this would be as good a place as any to take a break; there was nothing but sand and rock for miles around and there was not a lot of sense in trying to hold out for a Holiday Inn. Joni and I sat down on a rock to assemble our miniature transmitter and input our code.

If You Don't Have to Talk—Don't Talk

In business, silent individuals are commonly mistaken for intelligent individuals. Silent individuals are assumed to be engaged in contemplative thought and analysis. Absent evidence to the contrary, there is no good reason to think otherwise.

Until you talk, there is almost a presumption, a default courtesy, that you are intelligent. The silent person need do very little to gain a lot of credit. In contrast, a talkative individual must, in fact, *be* intelligent to be thought intelligent. Once your mouth is open and your tongue is engaged, you proceed at your own, great, risk.

Speech is a minefield. Each word is a mine and conversation, uncharted land. The more you talk, the more likely you are to set off an explosion.

We were facedown, kneeling over a blanket we had spread out on the sand next to the open back door of the Land Rover. We were deep in thought and completely engaged in assembling our "burst" transmitter. The burst transmitter was an old and cumbersome technology. Its basic design had not changed in ten years and it showed it. In a nutshell, it was a radio transmitter that collected

and bunched together the data we input and then, with a push of a button, it sent the entire data package out as one condensed, indecipherable, and untraceable radio broadcast. At the moment, we were focused on the chore of selecting and inputting the correct code into the transmitter, an extremely labor-intensive chore.

First, we had to write out the entire message in longhand. We then had to rewrite the message backwards. After that, we typed the backwards message into our transmitter, skipping vowels and double letters. We then selected a special predesignated encoding "crystal" (which physically resembled a transistor) from our crystal box. Each crystal was marked for a particular day and hour and each was disposed of immediately after its use.

Once we selected the appropriate crystal, we had to fit it into the transmitter. Most times the crystals fit but sometimes they didn't. If the crystal did not fit, we would have to wait an hour in order to try the next crystal. If the crystal did fit, we would switch the transmitter to "locked" mode and then we would push the "scramble" button. In "scramble," the transmitter would jumble up our message in accordance with an established, yet random, encryption method. Since Samson had the twin crystal to ours, our random scramble would be exactly replicated on Samson's receivers. After scrambling, we reviewed the message, painstakingly, letter by letter. We had to confirm that the scrambling had occurred. It had to be like a perfect shuffling of a deck of cards: No two letters could have anything but a random connection. If any two letters did, we had to wait an hour, change crystals, and reshuffle the "deck."

Here, too, was an instance where we knew little about the device or its internal workings. We couldn't jerry-rig it if we wanted to. All we knew was that it was a bear to operate and that, ultimately, it was totally dependent upon, believe it or not, sunspots and sun storms. I doubt

Mr. Riley (ace of spies) ever had to contend with such
challenges.

Once the mechanics of coding were complete, we
spread a large wire array on the ground. It looked like
an overgrown spider's web. It was our VLF (very low fre-
quency)/VHA (very high amplitude) antenna: We referred
to it as the "black widow." Once our antenna was out
and hooked up to the transmitter, we hit the "send" button and our message went out into the wild blue yonder
to Tel Aviv, via, I guess, the sun.

ALL OK. PROCEEDING AS PLANNED.

Awkward Silence Belongs to All;
Awkward Speech Belongs to Its Author Alone

Talking in the absence of necessity can be viewed—and often is—
as a sign of weakness and insecurity. This is so because for most,
silence in the presence of another is uncomfortable. It is considered
a problem that requires a remedy. It is deemed an unnatural experience that speaks poorly of those in it. And since those individuals
who are uncomfortable with it extrapolate the other party's discomfort from their own, they attempt to relieve it. And so, in an attempt
to relieve the discomfort and tension or in an effort to cater to the
other person's concerns, the anxious party will speak.

It is a nervous reaction to an awkward situation. And, ironically,
instead of suggesting to the listener that you are being polite, it
broadcasts to the listener that you, the speaking party, place the listener's social comfort over your own sense of dignity. It sends the
message: I am here to serve you.

Do not fall into that trap.

If the situation is awkward and calls for small talk, let the other
side carry the burden. By allowing the other party to fill the silence,
you make that side responsible for your social comfort and, thus, by
extension, responsible for your satisfaction with other aspects of
their presence, for example, their business conduct.

It also forces the other side to either consider what it says or run the risk of the "minefield." Here, too, you gain the strategic upper hand. And remember: While you are talking, the other side is thinking. In a business setting, allowing the opposition to think while you are not is rarely a desirable thing. Therefore, let the other side talk while *you* think.

A final point. This rule does not nor is it intended to suggest that you ought to be silent to the point of rudeness, "coldness." Rather, it is to say that you can convey warmth with a smile instead of a sentence; that you can convey kinship with a nod rather than a recitation; and that, in a nutshell, talk is not chatter.

When I looked up from the black widow, it was to look straight into the eyes of an officer of the Saudi army. I didn't know how he had gotten there, how long he had been there, or what would happen next. All I knew was that I was covered in sand, crawling on my hands and knees in an attempt to spread a lot of wire over some very thin ground. I smiled.

For a few long moments neither one of us spoke. He looked at me and at the wires. He looked at the sand-covered Land Rover. He looked at the remnants of a flat tire, now laying like a dead black walrus on a beach. Then he looked back at the wire. He was waiting for us to speak.

We didn't.

He did.

"Shiografia?" he asked in a soft tone.

I half nodded, half brushed some hair out of my eye. I had no idea what Shiografia was. I did know that it sounded nothing like one of the words I had learned in my intensive Arabic courses. All the same, it sounded a damn sight better than "spy."

"Shiografia," he said again, now nodding vigorously. "Nashional Shiografia?"

Of course. Nashional Shiografia. Or *National Geographic*. Same difference. The point is, this fine specimen of a Saudi military man concluded on his very own that

we were *National Geographic* **magazine correspondents rather than the Zionist agents we were.**

I thanked God for giving me the strength to keep my mouth shut. Even I would have failed to come up with such an ingenious explanation.

The tall officer knelt down and helped us complete the layout of the black widow. I couldn't resist having him push the "send" button on our transmitter. He thought we were measuring some natural phenomenon. And considering whether the sunspot activity would allow our message through, in a way, he was right.

If You Have to Speak, Say Nothing

When you cannot avoid the obligation of small talk, you should talk but say nothing. How to do so—without sounding stupid, that is—is easier than you may otherwise think:

Use the "open" question.

The open question is the simplest form of question there is. It suggests no answer and passes no judgment. It is the question used by children to elicit information. And children use it for the same reason that you should: It neither assumes nor suggests prior knowledge or conceptions.

"Where do you live?" "What is your name?" "What are you doing?" are classic examples of the open question. Look as you may, you will find nothing about the questioner—or the answer—hidden in the question. It is simply a big, lazy vessel waiting to be filled up any which way one wants.

"Do you live in Rome?" "Is your name Angelo?" "Are you eating?" are the exact opposites of the questions illustrated above. These are closed questions. They do not invite a lengthy response. They suggest the answer. They can be answered with a simple yes or no, a shake of the head. Indeed, a closed question not only suggests a yes or no answer, it almost demands it.

It is your enemy. Do not use it. Be a child. Be inquisitive.

The beauty and elegance of an open question, in contrast to the closed one, is that it cannot be answered with a yes or a no. Some original thought must enter into the answer, even if it is only a miserly "none of your business." But even that answer imparts more information than you would be likely to get out of a closed question.

In asking an open question you allow the respondent to choose any appropriate (and on occasion inappropriate) response and to expand upon it to his or her heart's desire. By asking a closed question, in contrast, you define the parameters of the answer that you will accept and, by so doing, intuitively suggest to the respondent a brief, narrow answer.

The sharp distinction between the two categories of question are most easily recognized in the legal setting, in court. The open question is used in direct examination when the attorney examines her own witness. The closed question is used (and in most courts can only be used) in cross-examination (or against one's own "hostile" witness).

In direct examination, the attorney wants her client to tell her story as completely as possible. Therefore, she will use an open question. In cross-examination, in contrast, when that same lawyer seeks to trap the other side's witness into an answer to her liking, she will use the "closed" question because the closed question, in turn, evokes the "closed answer," the answer suggested by the cross-examiner's question. The cross-examiner "force-feeds" the answer to the respondent.

You are not a cross-examiner. And you hope never to be cross-examined.

An open question opens the floodgates of speech. It allows you to float on someone else's waters. Ask enough open questions and you can conduct a lengthy one-sided conversation that appears to be flowing in two directions. When mastered, you need never impart information again.

An open question will never let you down. When you prefer to have someone else carry the conversation, just let the open question offer them the opportunity to do so. The simple reason for the success of this technique is that people, most people, like to talk about themselves. Given the opportunity, most people, even hard-nosed businessmen—in fact, especially hard-nosed businessmen—will tell their life story to complete strangers. The fact is that given the opportunity, most individuals will talk about themselves for hours, never once noticing that the other party has uttered barely a word.

> **The officer quickly gave up on his attempts at English and we reverted to Arabic. Captain Ahmed Salah wanted to know where we were going.**
>
> **"To the desert," I answered helpfully. "Where are you from?" I asked.**
>
> **"*Aiwa*. My father was born here, his father was born here, and his father's father was born here. My father's father's father was born farther to the south but they came up here—all of them, my father's father's father's wife, his animals, *kooloo* [all of them], they all came up here. . . ."**
>
> **I learned much about Ahmed's genealogy and he learned nothing about me, although I doubt that he noticed or cared very much. We left Ahmed as we found him, a stupid, talkative, vain soldier. Ahmed's report, if he made one, would say only that he assisted two *National Geographic* correspondents carrying out important "measurements" in the desert.**

Stockpile Information

The key ingredient to the success of the silence system is to use the "open" question and to use it often. This is so because in addition to its other virtues, the open question, in the broad response it elicits, allows you to build a stockpile of information directly from the horse's mouth. By listening to the speaker's answers and comments, given in his own words, in his own mind-set, without benefit of the suggested answer to be found in a closed question, you will gain insight to and understanding of the speaker's motives and ambition.

A conversation about a favorite restaurant, for example, can teach you about the speaker's culinary preferences, his preferred social settings, financial sensitivity, habits, and other useful data. This information, in turn, will assist you in planning your next move, your next question, and, in many cases, your entire negotiating strategy.

The Neutrality Rule

If (and, inevitably, when) you are called upon to contribute something original to the conversation, do so by discussing the most neutral of all subjects in the most neutral of all tones. This is an art and should be practiced before tried. Your goal is to be able to discuss a city, restaurant, sports team, or other "inanimate and unemotional item" without the listener being able to determine your position on that item.

"Berlin is quite a city. Truly something. Of course, when it was divided, it was completely different."

Consider these sentences. Together, they are a prime example of the Neutrality Rule. You have spoken, you have "occupied airtime," but you have said nothing. Can the listener divine from your statement whether you like Berlin? Hate Berlin? Do not care about Berlin?

By employing the Neutrality Rule, you shall be able to carry on the fine art of talking without actually saying anything for hours on end. And this form of chatter *can* be extremely useful if and when employed properly.

The Neutrality Rule is not used to curry favor with someone. Rather, it is used to acquire information about that someone. After you have done so, it is up to you to determine how to use such information. In some cases you may indeed wish to adopt a harmonious position with the other party. In other instances, you may wish to adopt a contrarian pose. The important factor is that whatever position you ultimately adopt, you adopt with forethought and calculation—not by chance.

Before entering Iraq, I had to receive a business visa. But visas were notoriously hard to come by. The country was in the grips of its war with Iran and they weren't quite sure how inviting they should be to Western businessmen seeking to feed on Iraq's ravenous military demands. I

decided to try my luck in Rome where, word had it, the Iraqi envoy was quite fond of a stiff drink and a few extra lire.

Over a superb Chianti, his excellency and I shared Italian cuisine and the meaning of life. I encouraged Mr. Mahmoud to assume that this dinner was simply a prelude to the more intimate sharing of my substantial resources. After all, he held my key to Iraq, and I, a Western businessman, possessed of some preposterous notion of money to be made down there, wanted in.

Then, out of the blue:

"Jews, you see, Mr. Templer, Jews . . ."

"Jews, indeed," I responded, curious to see where he was going to go with this.

"Yes, yes. Jews. It is only, only for the Jews. Would you agree, Mr. Templer?"

"Please, please, your excellency, call me Alain."

"Alain. That is a Jewish name?"

"Well, hardly, I suppose. No more than others perhaps?" I was getting distinctly uneasy. But damn if I would show my hand before he revealed his. "Jews, however, sir. I would quite agree. Quite so."

"So, so, rightly so. Never do business without a Jew on your side. Do you have a Jew on your side, Mr. Alain?"

"Well, my dear friend, I have a lawyer, and I am told that all lawyers are Jews, so I suppose I do now, don't I?"

I looked deep into his eye, and for an awkward moment I had no sense of which direction this was going. If he was probing, I gave him nothing. If he was joking, I gave him one to laugh at. If he was Semitically possessed or obsessed or just an average Arab diplomat espousing the Arab League's party line, I surely gave him no offense. The awkward moment lasted one awkward moment longer. Then he laughed and I gladly joined in.

Never Volunteer Information

There are at least two positions on every issue. In most cases there are more. During courtship you want your positions to align perfectly with those of the object of your desire. Therefore, speak last. Otherwise, speak, but say nothing. Remember: The odds that the partner to your conversation will agree with you—even on something as mundane as the weather—is at best 50 percent and in all likelihood far less.

The greatest mistake a negotiator—indeed, anyone—can make is to "volunteer" information. That is to say, to tell your adversary or potential business partner something that he did not already know and that he did not specifically, and directly, ask for.

While this rule might seem obvious, this is without a doubt the most common and oft-repeated mistake made. Breach this rule and pay the price. And mark these words, there will always be a price.

Do not, when asked for your name, offer your address.

Do not, when asked your nationality, offer your place of residence.

Do not, when asked for your proposal, offer the rationale for your proposal.

Parse every question into its most narrow, singular query. And then answer that question and that question only.

Information is knowledge and knowledge is power. Knowledge is the most powerful weapon in your arsenal. Once delivered to your opponent, it becomes part of his arsenal, not yours.

Knowledge is not power when shared widely. In fact it is *only* because of the ignorant, those lacking knowledge, that knowledge itself is power.

Consider if you will the oft-cited example of the police officer asking the motorist if he knew how fast he was going. The only response to such question should be no. Yet many motorists will actually answer yes and proceed to recite some speed that is well over the speed limit.

My instructor, Ben, was still a rookie Combatant when he saw the operation of the rule on one who should

have known better. It was his third month in Egypt. An Egypt still under the iron rule of Gamal Abdel Nasser, the nationalist leader and Egypt's hero of the Suez campaign. Ben was sent to Egypt to establish himself as an "early warning system." Nothing particularly exciting or daring, as indeed it should be for a first assignment. Rather, he was simply to live in Cairo and be on the lookout for signals that the unusual was becoming routine; that the ordinary was becoming extraordinary.

It was Ben's job to look for all of the small signs of early mobilization for war, those signs that cannot be detected by satellite, electronic eavesdropping, or high-resolution photography: an unusual absence of men on the streets, a son called back from military leave, food staples disappearing from the grocery shelves. Small yet telling things.

Every two or three days Ben was also to walk by a residential villa in Heliopolis, once a garden suburb of Cairo now long devoured by Cairo's urban sprawl, to take note of any unusual activity outside of a particular villa and to report his observations to the Office. He did not then know that the villa was occupied by Israel's premier Combatant in Egypt, Mr. Wolfgang Lutz, and that he was being asked to be a second pair of eyes for Mr. Lutz.

Samson had become concerned that Mr. Lutz (who later become widely known as the "Spy on the Horse" because of his equestrian escapades with his good friend and confidante Colonel Nasser himself) was "losing it." In other words, Samson was concerned that Mr. Lutz had contracted Combatant's syndrome, a condition in which the Combatant—out of fatigue, arrogance, or a combination of both—drops his guard and essentially challenges those around him to catch him.

As Ben tells it, on one fateful day, albeit for Lutz not for Ben, while passing by his villa, Ben found himself in the midst of an Egyptian police raid. In moments, the villa and its entire surrounding area were swarmed upon by police circling the villa's compound, seemingly surrounding it to lay siege. Ben quickly left the site and got off a message to the Office. At the time, Ben had no idea that what he had just witnessed was what had to be and what must continue to be the most pathetic capture of a secret agent in spy history.

After Ben had left the villa, Mr. Lutz, its owner and resident, arrived home in his trademark Land Rover only to find his house surrounded by Egypt's paramilitary police. Unfortunately, instead of approaching one of the officers on the scene to innocently inquire what was going on, instead of just turning around and driving away, Mr. Lutz approached the highest-ranking officer on the scene and said: "Game's up. That's it. You caught me."

Lutz was promptly arrested, questioned, convicted, and sentenced to a long and lonely life sentence in an Egyptian prison. He was lucky to be alive. And but for Nasser's disbelief that his good friend and confidant could indeed have been a Mossad Combatant, Lutz would have flared. Instead, Nasser exiled his former friend to Germany, Lutz's fictional Mossad home.

Later, Ben and the rest of the world learned that the Egyptian police were merely responding to a burglar alarm in the Lutz household. No one—least of all the Egyptian counterintelligence organization, the Mukhabarat—would have suspected Lutz of being a Combatant. After all, as a married, philandering, high-profile man about town, Lutz certainly did not fit anyone's stereotype of a Combatant. Which, of course, is what made him the perfect Combatant.

The Rule of Inaccurate Precision

Learning to avoid the disclosure of "excess" information is a necessity. Learning to do so elegantly—without affording the appearance of evasiveness—is an art.

Answer only, and exactly, what was asked. Never, ever, more. And answer the question as *in*accurately as possible.

Consider this: Under the Rule of Inaccurate Precision, the answer to "What is your name?" is not "Joseph Ben Hannan" but "Joe."

The answer to "How old are you?" is not "forty" but "middle-aged."

The answer to "How long have you known him?" is not "ten years" but "a long time."

When asked how many people work for you, do not provide the number of your employees. That is *not* the question. In fact, consider: Is the number of your employees equal to the number of people who *work* for you? Of course not.

If you seek to impress, then the number of people "who *work* for you"—which is, after all, strictly speaking (and we are always strictly speaking) the question asked—include your outside lawyers, your accountants, your consultants, your wife, and anyone and everyone else who does something of any value to you at some point during the day, any day.

If you seek to diminish your organization's size, then the people who "*work* for you" do not include all of those slackers who may be on your payroll but in fact do little, if any, "work."

So note: When asked where you live, name the country, not the state; the state, not the region; the region, not the city; the city, not the neighborhood; the neighborhood, not the street; the street, not the number.

The *less* information revealed, the more flexible and creative your subsequent answers may be. The *more* information revealed, the more captured you are in a sticky web of facts.

The Rule of the Questioner's Quota

There is an allowable, socially tolerable amount of information that may be gleaned from an individual in any one setting without appearing to be prying into that person's privacy. Go beyond your quota and you will quickly fall from favor in the community's eyes. Go beyond your quota and the subtle dynamic of a relationship swings against you.

The beauty of the rule is that it works. Most often, that feared follow-up question, that question seeking to elicit more information, the information you cleverly withheld upon first inquiry, never comes.

The dreaded question never comes for a whole host of reasons, among which is the fact that people do not like to appear nosy. And if your questioner keeps coming back at you with follow-up questions for more and more details, make *him* look nosy and he will forget that *you* were obtuse.

Therefore, if you force your interrogator to ask a question for each tidbit of information that he or she wants (and needs), he will quickly use up his quota and will have to drop it or wait for another day. The more "answers" you volunteer, the greater his remaining quota and the easier his work.

The Rule of the Unasked Question

A close corollary to the previous rule against the offering of information is the Rule of the Unasked Question.

An unasked question is one that, like a mirage, exists only in the mind of the person hearing it. It is a question that *appears* to have been asked and, therefore, seems to require a response. The unasked-question phenomenon is itself quite harmless. It is the uncalled-for response to the unasked question that is damaging.

As a general observation, women are more likely to violate the rule than men. Therefore, women Combatants must take especial notice of the operation of the rule.

Out of a desire to please, to be chatty, or otherwise to be friendly, we sometimes "preanswer" questions. In other words, in your mind you have "heard" the next question. In fact, as most intelligent people do, you have simply guessed what the next question will be. And so to "save time" or otherwise show your interrogator how clever you are, you answer the unasked question.

Wrong move.

By answering an unasked question you have volunteered information that may have been unknown to the questioner and that the questioner might never have asked you had you not volunteered the information. By answering the unasked question you increase the questioner's quota, thus allowing him or her more freedom to continue to probe. And by answering an unasked question you have shifted the pendulum of the conversation's control from you to your questioner because it is now you who appears eager to please rather than vice versa.

So if asked your name, your name will suffice; don't follow up with "what your friends call you." If asked what you do, give your job title; do not follow up with your job description.

And if asked "your bottom line," provide it (if you wish) but do not add that a substantial portion of it came from the extraordinary sale of an asset. That information warrants a separate question. By forcing the questioner to ask each question you wear down both the questioner and the questioner's right to ask yet another question. You exhaust both process and substance.

Note the subtle yet significant difference between the operation of this rule and that of the Rule of Inaccurate Precision. Under the former, you simply follow the questioner's requests, no more no less; under the latter you actively subvert the questioner by tailoring your responses to be unresponsive.

Use both rules often and intermittently.

Fanning the Flames

THE HIDDEN COST OF ASSUMPTIONS

■ASSUME NOTHING

> *"Ve Natati Lekha . . . Et Kol Eretz Canaan."*
> *"Ve Moshe Shalach Otam LeRagel Et Eretz Canaan. . . ."*
> "And I Will Give unto Thee . . . All the Land of Canaan."
> "And Moses Sent Them to Spy Out the Land of Canaan. . . ."

Ve Natati Lekha . . . Here we have a peculiar story. God the Almighty promises Abraham and his progeny the Land of Canaan. Moses, Abraham's progeny, one to whom God has promised the Land of Canaan, one to whom God was revealed and one for whom God performed miracles, seems to want to "double-check," so to speak, God's promise. Moses sends spies into the Land of Canaan, as the Torah (the first five books of the Old Testament) says, in order to "[S]ee the land, what it is; and the people that dwelleth therein, whether they be strong or weak, few or many; . . . whether it be good or bad . . . ; whether it be fat or lean. . . ."

Why? Why does Moses spy on the land if he believes God's promise that the land shall be his and his people's? Does Moses doubt God's ability to deliver the Land of Canaan to the people of Israel? Does Moses doubt God's choice of the Land of Canaan as a worthy patrimony to the people of Israel? If not, what then is the Bible's message?

Assume nothing.

"The Sudan is sand. Hot dry sand. Arid. Barren. It has nothing. It produces nothing. It offers nothing. Gordon lost his head over it in more ways than one. . . . It is the land of the original ten plagues: locusts, pestilence, blood, first-born, you name it. There simply is no commercial cover we can think of that will justify your presence in the south. Our suggestion is to scrap Sudan. We suggest that you try and meet Garang in Europe."

I was being briefed by Neta, a senior analyst of Mossad's Mission Planning Division, also known internally by its code name: "Studio." It was Studio's mission to assist individual Combatants in planning their cover stories. Studio was supposed to be able to create its own plausible covers as well as objectively analyze and criticize Combatants' homegrown schemes. Studio was analyzing the prospects for my meeting with Colonel John Garang, the Sudanese rebel leader of the Sudan Patriotic Liberation Front, the SPLF.

Studio was not a big fan of my proposal for a clandestine meeting in the Sudan. Studio could see no way for me to get into Sudan, let alone hook up with Garang. Unfortunately, if Studio was right, that meant that there would be no way for Israel to try and enlist Garang in its effort to curb Libya's expansion into Sudan. And that, in turn, meant the destabilization of the entire Middle East.

The Sudanese government was flirting with Libya and Ghaddafi in the hope that it would assist it in its ongoing border war with Ethiopia and in order to bring political pressure on Egypt, with which it had a falling-out over the latter's peace treaty with Israel. So long as Garang did not make his objections to Ghaddafi's engagement in Sudan clear, the delusional government in Khartoum actually believed that Garang would not obstruct the government's efforts to pique Egypt and anger Ethiopia. The government apparently believed its own propaganda that its war with Garang was a "civil" war and that Garang, as a "son of the Sudan," would somehow rally around the very government with whom he had been in life-or-death combat for over two decades.

It was imperative that we persuade Garang of the seriousness of his government's intentions vis-à-vis Libya. It was equally important that we persuade Garang to send a loud-and-clear message that he would not stand for a Libyan invasion, however benign, of Sudan. Problem was, up until now, no one could get to Garang.

Given that Garang had not left the Sudan in twenty years, the thought that we should wait until he was in Europe was a bit like waiting for global warming to cook your goose.

The difficulty with challenging Studio's assumptions, however, was that these guys carried a lot of credibility. Moreover, they were not known to shy away from a challenge. After all, it was Studio that conceived of the kidnapping of the arch-Nazi Eichmann from Argentina, the theft of a spiffy new MiG-21 from Iraq, and the assassination of known terrorists in the comfort of their own homes (the terrorists' own homes, that is). In other words, if there was a will, Studio had the way.

But what if Studio didn't have the way? Should one assume that there was none? I could not. Getting to Garang was far too important a mission to abort for lack of cover. That would have been the true confusion of procedure for substance. It is the cover that serves the mission—not vice versa.

I persuaded Studio that given Sudan's civil war with its accompanying famine and overall human misery, simple bribery would see me safely in and out of the country.

Make No Assumptions

The greatest pitfall any executive faces is the one he does not know is there. And the reason the executive does not know of the pitfall's existence is his reliance upon someone else's incorrect assessment of the situation or his assumption that one of his directives had been fulfilled when it wasn't. When it's important, make no assumptions.

Can you assume that an important message will be relayed as you requested? No. Can you assume that others will complete a transaction as you planned it? No. Can you assume that your directions will be followed just as you carefully outlined them? No. Does this mean that you should do everything yourself? No.

If it is of primary importance, perform the task yourself. If it is of secondary importance, allow another to perform it but verify yourself that it has been performed before acting upon the assumption. If it is of tertiary importance, allow another to perform the task but act upon it with the knowledge that the task may well not have been done.

A task of primary importance is any task that if not correctly performed the first time will lead to consequences that cannot later be corrected. A task of secondary importance is a task that if not correctly performed the first time will lead to consequences that can later be corrected but only at great embarrassment, cost, and delay. A task of tertiary importance is a task that if not correctly performed will lead to consequences that can later be corrected at modest cost.

Federal Express built an entire business on selling itself as the answer to tasks of primary importance. But if it truly does have to be there overnight, that is, if failure to have it there overnight is not correctable, should you send it Federal Express? No. Fly it there yourself.

There are no hard-and-fast rules as to what are primary, secondary, or tertiary matters of importance. Each business and each episode stands alone. The point is to analyze each situation and classify it for yourself as one of the three categories. Then determine for yourself whether you should assume the veracity of matters relayed to you or performed by another party.

Examples of matters of primary importance to your business are: the scheduling of meetings with individuals upon whom you are dependent; the making of payments to individuals upon whom you are dependent; or the performance of tasks upon which others are depending.

Limit Your Assumptions

Everyone assumes something. We could not function if we did not. You assume that the sun rises in the east. You assume that thunder follows lightning. You assume that night follows day. And you are not likely to be harmed by your reliance on these assumptions, even though assumptions they are.

But what of assuming that a man loves his wife? That a child shall die before its parent? That a professional knows the right course of action? That an agreement shall be fulfilled?

Well, here, as the saying goes, proceed with caution. And the best way to do that is to limit the number of assumptions you make. We must, of course, embrace a whole panoply of assumptions if we are to set one foot before the other. We assume that phones work, that packaged food is sanitary, and that water is potable. Sometimes our reliance is well placed and other times it isn't. But if we did not assume these things, if we had to confirm, test, and verify each and every action that we take in reliance upon past experience, we would not be able to function as citizens of a civilized world.

We decide that given the alternative—a breakdown of civilization—and in light of our experience, the making of certain fundamental assumptions is a reasonable risk to assume. A fisherman must assume that the tide will come in just as it goes out. Of course, he could just wait each day to see that it actually was so, but then he would do no fishing. A navigator must assume that the sun, which has risen since time immemorial in the east, will tomorrow, in fact, rise in the east.

This approach is fine when the assumption is one that has proven itself since time immemorial and is based upon a substantial body of knowledge; knowledge that we have every reason to continue to regard as true.

But when the assumption is one for which you have no independently gained experience and when the consequences of a failed assumption are significant and costly, you should not substitute someone else's experience and knowledge for your own.

The Sudanese civil war has been ongoing between the government in Khartoum and Garang's SPLF for the past

twenty-some-odd years. It was a nasty affair, being in its essence a racial conflict disguised for the sake of "culture" as a religious war. While the north of the country was overwhelmingly Muslim, the south was "Christian"; which is to say that the southerners held African spiritual traditions that had been adapted to Christianity in order to placate the missionaries of the time.

But the north was also "Arab," that is to say Semitic, whereas the south was African, that is to say Negroid, and therein was the true casus belli.

At the time, Colonel John Garang, the determined tribal warlord who had been driving, guiding, and sustaining the insurrection for all those years, was in control of Juba, a city in Sudan's deep south. "City" is somewhat of a charitable word for Juba. It was more like a large mud pie with tattered huts around it. Of the several brick buildings in town, only a few were left standing. And those were works of architectural wonder: They held more shrapnel than cement.

Garang, a decent fellow by rebel warlord standards, certainly, was always willing to turn a blind eye to strange happenings in his neighborhood provided the price was right. And seeing as the price was always set by Garang, the price was always right. One could hardly fault Garang for his extracurricular dealings because the whole world had turned a blind eye and deaf ear to the plight of the southern Sudanese, his constituents, for decades. The truth of the matter was that he held his ragtag troops together by whatever funds he could get and by the sheer force of his personality. As far as I was concerned, the man was entitled to a great deal of credit.

The only way to penetrate Sudan's south was with the Red Cross. With some pull, push, and fifty-five thousand dollars in a "donation" I purchased safe passage to Juba, the important provincial capital of Eastern Equitoria Province and the first point on the Bahr al-Jabal river (otherwise known as the White Nile), on a Red Cross

flight out of Zurich—no documents required. How I
would make contact with Garang I did not yet know. I
just assumed that in Juba, somehow, somewhere, I would
find a way to him. After all, if journalists could find him,
how hard could it be?

Gutenberg provided me with a passport in the name
of one Art Deco. I laughed out loud when I got it because
I was sure it had to be some bad joke. But much to my
surprise, if it was a joke, Gutenberg didn't get it. The
document already had a Sudan entry visa affixed to it,
and all of the necessary internal Sudanese travel documents were made out to Art Deco. My protestations fell
on deaf ears. I was apparently going to be Mr. Art Deco.

At Samson's direction, I was to use the Gutenberg
documents, passport included, only "if I had to," which
meant that I could show them at my wake. Samson's
reluctance to have me use the documents meant that they
were most likely "paper cover": documents Gutenberg
would have printed at home, on-site. These were mere
fiction, creatures of Gutenberg's own printing presses.
The documents themselves would have no substance, no
backup, and no reality other than the paper they were
printed on. Any routine police inquiry would suffice to
expose them as forgeries or at least raise questions about
them and their bearer. Combatants called them "Stretch-
ers" because if you were caught with one, your neck
would be lengthened by the hangman's noose.

The Red Cross had its own terminal where its char-
tered planes left for every one of earth's disaster zones;
one thousand points of blight. You had to hand it to these
guys; after all, they were Swiss, they could have been
bankers, for chrissake. Before boarding, Phillipe, my
Red Cross contact, told me that the government's troops
had retaken Juba, our destination, the night before.

Juba's change of hands complicated matters. First, I
would now have to find a way to cross the warring fac-
tions' front lines in order to go from government-con-

trolled Juba to the surrounding rebel territory. Second, landing in government-controlled Juba meant that I would have to enter through official government border controls with my rinky-dink Art Deco passport. I was worried about using paper cover to enter hostile territory, but then, a good Combatant is always worried: A calm Combatant is a dead Combatant.

We would be flying in on an old Boeing 707 that the Red Cross converted into a sort of flying hospital. Since most of the available space was occupied by medical equipment, the Red Cross team and I, a total of twelve men and three women, had to crowd into a small area near the cockpit.

At late afternoon we arrived in Juba. We were just in time for a heavy artillery pounding of the city by government forces. During our flight, the rebels apparently retook Juba. Our plane circled the makeshift runway waiting for ground control, if anybody was in control, to give us the green light to land. From the plane we could see black puffs of artillery smoke. The government would certainly not be pleased that the Red Cross was landing its hospital ship in rebel hands. So I assumed that they would continue pounding the airport until we ran out of fuel and crashed. I went to talk to the pilot.

"You've got to put this plane down," I said to the two young pilots.

They looked at me in bewilderment. I knew what they were thinking: Who the hell are you?

"You've got to land the plane. The government won't stop its artillery because they don't want you to land in rebel territory. How much fuel do you have?"

"We have enough to get us to Nairobi," said the pilot.

"Yea, but we're not going to Nairobi. We're landing here, now."

Some of the other Red Cross guys came into the cockpit to see what was going on. Once they understood my point the fight began in earnest. Most of the Red Cross team were on my side; they were willing to take the risk and get the plane into Juba. But the pilots and three Red Cross team members were not. They wanted to fly on to Nairobi in order to attempt to coordinate a different landing site with the Sudanese authorities several days hence.

I was getting nowhere.

I went to the back of the plane and came back with my backpack.

"Okay. No more bullshit, you assholes. Do you understand? I'm with Colonel Garang. I am the fucking SPLF. Unless you land this plane here and now, I've got enough explosives in my bag to blow you fuckers all the way to Nairobi. Understood?"

The Red Cross team scattered to the back of the plane. I held the bag's drawstring in my hand over the copilot's head. The pilot looked at me and calculated his odds of my pulling the string versus those of getting hit by artillery. He banked the plane to the right and came down low for a landing.

The artillery was close and a few rounds had hit the field, which made for a bumpy ride, but the plane landed without incident. Rebel troops ran up to the front of the plane as soon as it landed. Holding the bag in my left hand, I pulled the emergency door on the aircraft. It opened easily, and the heat of Africa steamed into the plane. The rebels had pushed a stair ramp to the exit. While the others were still digesting what they'd been through, I grabbed my stuff and went down the stairs. Ignoring the rebel troops who in fear of the incoming rounds had left the ramp at the exit and run back to the relative safety of the terminal sandbags, I walked straight to the rickety terminal and out to the street. This was rebel country, and my law was as good as anyone else's.

I quickly found my way to the local "pub," a dank, smelly hut where rebel soldiers and children, toting Kalashnikov semiautomatic machine guns, were drinking, shooting the breeze, and shooting at the occasional bird stupid enough to try and grab the seeds from the dirt floor. They all turned to me when I walked in as if waiting for an explanation.

"I'm looking for Colonel John Garang," I said with as much baritone in my voice as I could muster.

The rebels didn't stir. It was almost as though they were saying "wrong answer."

"I am looking for Colonel Garang. I have brought him money and weapons." Money and weapons are words that resonate in Africa, and it is virtually always the white man who utters them. So my words carried some credibility.

I was hustled into a Jeep by an armed rebel soldier. We drove off into the bush, and after twenty minutes or so the soldier next to me pulled the bandanna off from around his neck and very carefully tied it around my eyes. There was no point in even trying to guess which direction we were going in.

Several hours later, deep in mountainous terrain, with Mount Kinyeti, Sudan's highest mountain, clearly visible to the south, we stopped. It was ironic that of all the places in Sudan that I could have been taken to, I was brought to the one place where the topography was so distinct that I knew exactly where I was. We had stopped in the Immatong Mountain range on the Ugandan border.

Several minutes later, Colonel Garang himself appeared driving his own Range Rover. He was a warm and likable man. He showed none of the signs of wear one might have expected from waging a civil war for so many years against such formidable odds. I got right to the point.

"I am from Israel's Mossad, Colonel. We have information that Sudan's government intends to invite the Libyans into the country. That action, as bad as it is for us, would be a disaster for your cause. With Libyan

money, the Libyan air force, and Libyan so-called 'volunteers' assisting the government with its troubles in the
north, the government will be free to turn its efforts to
you, here in the south. We want you to send the government a message. We want you to make them understand
that if they bring Ghaddafi into the north, you will
expand your war into the north. We want you to let the
government know that you can hit them in the north just
as hard and as effectively as you hit them in the south."

"What do you suggest?" Garang asked. The man had
not survived all these years by acting precipitously.

"A bomb, Colonel. A bomb at Ar-Rusayris Dam. You
make it, I'll deliver it, you claim responsibility."

Garang looked amused. I sort of hoped that my offer
would grab his attention. Ar-Rusayris Dam was one of
Sudan's four principal dams on the Nile. It was way out
of Garang's domain. After all, Garang had not taken his
war to the north because of Christian charity but because
he couldn't. He did not have the capacity or capability to
threaten anyone north of Wau, and even Wau was
stretching his lines to their snapping point. Garang's
poorly equipped and educated men wouldn't survive
north of the Junglei Canal. With their dark skin and
their tribal and ethnic features, they could not blend in
with the more Semitic, Arab North. They were also not
sophisticated enough to talk their way into a military
target. So the opportunity to get a bomb to Ar-Rusayris
was not something that Garang was likely to pass up.

The SPLF equipped me with the sorriest-looking
explosive device I ever did see and my own Land Rover,
which was no doubt stolen from the Red Cross, given
that the vehicle still had the Red Cross emblems painted
on its doors. They also provided me with food, water,
beer, and jerry cans of diesel fuel. The SPLF would
accompany me and see me through to the outskirts of
Malakal, the one-time capital of Sudan slavery, which
was a good thing because traversing the Sudd was not

something that I relished doing on my own. The Sudd was that great swampland north of Juba and east of Wau. It posed a serious obstacle not only as swampland but because its papyrus islands had a nasty habit of shifting on you just as you thought that you had your path all figured out.

When I reached Malakal and the Sobat River, I was on my own. In Malakal, I found a "hotel," so to speak, and crashed. I slept for over a day. It was my first shower in over a week. I left my Jeep at Malakal and got on the Nile steamer to Kusti. There was no point in trying to traverse this difficult terrain on my own. Also, I had already decided that rather than go after Ar-Rusayris, I would deposit the payload at the Sannar Dam, a less important dam north of Ar-Rusayris and more important, closer, by far, to Kusti.

It would have been foolhardy for me to go after Ar-Rusayris. I had no reason to trust Garang's forces, and for all I knew, one of them was warning the Sudanese garrison at Ar-Rusayris right now. Second, Sannar was literally a stone's throw from Kusti, and from Kusti I had a much easier shot to Khartoum and the airport. Finally, and equally important, for Garang's purposes a bomb at Sannar was just as impressive as a bomb at Ar-Rusayris.

I hot-wired a local vehicle and made my way to Sannar. As I approached Sannar, I was stopped at several military barricades. I had my cigarettes prepared for handouts and my explanation—that I was an important person from "Anglia" who must see the dam—all ready. Anglia still carried more of a cachet than any other country in postcolonial Sudan, the home of the British-humbling Mehdi. When the dam was in plain view, I got out of the car with the device in one hand and my camera in the other and approached the last roadblock.

The soldiers at the roadblock were clearly befuddled. No European had ever come to Sannar before, certainly not unaccompanied. They stopped me and asked who I was and what I wanted. First things first. I pulled out two packs of cigarettes and gave one pack to each of them.

"Ana doctor. Ana doctor el maya. Tifham?" (I am a doctor of water, do you understand?)

The men moved aside and let me through. Clearly, I was there to cure the water of whatever ailment it had. I continued undisturbed to the edge of the dam. I decided against placing the device in the water because I had to assume its fuse would not survive the water. I also did not want to do any more damage than was necessary. So I walked back a bit to one of the guard towers. I climbed the ladder into the empty tower. I left the bag in a cozy nook inside the tower. I tripped the timer. If Garang's men were halfway competent, the tower would soon be history. The only remaining task would be to get out of the country quickly.

The explosive didn't go off until three days later, but it did go off. The tower came down and Garang's message to the Islamic regime was delivered loud and clear: "Bring in Libya and the next bomb will be in Khartoum."

Assume nothing.

SEALs, Spies, and Surf

OUT-OF-THE-BOX THINKING

OUT OF THE BOX

> "*Ve HaMetim Asher Hemit BeMoto Rabim MeAsher Hemit BeHayav.*"
>
> "So the Dead Which He Slew at His Death Were More Than They Which He Slew in His Life."

Ve HaMetim . . . Conventional wisdom has it that the story of Samson is a story of great courage: a story of one man's willingness to sacrifice his own life for the good of his people. And that it is. But the story of Samson is more profound than that. The story of Samson is about unconventional thinking. It is about one man's ability to devise a unique, unpredictable solution to a serious problem. It is about creativity.

Anyone can fight in life; Samson fought in death.

Samson is blind and bound. He is a captive of the Philistines. He is apparently helpless. Tied as he is to the coliseum's columns, it would appear that Samson cannot harm himself, let alone others. And, conventionally speaking, that view is correct.

Unconventionally and, therefore, unexpectedly, Samson pushes the columns apart and causes the collapse of the coliseum, the destruction of thousands of Philistines, and his own demise.

Before Samson, the destruction of others through the destruction of self is unknown. After Samson, it is unforgettable.

Think outside the box. Or lose the box.

We had all the pieces of the puzzle. What none of us had was a way to fit them together. In a way it reminded me of the psychological testing I underwent as a Combatant candidate. The Mossad's psychiatrist presented me with a twelve-piece puzzle that, when fully assembled, comprised a perfect square. Before leaving the room, the doctor explained that I had ten seconds to study the puzzle and sixty seconds within which to assemble it.

I studied the puzzle during the brief time allotted and then, in just a few seconds, I assembled the square. Problem was, I had used only eleven of the puzzle's twelve pieces. And for the life of me, I couldn't figure out where the twelfth piece was supposed to go.

Time was running out and I did not want to fail. I put the twelfth piece of the puzzle in my mouth and swallowed it.

The psychiatrist returned to the room. He slowly walked around the table, looking all the while at the puzzle. He had that "what's wrong with this picture?" look upon his face. He stopped behind me. Reaching over my shoulder to touch the puzzle, he counted the pieces in a puzzled mumble:

"Eight, hmm . . . nine, what?, ten, eleven . . . But you are missing one piece. No? Six, seven, eight . . . How is this . . . ? Where is the other piece? You are missing one piece!"

"No I'm not."

"Yes, yes, you are. You are missing one piece. This puzzle has twelve pieces. Here you have only eleven. One is gone. Where is it?" The doctor, now quite agitated, moved the puzzle aside, seeking the missing piece under it. He also looked under the table and on my chair. He was exasperated. I doubt this had ever happened before.

"With all due respect, Doctor, there was no other piece. This is it. This is your puzzle."

Several days later, I received the phone call accepting me into the Combatants' training program. I never found out if I was selected because of—or in spite of—the puzzle incident.

Perhaps that's what I had to do now. Perhaps I had to toss away a piece of this puzzle in order to solve it.

Creativity

The ability to produce original ideas, the knack to do what others do not and the insight to conceive what immediately after conception will seem to have always been there. That is creativity. It cannot be taught and it cannot be bought. It is as much a given as the color of one's eyes. It is as tangible as strength, agility, or intelligence. It is as much a factor in human interaction as are money, power, and knowledge. The power of a creative mind should never be ignored. And a creative mind should always be on your side.

When Samson took down the Philistines in Gaza, he was able to do so because of his ability to see the plan for his destruction as a blueprint for the destruction of the planners themselves. It was a creative solution to an apparently insoluble problem.

How do you assure that your arsenal contains creativity? You cultivate it. You encourage those who have it to use it. You allow the creative team member to think differently and, if necessary, to be different. You do not force the square peg into the round hole. You do not scorn creativity. You do not ridicule it. You do not stifle it. You embrace it, encourage it, and invite it into your home. You allow that every problem can have more than one solution and that the best solution is often not the most obvious one.

Encouraging creativity requires that you first recognize your own limitations. If you are born with brown eyes you will die with brown eyes. Accept it. But learn to accommodate it. In other words, if you are short, don't try to grow—get a ladder.

The best quality a noncreative mind can have is openness, a willingness to hear and consider other people's ideas. An open mind will listen to a creative proposal without interruption and without dismissing it out of hand. An open mind can embrace the creative one. When it does so, the open mind becomes a creative mind. And by so doing, it adds a positive element of success to its arsenal.

You must keep an open mind.

There were thousands of Jews dying in concentration camps. There were tens of thousands more awaiting death in remote provincial villages. Yet this was 1980, not 1940. How could this be? Where was the world? Where was Israel? Where, oh, where was Mossad?

We were in a Tel Aviv hotel room trying our best to assemble the puzzle.

The "Falasha," the Jews of Ethiopia, had been targeted for death by the Ethiopian Marxist dictator Mariam Mengistu. Those lucky few who managed to escape from their remote mountain villages to the Red Cross refugee camp in Sudan were quickly cordoned off into a modern-day concentration camp where they were denied both food and medical care.

An overt relief effort would be useless because both Ethiopia and Sudan were in an undeclared state of war with Israel and the West. A covert relief effort would be impossible because it would take a small army to free the Falasha. Yet Combatants rarely, if ever, worked in numbers exceeding the digits of one hand.

Discarding Limitations

The challenge in solving a difficult problem is finding the way over and around the obstacles that cause the problem to appear intractable in the first place. One facet of the creative mind is the ability to do so. How does it do so? By ignoring the obstacles, by discarding limitations. The creative mind will ask: "How would I approach this problem if, in a sense, it were not a problem? What path would I take if there were no obstacles?"

By ignoring the obstacles at the early stage, one often finds that the obstacles previously considered are in fact not on the *best* path toward the goal anyway.

Your company has an excellent product. You do not, however, have any distribution for it. You have adequate funds to develop your company and your product, but without an ongoing stream of revenue you will not be able to sustain your company for long. Your competitor has an inferior product but his distribution is nonpareil. The competitor's distributors will not distribute your product for fear of losing his product. Their fear may or may not be grounded in fact. For all practical purposes, it does not matter. All that presently matters is that you cannot now distribute your product. Moreover, given that you have no product sales and consequently no revenue, building a new distribution network for only your product will cost your company more than it can bear.

To the uninitiated, it would seem that you are trapped in a "lose-lose" situation: good product, no distribution. No distribution, no ability to sustain company growth. No company growth, no more products. No more products, no distribution.

Scrap the paradigm. Ignore the obstacles. Create your own rules.

Buy your competitor. Continue to sell its products while phasing in your products. Then once your product has captured the market, position your product in a different segment of the market than that of your competitors: a Cadillac and a Chevrolet, if you will. Now you have two products in two markets and distribution for both.

Find the solution, then redefine the problem.

Refuse to Surrender

One little recognized element of creativity is obstinacy—refusing to give up. The insistence upon finding a solution to an intractable problem will force you into more and more creative ways of examining the problem. And as you do so, you will stumble upon more and different ways to solve the problem.

When a major hospital IV pump and medical solution provider sought to increase sales to an already saturated hospital industry, and when the old and tired method of marketing a "new and improved" version of its hardware failed, the provider stopped selling its hardware altogether. Instead, in a novel twist to an old market, it began to "lease" its new and improved hardware to the hospitals in exchange for each hospital's commitment to purchase a fixed monthly amount of its solution.

In discarding its traditional method of doing business, in refusing to give up on its scheme to place thousands of new hardware units in hospitals, and in accepting that there is more than one way to arrive at the same bottom line, the manufacturer transformed itself into its own banker. In so doing, it expanded its product placement far beyond its hoped-for business model while tying its new and old customers up in long-term supply contracts.

In refusing to surrender it won.

"As I see it, the facts have no bearing on reality."

Davie, a veteran who had somehow maintained his zeal for undercover work over a long career, offered his analysis. This would be interesting. Davie's thoughts always were.

"It doesn't matter what the objective conditions for this operation are because given those conditions there just is no way to pull off this kind of operation. So, I figure that we have to create a different reality. First, we'll need Combatants, a lot of them. Without them there is no way to carry out a massive jailbreak. Second, we'll need trucks, because we'll have to move these folks from wherever they are to somewhere else. Third, we'll need boats, because once we free the Falasha, we'll have to get them to Israel. Sudan, Ethiopia, and Israel are all on the Red Sea, so once we get them on a boat, they're as good as saved. Fourth, we'll need a place to land these boats or at least a place to get the Falasha from the shore to the boats, so we'll need a seaside base of operations. Therefore, it seems to me, ladies and gents, that we now all know the answer: We

must create a fully equipped base of operations capable of providing both ground and sea logistical support. And the base must be on the Red Sea coast. What we need, my friends, is a fishing village."

Davie's idea was an essential first step. He shifted our focus from the problems confronting us to the solutions we were seeking. Of course, in typical Davie fashion, a fisherman's village was way "over the top." It was quite unlikely that out of the blue a horde of foreigners would simply descend on Sudan and establish a fishermen's village. But it was also quite unlikely that we would be capable of preventing a second Jewish Holocaust unless we embraced the approach Davie described.

As fate would have it, several weeks later, through a completely fortuitous turn of events, the details of which must still remain secret, we would find the perfect key to the impenetrable lock. A key far more outrageous and unbelievable than even Davie considered: a divers' village, an ersatz "Club Med," managed and operated by Israeli spies and Israeli SEALs (frogmen). A true mirage in the Red Sea Hills of Sudan: Club Med by day, Club Dead by night.

Over the course of five long years, we, Mossad Combatants, men and women, supported by the elite of Israel's armed forces, its Navy SEALs, ran a full-fledged divers' recreational village in Sudan. We did so in full view of the militant Islamic Sudanese authorities who frequently provided us with assistance and support without recognizing the true import of their actions. We did so under the nose of our guests. Guests who at times included Carlos, the infamous international terrorist, Muammer Ghaddafi, and other luminaries of the Middle Eastern underworld. And in so doing, we rescued tens of thousands of Jewish refugees from the hellhole of their Sudanese captivity and brought them to the safety of a new home, the state of Israel.

We were so far outside the box we couldn't even see it.

PART 2

PREPARATION

To Kill or Not to Kill

THE ELEMENTS OF A WINNING TEAM

■ THE WINNING TEAM

> *"VaYa'asof David Et Kol Ha'Am VaYelech Rabata VaYelachem Ba VaYelkeda."*
> "David Gathered All of the People, Went to Rabbah, Fought Against It, and Took It."

VaYa'asof David . . . The city of Rabbah is the last of King David's military conquests. It is therefore significant that the Book of Chronicles makes specific mention of the fact that David gathered *all* of the people *together* in order to attack it.

David, of course, was a mighty warrior. Moreover, Yoav, his chief of staff, was already encamped outside the city and could have easily conquered it. Why then does David gather *all* of the people *together* before attacking?

Precisely because he does not need to do so. By assembling a team where one is not necessary, on the eve of his last military conquest, David leaves a legacy for his people: strength in numbers, victory in cooperation.

The "object" was hurrying out the door and into a car. He would be gone in minutes. I had no way of knowing whether he had a backup entourage. I made a quick

decision: Instead of keeping our numbers to a minimum as one usually would during a "tail," we would tail him en masse.

Strength in numbers.

Strength in Numbers

In business as in war, there is strength in numbers. In war, numbers play an obvious advantage. Better to have reinforcements than not. Better to strike awe in your enemy than not. Better to have flanking ability than not. Better to inspire confidence in each one of your warriors through the presence of a brother warrior.

So too in business. The presence of numerous professionals on one side, preferably your side, delivers a compelling message of superiority to the other side. First, it demonstrates unequivocally that you take this matter seriously. Assembling a team (rather than one or two professionals) requires time, effort, and resources. You do so not out of choice but out of an understanding that it may be wise and necessary to do so. You do so when one takes the matter with gravity and when you want the other side to know that.

Second, assembling a team demonstrates a resolve to prevail and to spare no expense or effort to prevail. True, you may reasonably assume that the other side knows of your desire to achieve your goal. But knowledge of your desire is not enough. You wish to impart to the other side the *depth* of your desire to achieve your goal. One way to do so is to assemble a team—a large team—perhaps completely out of proportion to what is required for the performance of the task at hand in order to simply obtain the right to perform the task at hand.

So did King David at Rabbah. And so should you.

The object, nom de guerre Fatwa, was a tall, dark-skinned man of about sixty years. He was an ordnance specialist, a graduate of the PLO's Lebanese "School of Mayhem" in the Shouf Mountains. (The school, which was described in incredibly accurate detail in Le Carré's *The Little Drummer Girl,* does exist and does train the

international outcasts of the world. The Japanese Red
Army, the Italian Red Brigades, the IRA, the German
Baader-Meinhof Gang, all at one point or another had
representatives training and being trained at this infamous school of lower education.) Fatwa was so called
because of his eagerness to carry out the edicts (a
"Fatwa," in Arabic) of ayatollahs and such. Fatwa's own
nationality was unknown and, frankly, irrelevant. What
was relevant was that he was currently in the employ of
radical Algerian Islamists.

Fatwa was a member in good standing of the Armed
Islamic Group (the GIA), the more radical of two radical
Islamic groups who were on the threshold of an all-out
campaign of terror to oust the country's military regime.
To the GIA, westerners who worked in Algeria were per-
force in cahoots with the regime and, as such, fair game.
But, then again, to the GIA, anyone was fair game.

I had recently opened an office in Algeria for one of
the Office's fake companies, "Chemonica." The point of
the exercise was to provide my fellow Combatants with
as real a business presence as was possible under the
circumstances in Algeria's capital, Algiers. Chemonica
was tangentially related to Algeria's liquid natural gas
industry. This provided our Combatants with relatively
unfettered access within the country and to the country's
primary strategic asset.

Although the Office had no Algerian work in
progress— that is to say, there was no ongoing or
impending Algerian operation—the Office planned for
the long term: One never knew when a Combatant's presence in Algeria could be useful.

Our presence in Geneva was warranted by the fact
that Chemonica had a Geneva office. That presence,
however, made Chemonica a legitimate, indeed a prized,
GIA target.

Ironically, in this instance we were a target for simply
being westerners. Had the GIA known that we were not

westerners in the true sense but rather their Middle Eastern "cousins," they would have, no doubt, bumped Chemonica up to the top of their international "hit" parade.

Samson had received word from Siren, the semi-autonomous Mossad agency that tracks the movement of any and all unsavory characters worldwide, that Fatwa had arrived in Geneva the night before last. Since Samson knew that we had incorporated Chemonica in Switzerland and that Chemonica's registered offices were in Geneva, she immediately alerted us to Fatwa's travel to Geneva.

Fatwa's presence in Geneva, the city in which Chemonica had its office, might have been just a coincidence. But then again, it might not have. Samson's approach was, why risk it?

As Chemonica was my creation, Samson wanted me to run the check on Fatwa. As a general rule, I would never have intervened in the goings and comings of Fatwa or anyone like Fatwa in a European city. My current mandate extended to "target" countries, that is, countries in a declared state of war with Israel, not beyond. As a matter of mandate, Geneva was outer space and Fatwa was the man on the moon.

This case, however, was not one for the "general rule": My business offices were in Geneva. In Geneva, my colleagues and I were model citizens. If I had a bomb blow up on my office doorstep, someone might take a closer look at Chemonica, a liquid natural gas broker with nary a client in the world. A pesky journalist, an inquiring police officer, a sordid politician, all likely to be drawn to me by an unwelcome bomb and all of whom would be unwelcome intrusions into my world.

So I had to make sure that Fatwa was not interested in Chemonica. And if that was indeed so, why, then, Chemonica would not be interested in him. But since tracking was not my bailiwick, I brought in "Flat Feet," the Office's expert team of "followers."

Flat Feet team members are trained in little else but following "objects" from one point to another. To Flat Feet, there were no identities, no names, no nationalities. Everyone was an object and objects were fungible; nothing was personal. Flat Feet's mandate was simple: follow and report. It was the ultimate "shadow" job; Flat Feet was not supposed to influence an object's actions. If it did, if the object did something it would not have done unless it had sensed a tail, then Flat Feet had failed.

On the rare occasion, in the face of certain, irreversible harm, Flat Feet was authorized to step out of the shadows and "intervene": either kidnap or assassinate an object.

Flat Feet's action in such cases was frowned upon. The Office had a hearty distaste for unnecessary violence. In its books, a spy who left "litter" (traces) was no spy at all, and a dead body was the worst kind of litter one could leave. And, finally, if violence was somehow called for, the Office wanted it to be a decision properly made with due consideration—not one made under duress or on the spur of the moment. All the same, reality occasionally interfered with the Office's theories and Flat Feet did leave its share of "litter" around the globe.

I had Flat Feet tail Fatwa from the airport to his downtown hotel, where for the past twenty-four hours he had not left his room. By my estimation, if Fatwa was going to do anything naughty in Geneva, we were now in the "naughty zone." Twenty-four hours in the hotel would have been ample time for him to assemble whatever required assembling and for him to contact whoever should have been contacted. His next move, I guessed, would be a significant one.

The Benefits of a Team

Before assembling a team and before committing to a team, you should ask what benefit is to be had from a team. If you cannot accurately identify and articulate the benefit to be had from sending a team to perform a task that one individual might possibly perform, there is no benefit in having a team.

Each challenge is different, and in each case you should analyze the value of a team in that specific context. Some general rules, however always hold true:

- *A team provides morale to the individual team members, and strong morale can be the difference between success and failure.*

  When you alone or anyone on your behalf is facing a phalanx of attorneys, salespeople, or corporate executives, it is difficult to maintain an upbeat confidence even when you hold more cards than the other side. When you are with a team, whether or not the team has immediate relevance to your task, you are more likely to feel confident and therefore to be confident and positive in your ability to succeed. This mental advantage is likely to translate to real advantage in the negotiations ahead.

- *A team allows you the ability to recover from a minor mishap that could otherwise lead to defeat.*

  In business negotiations and in other business practices, it is difficult to never miss a beat, commit a mental error, bobble a pass, if you will. When you are alone, even if you are perfectly matched with the other side and even if your individual performance is at 99 percent efficacy, one mistake or momentary inattentiveness can lead to failure. With a team, one of your team members can help you recover from the mistake, settle the ball, and get to the goal line.

- *A team allows you to assume a persona, which is useful to obtain what you want but which might otherwise be impossible for you to assume.*

  In a sales meeting, you may want to be a cheerleader to your sales force. But you also have to convey a stern, skeptical message to your sales force. One that will not mix with the upbeat message you ultimately wish to convey. Although in theory there is nothing to preclude you from being first the good cop and later the bad cop, in practice such personality shifts rarely work and more often than not result in a confused audience. A team allows you to choose the role you wish to play while assigning the other roles to your team members.

Following, or "tailing," an object was never my cup of tea. Tailing requires patience, deliberation, slow and precise moves, none of which were my strong suits. Fortunately, I was not required to do the legwork myself. Flat Feet would cover all of Fatwa's movements. And the larger the team and the more specifically tasked it was, the less likely Fatwa was to detect the tail.

Use Your Numbers

The proverbial hordes of lawyers, bankers, accountants, and other so-called essential deal makers entering a room to do battle is a common business phenomenon. It is also quite a useless one. Useless, that is, unless each and every one of those professionals is specifically "tasked"—that is to say, assigned a role for which that individual is not only qualified but, indeed, uniquely qualified. Otherwise, you have accomplished nothing but increased overhead and reduced efficiency while gaining none of the value of having a numerous team.

Numbers alone—sheer mass—have never guaranteed superiority. Nor is there any reason to believe that they ever will. Numbers, however, employed with purpose and mission will defeat a less numerous opponent every time. The Nazi German war machine could cut through the best armies of Europe in battle after battle because it was both larger and better disciplined than its opponents. Discipline in the German sense of the word was more than obedience; it was a task. Indeed the word *discipline* itself has become synonymous with profession, avocation, one who is "tasked."

The American troops in Vietnam were numerous but undisciplined, as were the Russian troops in Afghanistan. The Americans in the Gulf War, in contrast, were a model of "tasked masses." The Gulf Alliance soldiers, led by the Americans, were mostly all volunteers and far outnumbered the Iraqi enemy. But more important than that, they were tasked. They each had a purpose. They did not stand—as did their historical predecessors—idly by during battle.

The shepherd David defeated Goliath and the Philistines because the Philistines, while numerous, indeed far more numerous than David and the Israelites, just stood there. Instead of pushing their quantitative advantage over the Israelites—an advantage to which the Israelites had no response—the Philistines foolishly gambled on a qualitative advantage—that of Goliath over David. But with strength in numbers, the Philistines should have battled the Israelites by pitting their sheer force against that of the Israelites rather than battle them on a contest of individual warrior skills.

In business the lessons are no different. If your employees are not individually tasked, chances are that no one is doing that which you think he is. If you have more than one person assigned to a task, then, in fact, you have assigned no one to that task. Individual assignment is the prerequisite to individual responsibility. And individual responsibility is the essential ingredient to team performance.

While teamwork is a much ballyhooed cliché, and team effort, team spirit, and winning team can be found emblazoned upon T-shirts and inspirational posters from the Halls of Montezuma to the Corridors of Monsanto, in the final analysis a team is a gathering of individuals. If each individual has a specific assignment, knows his assignment, can perform his assignment, and can, if and when necessary and only if and when necessary, fill in and support a fellow team member, then one has a winning team.

For a surefire prescription for failure look to those companies where more than one individual shares a title, a role, or a field of influence. Does a company need a copresidency? Does a company need a cochairman? Did Disney need Michael Eisner and Michael Ovitz? Did Disney or its shareholders receive any benefit from Ovitz's term at Disney? Did they receive ninety million dollars' worth?

One task, one person. Many tasks, a team: an individually tasked group of individuals.

Tailing is an elaborate game of skill. The "tails," those individuals attempting to follow the "object," are like a professional sports team: Each player on the team has a specific role in the game; each player on the team can, if necessary, fill in for an indisposed fellow player; and all the players together form a seamless entity. The team has but one problem: Unless it is extremely lucky, it does not know where its next game is being played.

The object chooses the "field," so to speak, because only the object knows where he will be going. The team must therefore take things literally one step at a time: It can only prepare itself to cover the object, that is, tail him, in the immediate vicinity of the object's home base. So a good team will station its teammates at each major intersection in the vicinity. It will position a team member at each of the public transport stations. It will post lookouts at each strategically located building. But once the object leaves home base, the team must react and respond immediately. Failure to do so is to forfeit the game.

The only way to effectively blanket the object without alerting the object to the tail is through specifically tasked team members. Each and every one should have a role and the object should never see the same face twice. The object should be handed off, relay-race-like, from one team member to the other until he, the object, reaches the finish line.

Leading each team, and mine was no exception, is the captain. The captain is the tactician, the player who decides how to track the object. You can't run a tail without one. But the captain is not the team commander or Pod leader. That role is a strategic one. The Pod leader decides when to cease the tail and when, if at all, to "litter."

My captain was Zak, a seasoned veteran who would rather stalk an object in pouring rain than lose him. Zak was a professional—to him being a Flat Foot, let alone its captain, was the highest calling. In another life, Zak would have been a detective or a cop. In the Middle East, he was a spy.

Placement of team members was critically important. This is where Zak's experience and sixth sense was crucial. If, perchance, Fatwa spotted the same face in a different "zone," that is to say in a neighborhood or area that was different from that where he first recalled spotting that face, he would assume that he was being followed and either cease all clandestine activity, if that was an option, or "shake" the tail, by taking extreme action, such as a U-turn on a crowded street or heading into a dense crowd (like those that public markets and bus and train stations offer).

By moving his team members as soldiers on a chessboard and by allowing each of them to use their peculiar strengths, Zak would be able to minimize the exposure of any one of them. What Zak had to do was to guess accurately and intelligently where Fatwa would next go and what he would next do based upon his previous step, his operational history, and the likely targets of his current employer.

Most people would not stand a chance in this game against an object with the skill and experience of Fatwa. With Zak in command, I felt Fatwa deserved a head start.

Fatwa was carrying an oversized attaché case, a Zero-Halliburton-type valise. He headed to the bus station near his hotel in the general direction of downtown. Zak had someone already positioned at a bus station one stop west of Fatwa's hotel. Her instructions were to board the bus on Zak's signal. Upon seeing Fatwa go to the station, Zak gave her the signal. When the bus heading downtown arrived at Fatwa's station a few minutes later, Flat Foot team member number one was already on it. Fatwa would have no reason to suspect her of tailing him. All the same, one could safely assume that Fatwa would catalog her face along with those of all of the other bus passengers.

Fatwa got off the bus several stops later. Since Zak had his team cover each of the stations along the bus's route, Fatwa was "picked up" again as soon as he got off the bus. Unfortunately for Zak, he was about to waste two team members because Fatwa immediately hailed a taxi, which was normal practice for someone as experienced as Fatwa and an act that was anticipated by Zak. Nonetheless, two team members were exposed to Fatwa with no apparent gain.

Zak had several cars on hold, and one of them tagged Fatwa's moving taxi. Car number one followed the taxi until it turned off the main road. Cars three and four were paralleling car number one so with the first turn it was simple for car number two to pick up where car number one left off. In the meantime, Zak advanced his other team members to Chemonica's office.

Fatwa got out of the taxi several blocks before Chemonica's office. He continued to walk in its direction. He stopped at the street's corner and looked around him. He then crossed the street to enter a bar. Zak, anticipating Fatwa, had already positioned a couple in the bar. He gave the couple a "head's up" over the phonac. Fatwa entered the bar and ordered a beer. He stood at the bar for several minutes. He did not once touch his beer. Zak's couple were positioned in the bar's corner. Even Fatwa would not be able to see them. Zak was in no mood to waste any more players.

As it was now late evening, Chemonica's office would be closed. If Fatwa's Halliburton contained a bomb, he would have to throw it through the office's glass windows. That was not a very likely prospect given Fatwa's known preference for low-visibility actions. Therefore, I was rather skeptical of Zak's reports of Fatwa's beeline toward Chemonica's offices.

One thing I learned early on: Qualifying as an expert

in one discipline does not qualify one as an expert in all disciplines. Zak could tail better than anyone, but that didn't make him an expert on the GIA. I was duly skeptical that of all of the Western entities doing business in Algiers, our tiny Chemonica would somehow be targeted as a top GIA priority.

Fatwa was now at Chemonica's office block. He passed it by without a second look. Instead he walked up to the front door of the Air Maroc office that was just several doors down from us, pulled out a key, and opened the door. He disappeared into the office behind the opaque glass and the promotional posters. The lights remained conspicuously off. I was relieved but curious.

Quite obviously, Fatwa was not after Chemonica. But who was he after? Had Fatwa, unbeknownst to Siren, expanded his clientele to include the Polisario, Morocco's rebels fighting for the Western Sahara?

Moments later one of the team alerted Zak to the approach of a short, dark, Moroccan-looking male to the Air Maroc offices. The arriving subject, who was probably the station bureau chief, was dressed impeccably in a dark navy suit. Standing at the main entrance to Air Maroc's offices, he fiddled with a set of keys and then let himself in.

In a sequence that must have taken less than a minute, the lights in the Air Maroc offices went on, off, on, and then off again. From where we stood we could not hear a sound. My guess was that Fatwa's Zero housed a revolver and a silencer and that he used them to shoot the Moroccan airline executive on behalf of the Polisario guerrillas. The executive must have put up a bit more resistance than Fatwa had expected.

I knew that only one person would emerge from the Air Maroc offices and that that person would be Fatwa.

Zak began to order his team to move in in order to kidnap Fatwa. It would be a good move: Fatwa was oblivious to Zak's tail. Had he detected it, he would have

never gone forward with the assassination. Therefore, he
was expecting nothing but a safe and expeditious exit.
His defenses would be down, and he would be ripe for
the picking. Christ, I could have probably done it myself.
Since Fatwa was wanted by just about every Western
intelligence organization in the world, catching him and
bringing him to justice would be a major public relations coup for the Office.

Unfortunately for the world, I—not Zak—was making
the decisions.

I couldn't compromise the Office's Algerian operations
or Israel's diplomatic relations with Switzerland for one
rotten apple. If we kidnapped Fatwa and brought him to
trial, sooner or later the world would know where we
kidnapped Fatwa. That, in turn, would cause a huge public relations brouhaha and would piss off the Swiss no
end. They wouldn't be upset at the GIA or the Polisario or
even at Fatwa for that matter. They'd be pissed off at
Mossad for operating in their sovereign backyard. Yet, if
we simply alerted the Swiss to Fatwa's presence, they
would ask what the hell Mossad was doing tracking
Fatwa in Geneva anyway. And if we tipped them anony-
mously, they'd start looking for the tipsters—us—instead
of for Fatwa.

The Swiss are a bit peculiar that way. They call it neutrality.

I called Zak's team off.

"Go home, Zak. Bloody good job, mate. But it's over
now. Go home."

Zak wasn't happy with my decision, but Zak wasn't
calling the shots.

Iraq-Iran War

CHOOSING A TEAM FOR A HIGH-STAKES MISSION

CHOOSING THE TEAM

"Who Yehiyeh Lekha LePeh, Ve Ata Teheye Lo Le Elohim."
"He Shall Be to Thee Instead of a Mouth and Thou Shall Be to Him Instead of a God."

Who Yehiyeh Lekha . . . Moses stuttered. He was, as he tells the Lord, "slow of speech and of a slow tongue." Moses does not want to go to Pharaoh as an advocate for the Israelites. But God has little patience for his reticence. Deputize Aaron, your brother, to speak for you, says God; "Thou shalt speak unto him and put words in his mouth. . . . [H]e shall be to thee instead of a mouth. . . ." God has made Moses the team leader, "instead of a God," and Aaron the team spokesman.

God has chosen his team.

At headquarters I was known as the man who could interview a fly. My operators knew that arguing with me was an exercise in futility; the canard was that I could convince the pope of his fallibility. What can I say? It was a gift.

In addition to the gift of gab, I was creative; I could

spin a yarn like few others and invent entire odysseys out of thin air. Lying came naturally to me. Not because I particularly had anything to hide but because I found making things up usually more interesting than simply relating the truth. As far back as I can remember, I was inventing stories and imaginary events. A Freudian would have a field day with me.

The bottom line was that I was never at a loss for words, and if I was, I'd just make them up anyway. In this line of work, such skills came in handy.

There was never a doubt that I would be a team leader. The "mouth" is always team leader because the unspoken premise at the Office is that "mouths," by virtue of their creativity and gall, are better suited to lead a Pod out of trouble. In our business, of course, getting into trouble is a given.

We were the clever men in the proverb: "A wise man avoids trouble, a clever man gets out of it." Since trouble was our avocation, being clever was essential. Being wise—a luxury.

The Modern Rule of Limitations

Emerging from the Dark Ages, a revitalized Europe led by Italy introduced the world to the possibility of Renaissance man: a philosopher-prince who could teach medicine, invent submarines, design helicopters, and bring art to the privileged classes. In short, one who knew more than something about everything. Today, the Renaissance man along with the Renaissance itself is gone. If, in fact, Renaissance man ever existed, he did but in several exceptional individuals.

The twentieth century has brought us the opposite of the Renaissance man, the "specialist," one who according to lore knows virtually everything about nothing, or about such a narrow field that his knowledge is ephemeral, virtually useless. The specialist is a modern-day caricature of the modern world.

The true objective ability and aspiration of man lies somewhere in between the ephemeral Renaissance man and the modern-day specialist: Specialize in one thing but know something about everything.

The world is too complex and demanding for any one person to master every discipline. Excel in as many as you can but do not expect to excel in all. Even a gold-medal decathlete loses more events than he wins.

The Modern Rule of Limitations, therefore, instructs that in your profession, in your avocation, limit yourself to that in which you excel. Do not try and do it all yourself. Do not try and be a modern-era Renaissance man.

Better to focus and excel than to defocus and leave no mark.

The sooner you recognize, digest, and act upon the fact that no one person can competently perform every task, the sooner you shall succeed. After all, if Moses, the Lord's handpicked leader of the Israelites, required expert help, who among us will not?

Successful people will often attribute their success to their own ability to do everything better than anyone else. That belief is often the first step in their downfall. The business leaders who survive and display longevity are those who know their strengths, utilize those strengths, and delegate all other tasks to specialists trained or naturally inclined to perform such tasks better than the leader.

Can the leader perform the delegated tasks? Probably. Can he perform them well? Perhaps. Should he perform them? Not if there is someone, anyone, who can perform them better. Is there always such a person? More times than not. More times than most care to admit and acknowledge.

Why should you engage another person to perform tasks you can perform adequately, perhaps even competently? Because there are other tasks you perform better. There are other tasks that, in fact, no one can perform as well as you can. You should devote yourselves to those.

Better to excel in one task with a team member excelling at another than to attempt to perform all tasks by yourself. Failure to do so will result in mediocrity in all tasks and excellence in none. And mediocrity cannot succeed or survive for long.

My "first-round" draft choice in assembling my team was Albert, a handyman par excellence. Albert was like no one else I knew. He could repair anything, build everything, and break nothing. Give him a rubber band and he'd give you a motor; give him a paper clip and he'd return an antenna. Albert was a mechanical genius; he was a man who encouraged you to sneer at the otherwise scary phrase "some assembly required."

Albert's other virtue was that he could speak English, French, and Italian fluently. And although he never went to high school, he had read most of the great literary works in their original languages and could identify every major piece of classical music from its first four notes. Albert was the self-made Renaissance man.

Albert's one shortcoming, and in a secret agent it must be called that, was his shyness and his inability to "shmooze." In short, Albert was not a mouth. But I was.

Hanna, team member number three, was a "mouth" too. A big one. You did not mess with Hanna unless you had to. This had its advantages: Hanna could deliver messages with a finality. Other team members and outsiders would dare not challenge Hanna directly or indirectly. Hanna had that intangible quality—authority.

Hanna was also well-versed in breaking and entering and could get through any lock, whether mechanical, electric, or electronic. And on the off chance that she couldn't, she'd get in some other way. People like Hanna either work for the government or against it.

Team member number four was Yaniv: a chronic adventure seeker. Yaniv's c.v. read like a script for *Lifestyles of the Young and Restless:* Army Ranger, mountaineering in Chile and Peru, North Sea diver, and now this. Yaniv was continuously in search of "new ways to die." I had to make sure he didn't do so on my watch.

As our plans developed and our modus operandi became more clear, I added specialists and specialties to the team. My goals were to never have to drop someone

**from the team and to always anticipate the need for the
next team member and his or her specialty.**

Define Each Player's Roles

You might think it obvious that you perform one task better than
another person and that therefore, you should be assigned the performance of that task. But you would be mistaken. Nothing is obvious: Rarely do people believe that they are inferior to a colleague,
and never does a superior believe that a subordinate can perform a
task as well as he or she could.

After all, competition without conceit is impossible and brilliance without competition is improbable. Absent brilliance you will
fail.

The team leader's role is to ensure that the best player for a particular position plays in that position. The team leader's role is to
capture brilliance, lose conceit, and maintain competition. The
team's leader's role is to enable the team to win.

It does not matter where your players want to play. It does not
matter whether they have agreed amongst themselves what positions to play. It does not matter that they themselves are pleased
with whatever arrangement they have worked out among themselves. All that matters is that you, as team leader, know who on
your team plays best in what position, and that the best player for a
position is indeed in that position when the game whistle is blown.

**Albert could fill any number of roles and, hence, my
dilemma. The Office had recruited Albert as a "boy Fri-
day" to my Robinson Crusoe. The Office's expectation
was that, lacking in formal education, Albert would fetch
the proverbial wood and pump the proverbial water.
What the Office at the time did not know was that Albert
could have stepped into almost anyone's shoes and tap-
danced his way to the Spy Masters Hall of Fame. Albert
could do almost anything.**

**Yet despite his talent, Albert was content in his jack-
of-all-trades role, and he would have liked to continue**

to serve as the "default" Combatant—the one to whom every job not specifically assigned to someone else goes. But Albert's utility was far greater than that. And by allowing Albert to flit around various tasks, I would lose Albert's core genius, which was making things work and keeping them that way. Moreover, in the absence of a "title" and a well-defined job, the other team members would not give Albert his due. To them he would be just another wise guy with an idea.

So however reluctant I was to lose Albert's input on everything, I had to have his mastery of something, one thing—things that moved, mechanics.

"Albert, you get mechanics. As far as I'm concerned, from now on, if it moves, it has Albert stamped on it. Anything with a part is in your domain. I'll look to you for inventory reports, equipment requests, spare parts, maintenance updates, the usual headaches."

"Why me?"

"Because you're good. You're reliable. Because you can do it."

"Yeah, but I can also do other things. Why limit me to this stuff? I can do this stuff in my sleep."

"Yes, Albert, that's probably true. But you'll need your sleep. Anyway, you're far too valuable to be unassigned. If you remain unassigned, you know that you will be the first Combatant to be pulled off this operation, don't you? You know that if Samson decides to move a Combatant from this operation to another, for whatever reason, she'll go first for whoever is unassigned, don't you? And you know, don't you, that no matter how forcefully I argue that you are unassigned because you provide input to everyone else, she won't care? Albert. My friend, you're assigned."

"Screw you."

I didn't have the luxury to worry about Albert's attitude. I had a mission to plan and the comfort of knowing that Albert could be counted on to come around.

Right now my prime concern was to find a way to get the four of us into Iraq.

In a memorable quote, when asked, "What was the West's interest in the Iran-Iraq War?" Henry Kissinger replied: "That it continue forever." When I was tasked with supporting the Iranian effort in its war with Iraq, the war between the two Moslem, anti-Israel, anti-Western countries had already been raging for over two years. My job was to try and bring about Dr. Kissinger's wishes.

Entering Iraq at any time is difficult. Saddam Hussein's regime elevated customary Arab dictatorship paranoia to a new level. No entry visas were granted unless one had a written invitation from an Iraqi national and an Iraqi company. The bona fides of such invitations were uniformly and, as best we could tell, comprehensively verified. Except in the most peculiar situations, entry was limited to periods of ten days or less and renewals were less a matter of "how long" than "if." Once finally in the country, it was not uncommon for expatriates, even those in Iraq at the express invitation of the government, to have their hotel rooms and private residences brutally, openly, and destructively searched by Saddam's secret police. And a search by the secret police, however unpleasant, was preferable tenfold to a search by the Intelligence Regiment of Saddam's Imperial Guards. Those frequently and unpredictably ended in death or mortal injury to any innocent bystander who happened to get in the way. And one always happened to get in the way.

Entering Iraq during its war with Iran was virtually impossible. Yet enter Iraq was exactly what I was tasked to do, and I would have to bring in my Pod with me.

After an initial wave of success in 1980 and early 1981, Iraq's troops had faltered. Iran, despite all of its post-shah revolutionary upheaval, somehow managed to rally its people around the solidarity of a nation under

attack and stymied further advances by the Iraqis. The
war seemed to be settling into a prolonged World War I,
Maginot Line, pattern. And for Israel, that was good.

Although neither Iraq nor Iran shared a border with
Israel, and although neither had a substantive dispute
with Israel, both countries provided ideological and
monetary fuel to the Arab war effort against Israel. In the
convoluted politics of the Middle East, this was not altogether surprising.

The Ayatollah Khomeini and the Iranian mullahs
were relentless in their support of anti-Israel terrorism
and war because their predecessor in power and their
mortal enemy, the shah of Iran, had been an ally of
Israel. The shah had recognized Israel diplomatically
and had committed the unforgivable sin of allowing
Israel to purchase Iranian, Moslem, oil. The shah did so
because he viewed himself and his nation as Persians,
not Arabs, and as such he had no cause for war with
Israel. In gratitude for the shah's nonbelligerence, and
with the desire to preserve his rule, Israel's own internal
secret police force, the Shin Beit Kaf (the Hebrew initials
for "General Security Service," a name that imparts new
meaning to the question: Was the service good?), trained
the shah's secret police, SAVAK, and thus managed to
inscribe Israel's name in Iranian infamy forever, which
is a long time in the Middle East.

Iraq was and had persisted in its anti-Israel stance
largely as a result of its desire to assert hegemony in the
Arab world. First, it was an easy way to coalesce unrest
and antidictator sentiment and redirect it against an outside threat, however unreal. Second, Baghdad and its
leaders saw themselves—not Egypt, not Syria, and certainly not Saudi Arabia, a backward feudal kingdom—as
the rightful leaders of the Arab world because of their
historical greatness as former Babylon. Finally, Iraq's
Ba'ath Party (the pan-Arab socialist party that sparked
the antifeudal revolutions in Egypt, Syria, and Iraq)

sought to claim supremacy over the other Arab Ba'ath parties by demonstrating its ability to be more extremely anti-Israel than all of the other Ba'ath parties combined.

Since both Iraq and Iran had oil, they carried clout far beyond their otherwise natural ability to hurt Israel. As totalitarian states, they could devote large sums of money and huge manpower toward fighting Israel without the risk of an opposition party questioning the folly of wasting each country's wealth and humanity on combating a Potemkin enemy who posed no threat to them, made no claim upon them, and wished them no ill will.

Over the past several months there were some disturbing (at least from Israel's vantage point) developments in the war. The Iraqis were in the process of rearming their army with newer weapons. Moreover, the Iraqis had expanded the draft in order to create a twenty-one-division monster of an army. This suggested that Iraq might soon be in a position to tilt the war in its favor. That outcome, however, would be a prescription for disaster as far as Israel was concerned. Not only would both Iran and Iraq be free to divert their attention once again to making Israel's life miserable, but the Iraqi army and their generals, with their twenty-one victorious, restless, and soon-to-be-unemployed divisions, would demand their pound of flesh from Saddam.

It was more than likely that Saddam would decide that a military march through Jordan to Israel was preferable than one from Basra to Baghdad.

Of course, what Israel did not know at the time was that the United States had decided to take sides in the war. The United States had decided that Saddam, the military, secular dictator, was preferable to the unshaven and unkempt religious zealots of Iran. So Washington decided that Iraq would be supported and the ayatollahs toppled. But in the Middle East snake pit, the best-laid plans turn to pandemonium.

We were to be the equalizers. We were to devise a

method to hinder the Iraqi war machine from inside the
country. Our stated goal was to hurt Iraq's effort in its
war with Iran. Yet, ironically, I had little doubt that if we
were successful and the tides of war shifted against Iraq,
our next mission would be in Iran doing the very same
thing for the other side. In fact, for all I knew, I already
had a doppelganger Combatant somewhere in Europe
readying himself to enter Iran.

Iraq-Iran War

WHY SIMPLICITY IS THE BEST STRATEGY

▮ SIMPLICITY

> *"Kol HaMosif Gore'ah."*
> "All Who Add, Detract."
>
> *Kol HaMosif* . . . Three simple words. Subject. Verb. Adverb. Not one
> word less than required to express the thought, and not one word
> more. Add to this and you detract.

Since the Iraqi lines were long and the terrain challenging, Saddam could not rely on his military truckers alone to supply his frontline troops. Our intelligence reports told me that Logistique, a French logistics company, was operating trucks in Iraq. Logistique, with its sophisticated tracking system and European expertise, was just the ticket for the beleaguered Iraqi support lines.

And, as such, it was just the ticket for me.

The Measure of Success

The measure of success is simplicity. The manifest elegance of a solution is its simplicity. The most reasonable explanation is the simplest one. The most important innovation is that which in hindsight is obvious. The most shattering action is that which can be grasped by a child.

To add to something which itself is whole is to detract from it. To elaborate on a theme is to risk the loss of the theme. If an action does not serve a clearly defined purpose, it is not required. If it is not required, it should not be taken.

> **I didn't need sophisticated bombs, assassination plans, or elaborately planned operations to stymie Saddam's war effort. The way I saw it, a flat tire would do.**

Simplicity First

Over time, most people will be able to devise a more simple solution to a challenge that was solved with a complex solution. The key to success, however, is to devise the simplest solution to the challenge when the challenge first arises. Doing so will distinguish you from the crowd; it will provide you with your competitive edge; it will give you your marginal advantage.

Do not seek a solution to a challenge. Seek a *simple* solution to the challenge. If it is not simple, it is complex. If a solution is complex, then it is simply a different challenge, not a solution at all.

Do not substitute one challenge for another.

> **Logistique had a Lyons office. Flat Feet surveillance revealed that a company executive regularly lunched at Pierre Rochault, one of the better restaurants in a city of better restaurants. By week's end, Hanna, attractive, bright, fluent in French, and a motor mouth, was waitressing there.**
>
> **On the Tuesday of Hanna's second week on the job, Marc Palleir, Logistique's personnel director, was seated at "her" table. Hanna small-talked her way into his heart. Palleir came more and more frequently to Rochault, refusing to be seated until Hanna's table opened up. Two weeks later, Hanna was working for Palleir at Logistique.**

Thanks to Hanna, acquiring the paperwork required to process our visa applications through the company was now a relatively simple matter. Similarly, Hanna's position and relative leeway to roam around the company's office at her leisure would allow us to dispense with the Office's cumbersome secret communications apparatus. What better, safer way to communicate than on Logistique's own telex lines? We could communicate with Samson directly through Hanna. We arrived in Baghdad four weeks from the start of the operation. Team member number one did her job. And no one among us could have done it better.

Hanna also advised the local director of Logistique's Iraqi operations of our posting. His name was "Mal Louis," and as far as I was concerned, the man was aptly named.

Mal Louis was a suspicious little bastard. First of all, he was an old Middle Eastern hand, having spent most of the past thirty years working in one Levantine country after the other. Second, he was among the many ex-pats who in the twilight of their lives question whether the quality of their ex-pat existence was worth the nomadic life they had lived. Third, Logistique Baghdad was his domain. And Mal Louis was not about to let three uninvited sojourners into his fiefdom without assessing their intrinsic worth.

The scientific axiom is: All else being equal, the simplest explanation is the correct one. Similarly in business: The simplest explanation, the simplest action, the simplest strategy is the correct one. Why? Because of the Rule of Errors.

The Rule of Errors

Simply stated, the rule says that the more elements to a component the more errors in the component. If I use a picture instead of a word, I can make no mistakes. If I use one letter instead of a word,

I can make only one mistake. If I use a three-letter word instead of a seven-letter word, I can make only three mistakes. If I make no mistake, the typesetter may do so. If the typesetter doesn't do so, the reader may do so. And if the reader doesn't do so, the person to whom the reader conveys the message shall surely do so.

If I can convey my message in a brief presentation, I should do so. If I do not, I am likely to commit an error, a totally unnecessary error. And since the gravity of any error can only be finally determined after it is committed, such assessment is always too late.

All who add, detract.

By adhering to simplicity, you avoid unnecessary errors. But equally important is that in so doing you also preclude all of the other "error carriers" in your chain from infecting your work with error. A simple command cannot be misunderstood. The eternal war command "Charge" is eloquent and elegant simplicity. It is precisely for that reason that it has stood the test of time and war in every language in every culture. It simply cannot be misunderstood. "Attack the gunnery position near the horizon, off to the left," as important a message as it may be, is not likely to be followed exactly as the commander had intended for it to be.

All of us, and businesspeople are no exception, have a limited attention span. After the first three minutes of listening to another, our attention begins to wander. Sometimes sooner. That means that you, the speaker, have very little time in which to get the thrust of your message across. If it is simple, you shall do so. If it is not, it is very unlikely that you will accomplish your goal in one meeting.

We are conditioned to suspect complicated messages. If you cannot explain or instruct in a simple statement, the listener will suspect that either you yourself do not understand what it is you are saying or that you are saying something you know to be false. Neither outcome is welcome.

Imagine you are seeking an investment in your company. Your investor, whether banker or potentate, will provide you with three minutes of attention and will immediately swoop down upon any unclear or confusing expression like a hawk on a pigeon. If your presentation is simple, meaning your plan is simple (or simply explained), you shall have no problems in addition to those of getting money out of a third party. But if it is not, you are likely to spend all of your time explaining matters that are tangential to the task at hand.

To keep matters simple, work at it. If you can express an idea with a picture instead of a paragraph, do so. If you can create a plan that a three-year-old would understand—"buy low, sell high" comes to mind—do so. If you can create something with two components instead of four, do so.

If you can destroy something simply instead of expensively, do so.

We based our cover stories on the job descriptions that Hanna fed us from inside the company. Since its earliest presence, Logistique Baghdad did not have an efficiency expert on-site. This was no great surprise, as there was little to be efficient about in a country where petrol is cheaper than human life. Since I knew nothing about transportation, I was the perfect candidate to use the "expert" cover. After all, the very definition of an expert is someone who knows everything about nothing and I fit that description to a T. Of course, as an efficiency expert, I immediately became Mal Louis's nemesis and his most hated employee.

As if that wasn't enough, as the only nonnative French speaker among us, as far as Mal Louis was concerned, I was barely civilized. To Mal Louis, a non-Frenchman was an abomination; a crime against the natural order. A non-Frenchman working for a French company was worse.

Yaniv was an easier sell. First of all, as a Tunisian Jew, he was fluent in French and in Arabic. Second, Yaniv's dark skin color, his dark curly hair, and his penetrating green eyes made him look the perfect colonial remnant—a genetic testimony to France's presence in Africa—which Mal Louis, despite his LePennist (rightist/fascist) leanings, immediately took national pride in. And, finally, Yaniv, now using the alias of Ali

Kemali, could drive anything with a motor. So, in accordance with the purloined Logistique personnel chart, he became Mal Louis's driving instructor.

Albert was the easiest sell of all. First of all, Albert was white. Like Mal Louis, he was a "true Frenchman." Second, Albert was young. He could have been Mal Louis's son or grandson, and Mal Louis treated him as such. And finally, Albert was a mechanic. And that, well, that, in Mal Louis's book, was as close to God as one got in this lifetime.

At the time, Logistique had its finger on the pulse of the Iraqi war machine. It operated as sort of a surrogate transport brigade for the Iraqi army. Troops had to be ferried to the front? Logistique. Ammunition was needed in Basra? Logistique. Pipelines to drain the southern marshland? Logistique. It was the perfect place to wreak havoc on Iraq.

"Ali" quickly took his job to heart. Ali made sure that whatever good sense the Iraqi drivers had about sixteen-wheelers, tank-haulers, troop carriers, you name it, and whatever natural driving instincts they had, were buried under the weight of his gobbledygook theories of driving.

"Clutch? What the hell for. Synchronize the engine's RPM and you can shift without the damn thing." "Brakes? Never waste them. Just downshift from ninth gear at eighty kilometers an hour to second. Ignore the noise, think brakes. And, remember, I'll be inspecting them to see who's been wasteful." "Headlights? Never, ever turn them on. Stay dark, your eyes will grow accustomed to the light. But do flash them as you approach another vehicle to let them know you're there. But then, of course, use your brights."

Ali did not merely preach these blasphemies, he actually took to the road to assure that they were being implemented. He would shout, hit, and cajole the drivers into taking reckless action, needless risk, and unnecessary chances every time they sat themselves down behind the wheel. He was Evel Knievel unbound. By the time we left Iraq, Ali himself had been in over a dozen accidents, destroying untold numbers of trucks, ammunition, and ordnance. He was, of course, indirectly responsible for thousands more. And for all I know his legacy survives among Iraq's drivers to this very day.

Several months after our arrival, we lost Ali to a severe concussion. He had flipped a tank carrier into a ravine. Mal Louis himself arranged for his emergency flight to Paris. Yet, team member number two met and surpassed my expectations. He did his job and he did it better than anyone else could have and better than I had any right to expect of him. Ali more than any of us left his mark on the Iraqi war machine. And the mark was a very costly one.

Albert's job was more challenging. Mal Louis hovered over him like a bee around honey. He either wanted to adopt Albert or make love to him and I wasn't sure which. Moreover, Albert was not a trained mechanic; he did not go to mechanic's school or work in a garage. His was a self-taught, intuitive, "kick-the-engine-and-let's-see-what-happens" approach. So when Mal Louis persisted in playing "guess the problem" with Albert, it was my turn to earn my keep.

"Guess the problem" had become Mal Louis's favorite pastime. He would take a part of a truck's damaged engine assembly, the air brake, the carburetor, something, and show it to Albert, asking in a childish, nursery rhyme, singsong voice: *"Quel la problem, mon Albert?"*

Albert then had to examine the part and declare the problem. Problem was, however, Albert did not know the source of the problem. Nor was he likely to find it by simply examining a part of a faulty assembly. So Albert did what we all had to do from time to time: He improvised. He would try and turn the inquiry into a joke. He would take wild guesses. When he was lucky and guessed right, he would play it to the hilt. When he was far from the mark, he turned it into a joke, as if to say: "Of course I know that the response I gave was incorrect." Unfortunately, there was no long-term strategy there.

So I went into action.

I concluded that if Mal Louis had less time on his hands, he would have less time to play spin the bottle with my Combatant. So I reverted to form and became the big-mouth efficiency expert I was supposed to be. I inundated Mal Louis with charts, diagrams, explanations, and analyses explaining why his system of transportation was all wrong.

I argued to cut truckloads by half and to increase truckloads by half. I argued to increase truck-driver sleep and to decrease truck-driver sleep. I demanded that we rotate tires to the left and cross them over to the right. And I had a theory for each demand and I insisted that Mal Louis hear each and every theory. By the time I got through with him, Mal Louis wanted only to be left alone to sleep. "Guess the problem" was least among his priorities.

My actions opened the road to Albert to do his magic, and magic it was. Albert, as Mal Louis's "master mechanic" and favorite son, had complete and unfettered access to all parts of the Logistique compound. He used it to our fullest advantage.

In principle, Albert wanted to garble the message—not to harm the messenger. So he devised methods to damage the cargo without harming the driver. After a cursory examination of the problem, he devised the perfect solution: "trip" the cargo holds and dump the cargo. Sixty to 180 minutes after a truck's engine had been working at above a certain RPM level, the truck's cargo area would either elevate on its own or its pins disconnect from the cabin. Simple and elegant. The cargo is either destroyed or damaged while the truck driver walks away to drive another day and inflict yet more damage through Ali's training or Albert's machinations.

Through Albert's inspired sabotage, the Office estimated that the Iraqi war machine lost over ten thousand
shipments of military matériel and munitions and ordnance in an amount equal to the entire payload dropped
on Iraq in Desert Storm.

Before too long, Logistique's accident rate was going
through the roof. Hanna sent us a coded warning from
company headquarters that Lyons was getting curious
about our incident reports (which we were required to
file on each mishap). Although through a bureaucratic
interpretation of the company's report codes Hanna was
able to keep the cargo destroyed by Albert's devices out
of our tally, Ali's dinky drivers continued to cut a wide
and deep swath. It was time to leave.

We made no fuss and said no good-byes. We simply
took our passports and work permits, commandeered
Mal Louis's personal Land Cruiser (I couldn't resist
doing that), and took off to the country's northwest, to the
Turkish border. Although Saddam had troops in the
north, to protect against possible Kurdish insurrection,
the Office had military advisors with the Kurds and
those were instructed to divert Saddam's troops from our
escape route.

Simple.

Lying in Libya

HOW TO MAKE PRETENSE REALITY

▌PRETENSE IS REALITY

> *"Hakol Kol Ya'akov Aval Hayadayim Yedei Esau."*
>
> "The Voice Is Jacob's Voice, but the Hands Are the Hands of
> Esau."

Hayadayim Yedei . . . Isaac, the biblical patriarch, is on his deathbed.
He is feeble. His eyesight has failed him. Before his death he wishes to
impart a special blessing, a blessing reserved for eldest sons, on his
eldest son, Esau. Unbeknownst to Isaac, however, his wife and his
youngest son, Jacob, have conspired to have him bless Jacob instead
of the rightful party, the eldest, Esau.

But Esau is big and hairy. Jacob is not.

So Jacob, at his mother's urging, covers his arm with sheep's wool and
approaches the weak patriarch. Isaac feels Jacob's wool-covered arm as
he draws him near. Jacob tells Isaac that he, Jacob, is Esau.

Isaac says: "The voice is Jacob's voice, but the hands are the hands of
Esau." Although in doubt and confused, Isaac nonetheless blesses
Jacob.

Pretense is reality.

I was bedecked in the uniform of an Italian Civil Aviator on my way to a Libyan air force air show at Umm Aitiqah, a military air base along the Libyan coast, just east of Tripoli. I was Rafaelo Tucci, a "dottore" (a "doctor," an Italian term of deferment to an educated or respected person) in Italy's Civil Aviation Command. I was also, of course, uninvited. I was simply counting on my uniform to get me in.

Why Italian? Because Studio guessed that Libyan security was not very likely to make a fuss over an Italian Civil Aviator showing up to the "invitation only" air show at the Tripoli air base. Italy and Libya had colonial ties, world war ties, commercial ties; Libya and Italy went back, so to speak, a long way together. Libya understood Italy's "Westernness" and did not begrudge the Italians for it.

Why Civil Air Command? Because there was some internal logic to the premise that an Italian civilian aviator was for one reason or another invited by someone in Libya to the air show. After all, the Italian civil authorities, in contrast to their air force brethren, were one step removed from NATO.

Why this air show? Because the Libyans were showcasing the arrival of their most recent acquisition, two new MiG-29 aircraft.

Why me? Because I drove an Alfa Romeo. And given the state of the Office's Combatant roster that day, the Alfa made me the most qualified Combatant for the job. In fact, joking aside, I did speak some Italian, if haltingly, and I had worked out of Italy on previous missions. So, given that I was in Tel Aviv awaiting my new posting, I probably was the most qualified Combatant available, which is different from saying that I was the most qualified Combatant.

Act As Though You Are That Which You Wish to Be

Most people will accept a fictitious assertion, reasonably—yet forcefully—made, even if it flies in the face of everything they know. Even when the facts are in plain sight.

There is little that cannot be made to be "true" by a strong and well-presented pretense.

If persuasion of a particular reality is an important objective, do not let the facts stand in your way. If it is necessary to persuade someone of something, anything, which something has no basis in reality, act as though it does. If you do, chances are that that someone will then be persuaded.

The simple truth is this: If you act as though something *is,* the surrounding world must either accept it as being so or assume your insanity. In other words, if you behave in a fashion that presumes the existence of certain facts, then your willingness to accept the consequences of behavior predicated upon the existence of those facts compels the conclusion that those facts exist. Because if they, the presumed facts, did not exist, one would have to conclude that you were insane. And one of the strongest biases of civilized society is sanity. We all presume sanity unless given an overwhelming reason to believe otherwise. And since this presumption is so strong, relinquishing it causes dissonance. So to reconcile or avoid this dissonance, we prefer to grasp alternative explanations.

That is why, given the choice between accepting that someone who in all respects appears perfectly sane is insane and accepting that an assertion which strikes one as being questionable is in fact true, most people will choose the latter. Because doing so results in a lower level of dissonance to the individual. The individual will therefore accept your pretense in order to lower his or her anxiety. The individual then acquires a personal stake in your pretense, and this stake will allow you to continue the pretense at escalating degrees of divergence from fact.

Isaac knows that the voice is not Esau's voice. Isaac is aware of something strange going on.

Pretense.

But if this person is not Esau, why would this person be standing next to Isaac with an outstretched arm?

Dissonance.

Isaac feels the woolbound arm; the voice is not Esau's, but the arm is.

Desire to reduce dissonance.

Isaac blesses the pretender.

Pretense is reality.

Aside from the unlucky circumstance of this mission being in Libya, the mission itself was not complicated or particularly difficult. It merely entailed attending the air show so that AMAN would have a first-hand, reliable account of the MiGs' arrival. (AMAN is the Hebrew acronym for Military Intelligence. In contrast to Mossad, which gathers intelligence and carries out special operations, AMAN has the primary responsibility of analyzing all intelligence gathered.)

AMAN, as usual, had known for some time that the Libyans had acquired these aircraft from the Soviet Union. But AMAN realized only several days before the air show that the air show was being staged to debut Ghaddafi's new MiGs to the East Bloc military attachés in Libya and to announce their arrival to the world. AMAN had questions and it wanted answers. How many planes was Ghaddafi willing to display? Did the planes look new? Were Russian pilots flying the planes? Were Libyans?

So, armed with some rusty Italian phrases and memories of Rome, I was to become Italian. While I was somewhat concerned about the contrived Italian cover, Samson was apoplectic. In briefings, she cautioned me to not use Italian; to not use Italian unless I absolutely had no choice; and then, again, to not use Italian. I was cautioned to stay away from Italians, Libyan-speaking Italians, and anything remotely Italian. Christ, Samson didn't even want me eating pasta.

When it was certain that the mission was to proceed, Samson told me about the Office's Libyan "helper." I had never heard the phrase before and wasn't quite sure

what a helper was but I remember being relieved that we had one.

A helper, while not quite a Retailer, was someone who was willing to do a "friend" a favor from time to time. The helper was not in it for the money, and any rewards a helper received were sporadic and nonmonetary. The helper knew very little. Usually the helper didn't even know who the ultimate beneficiary of his efforts was. But so long as he broke no law, the helper really didn't seem to care. Sometimes helpers were regular people seeking a little adventure, sometimes they were just hospitable natives seeking to entertain and befriend ex-patriates. Sometimes they thought it might help their business, and sometimes they were people who disliked the regime enough to do a little something about it but less than that which might cause their sudden death. In sum, these were folks the Office couldn't always figure out, which made them somewhat dangerous, but, in a crunch, not beyond the pale. This apparently was a crunch.

My Libyan helper was Wafia Hallad. He was wealthy, he was connected, he would meet me at the Tripoli International Airport, and he would be my host.

I had four days to prepare. During the first twenty-four hours, with help from Studio, I scripted my cover story. I was Rafaelo Tucci, an Italian civilian aviation expert, a "dottore." Earlier in life, I had been a military helicopter pilot until grounded with a back injury. (Statistically speaking, there were fewer helicopter than airplane pilots in the world, so when pressed to fake something, we always went with the numbers.) I served in Italy's Ministry of Civil and Military Aviation General Headquarters in Rome (where there were so many people it would have been impossible for anyone to state with certainty that there was no Rafaelo Tucci, as it would be okay for me to say that I didn't know someone who worked there). I was the ministry's representative to the

air show. I was directed to attend by my superior officers. I grew up in Milan. I did this and I did that. In sum,
I had a life and I knew all about it.

After the cover story, I was handed over to AMAN.
There I was briefed by a colonel. He was supposed to
alert me to those specific questions that AMAN sought
answers to. As I quickly found out, however, he wanted
to know everything there was to know. His questions
were so numerous and so detailed that, given the time
constraints, I wasn't even going to try and remember
them. I'd get what I could and that would be the most I
could get anyway. The colonel then turned me over to the
Israeli air force. The IAF officers first taught me what
they thought a former Italian helicopter pilot might
remember about flying from training that was supposed
to have taken place ten or more years ago. Then they
taught me about MiGs in general and the MiG-29 in particular. I had one-half of a day left for brushing up on
my Italian.

Wafia Hallad was in the oil business. He monopo-
lized the Libyan market for drilling equipment. The
Office somehow got its fangs in him during one of his
European trips. His "mission," as I was told he understood it, was not so much to spy on his country but
rather to help "the West" effect some positive degree of
influence on Libya. In other words, his treachery was for
Libya's own good, or as the Untouchable who recruited
him must have put it: "It's like going to the dentist. It
hurts, but it's good for you."

Interestingly (for me, at least), Hallad did not know
that he was working for the Office. The Untouchable
who recruited him never identified himself as Mossad.
For that matter, he didn't identify himself as anything.
Rather, in the best Office tradition, he let Hallad believe
what Hallad wanted to believe, and Hallad wanted to
believe that the Untouchable was from an important
"Western intelligence agency." Hallad also wanted to

believe that with very little effort, Hallad could do for
Hallad, that Western agency, and, most important, Libya,
an important service.

Hallad lived in great luxury. He had a resplendent
home with every creature comfort that would have been
available in a western European capital. Clearly, he was
favored by the regime. In Libya, one does not attain
wealth, let alone hold on to it, without the Great Leader's
blessing.

So whatever it was that led this wealthy man to offer
his services, however limited they were, to an enemy
organization (for the "West," too, was Libya's enemy, in
many regards, even more so than Israel) I did not know.
But I knew that whatever "it" was had to be either very
noble or very sordid, for money meant nothing to Hallad.

Hallad's tasks for the Office were minimal. On his
European trips he was expected to have dinner with
Edward, his Untouchable contact, and report about
unusual goings-on in Libya and on the presence (or
absence) of certain of the usual suspects in world terrorism. And there was the occasional hosting of a "westerner"
like me. Edward would tell Hallad that a close,
Italian friend of Edward's would be coming to Libya for
a brief visit. Hallad would be asked to assist Dottore
Tucci, the friend, while in Libya. No more would be said
and no more needed to be said. Hallad would know what
to do and, if the past was any indication, Dottore Tucci
would receive the "red carpet" treatment.

The Air France plane landed in Tripoli on schedule. I
deplaned with everyone else, and right there on the tar-
mac, by the plane, was a chauffeur standing next to a
black limousine bearing a piece of cardboard with my
name scrawled on it. Hesitating for just a moment, I
walked over to the driver, who promptly took my carry-
on bag and let me into the back of the car.

The driver drove me to the VIP arrival lounge, where
I was met by a uniformed official who took my passport

and gestured at me to follow. The official walked me
through the border patrol, stamping my passport himself
and taking me by the hand as he took me toward the customs desks.

Ordinarily, the intrepid traveler would be delighted
at this kind of reception: waiting limousines, obsequious
officials. Not I, however. Nor, for the record, any other
spy with even half a brain.

Spies were never supposed to make themselves the
focal point, the main attraction, so to speak. To be center
stage was to look for trouble. Celebrity brings curiosity
and curiosity brings attention. And no spy can be the
focus of attention before sooner or later someone will
wise up to the substance behind the image. So all of this
VIP treatment was most unwelcome.

On the other hand, since I couldn't control it, I was
reconciled to enjoy it.

The government official took me over to a smiling
and welcoming sixtyish, white-haired, dark-skinned
gentleman. It could have been Omar Sharif, but it wasn't.
It was Wafia Hallad. Without much fanfare or undue
secrecy, Hallad handed the government official several
banknotes and embraced him warmly. Then he turned to
me with both hands extended and welcomed me to
Libya.

"El dottore? Dottore Tucci, si? Piacere."

Hallad was talking to me in Italian. With a British
accent but Italian nonetheless. This was not good.

"Parle Italiano, Signor Hallad?" I asked, dreading the
answer.

"No, no. I am afraid not, signor. Unfortunately that is
the extent of my Italian. You must forgive me, si?"

Forgive him? I wanted to kiss him. A load lifted from
my shoulders as I took in his answer.

"Of course, Mr. Hallad. Is not a problem, as you say,
si? Welcome to meet you too, piacere. My pleasure.
Please call me Rafaelo. I insist."

I was speaking the best Italian I knew: English with a Hollywood Italian accent. It was something that I had picked up watching *Godfathers I, II,* and *III.* Somehow, this seemed to work for everyone in the cast, and those guys won Oscars galore.

"And you, my friend, call me Hallad. Please. Welcome to Libya."

Hallad released one of my hands but kept the other. I had no bags save the carry-on, which his driver still had in the car. We walked through customs without being stopped and exited the terminal. Hallad's limousine was already out front, waiting for us.

We got into Hallad's limousine. Hallad told the chauffeur to drive away as he signaled to him to close the dark glass partition between the rear and front seats. As we pulled out of the airport roundabout on our way north to Tripoli, Hallad loosened his tie, opened a bar in the rear compartment, pulled out a crystal bottle of scotch and two Baccarat glasses, and poured a double shot for himself and for me. I sensed that this would finally be the day I learned how to drink scotch.

Hallad offered me a glass and we toasted one another: "salute." Hallad and I had a few drinks of scotch on our way into town. By the time we reached Tripoli, I was quite relaxed, although I am not sure that was the clinically correct term for my condition. Whatever it was, Hallad was in the same state.

"You, Rafaelo, will be staying with me. Si?"

"No, no, Hallad, I cannot. Thank you, but I have the hotel, is fine. *Grazie.*"

"No. no. no, Rafaelo. You stay with me, dear boy. No further argument. I insist. The hotel is not good, my son. Too many Mukhabarat, too much filth. Trust me, Rafaelo, you shall stay with me."

I resisted Hallad's offer because this was not the script that Studio had prepared for me, and as a general principle, I liked to follow the script. But this "movie" was apparently not turning out to be the one that Studio had prepared me for anyway. First of all, I was in no condition to argue with Hallad because there was little I could do to dissuade him from his offer. Second, my brief stay in the airport was enough to tell me that I could not hope to get around Tripoli unnoticed. Nor was I likely to go anywhere without being followed. The air-port alone had more secret policemen than Tel Aviv had police. It was clear, and Hallad left no doubt about it, that Libya was teeming—hotels especially—with big dark guys in big dark glasses.

Sure I'd stay with Hallad, why the hell not?

As we pulled up to Hallad's house, Hallad put the scotch away and straightened his tie. A galabiya-robed doorman emerged from a palatial house and opened the car doors. Two more traditionally garbed men took my bag from the trunk and Wafia Hallad's attaché case. We followed them into the house as Hallad put his arm behind me either steadying me or steadying himself. I entered the magnificent marble foyer of Hallad's house. It was like entering the Villa Borghese. I was glad to not be staying at a hotel.

Although it was still relatively early, the combination of scotch and travel combined to exhaust me. I would be happy to hit the sack and call it a night. But Hallad had different plans.

"Well, old boy, what say you freshen up a bit, change into something a bit, how shall I say, evening like, and I'll see you in the library. Say, forty minutes? We'll get something decent to eat. Ali, show Mr., no, el dottore Tucci to his room."

Ali took my bag from the doorman and walked off toward the home's west wing. I followed dutifully. We walked down a long, broad corridor lined with original works of Impressionist art. Ali opened an ornate door leading to a large spacious room. He carried my bag into the room and hung it up in the oversize closet. Then, like an experienced hotel bellboy, he pointed out the light switches, opened the window shades, and opened the door to the large balcony. Then he went into the bathroom and turned on the lights and the water in the bathtub. Ali bowed and walked toward the door. I honestly didn't know whether I was expected to tip him.

I threw myself on the bed and closed my eyes. OK, an early, quick dinner and to bed. I can handle that. I had a splitting headache. I dug through my shaving bag and pulled a pair of aspirin out of a bottle. I downed them on my way to the bathroom. I closed the bathwater and turned on the shower.

Forty minutes later, dressed in my nicest (and only) suit and tie, I joined Hallad, who was already sipping a scotch in a room that might have been moved from Mayfair: original leather-bound books in a leather- and oak-ornamented room. Hallad offered me a drink. In for a dime . . .

"*Si, Hallad, molto grazie.*"

"*Prego, dottore, prego.*"

Over drinks and cigars, I learned that Hallad made his first fortune after World War II. Barely in his teens at the time, he and his brothers claimed the remains of Rommel's desert tanks as their scrap metal. They dragged them piece by piece into Tripoli where they sold them to middlemen who resold them abroad. He estimated his wealth at the time as the equivalent of a Rothschild.

The family plowed its earnings into Libyan real estate, which soared in the years until Ghaddafi's military "revolution" and his subsequent ousting of the Americans from the Libyan oil fields in the 1960s. The family slowly disposed of their now-depressed real estate as it, led by Hallad, moved into the oil supply business. Today, apparently not one drop of oil came out of a Libyan rig unless it was using Hallad's hardware, mud, or drill bits.

"Well, Rafaelo. It is time to go. Tonight, Rafaelo, in

your honor, we shall have a lovely dinner, a special dinner. A surprise welcome from me to you." Hallad put his drink down, his arm around me, and led me out to the waiting limousine.

Hallad's limousine pulled up in front of an elegant though simple-looking home along the Tripoli waterfront. The chauffeur opened the rear door and let us out. Hallad took me by the hand and walked me into the building. We were met at the door by a beautiful woman in traditional Libyan attire. She greeted Hallad warmly. All smiles and greetings, she led us into what was a plush restaurant that resembled a cross between a fine Parisian salon and an elaborate Bedouin tent, the type that the Great Leader himself might have favored. As she moved deeper into the room, I wondered where she might be taking us. It was obvious that all of the tables were taken. There simply were no more empty tables. Much to my unpleasant surprise, she stopped at a table already occupied by two men in black tie and one sparkling woman in a silky black dress and a multiple-strand pearl necklace. Our hostess bowed her head and left us standing at the table.

The look of bewilderment on my face must have been obvious because Hallad grabbed my arm again and announced:

"You see, my dear Rafaelo. A delightful treat. The right honorable Italian ambassador to Libya, Salvatore Trastevere, and his wife, the lovely la signora Maria Trastevere. Also, my good friend the honorable Italian commercial attaché to Libya, Signor Luigi Francesi."

Being

To your business colleagues and competitors, you are that which you choose to be. If you follow an internal script and carefully note your words, your actions, and your mannerisms, only you will know that what is on display to the world is not what you feel inside. And if you consistently present the same externality to the world, that which you present will ultimately become that which you are. So while this may sound like psychobabble, it is not.

Most of your business cohort will know and can know very little about you. Therefore, even if you have something of a reputation, in your first meeting what you display is what will register most strongly. If you demonstrate charm, the assumption will be that you are charming. If you demonstrate resolve, the assumption will be that you are resolute. That is why first impressions are extraordinarily difficult to change.

So if, on your first meeting, you present defining character traits, for most people it shall be those character traits which define you. And they shall continue to define you in their eyes until stronger evidence—evidence acquired by them, first-hand—is available. Absent that, your reputation or rumors about you shall come a distant second.

"I say, Rafaelo, say hello to our guests. Salvatore, Maria, and Luigi."

My hand went uncontrollably to my neck. I supposed I wanted to feel it thinking that it might be soon severed from my body. All eyes at the table were turned up to me, but all I could hear was the beating of my heart. Although my mouth was moving, I had no idea what I was saying. I hoped that it was *"Buona sera"* or something like that.

After a momentary freeze, I snapped back and scanned my options. They were fairly limited. I could bolt to the door and try to swim across the Bay of Benghazi, I could swoon, faint, and hope to wake up in a Red Cross hospital, or I could take a deep breath and go for broke. Not surprisingly, I rolled the dice.

I conjured up every Italian phrase I knew and scanned them in my mind. After discarding those that I was not sure that I would be able to pronounce convincingly, I was left with about ten, fifteen minutes of material. If I husbanded the phrases carefully, I figured

that I could maybe stretch my material out to last
through drinks, appetizers, and at least part of the main
course. That's all there was. I knew it wouldn't work. I'd
have to think of something else.

*"Piacere, piacere. Mi chiamo Rafaelo. Come sta? Da
dove viene?"*

There, I blew about a good 10 percent of my best
material on the introduction, but experience has taught
me that first impressions are everything. If they bought
me as Italian now, they would be very hard-pressed to
change their minds later, even if I got up on the table and
sang "God Save the Queen," which given my level of
adrenaline and inebriation, was a distinct possibility.

I leaned over to kiss the signora on both cheeks and
warmly embraced the ambassador and the attaché. I
could tell that they were pleased with my performance.
Their compatriot had handled himself with the expected
Roman warmth and dignity.

The Rule of Immutable Opinion

Minds are a difficult thing to change. Opinions (and beliefs) are
like clay; at first they can be molded, even washed away, but with
the progression of time they harden and turn to stone.

If people hold the opinion, have "formed" the opinion, that you
are honest, then regardless of who you steal from and how much
you steal, you are "honest." If people hold the opinion that you are
unreliable, then regardless of how often you perform completely,
competently, and on time that which was requested of you, you
remain, in the eyes of the opinion holder, unreliable.

Couple this reality with the fact that opinions are formed very
early on in the course of human interaction and you understand
why first impressions are of paramount importance. It is easier to
impress someone that black is white on a first date than to persuade
them that white is off-white on the second.

Causing one to change an opinion is like causing one to relin-
quish a beloved child. And like one's love for a child, the commit-

ment to it increases geometrically with the passage of time. The longer an opinion is held and the greater the investment one has made in it, the more one will wish to continue to hold it. This is so because the longer one has acted, defended one's action, and, perhaps, has caused others to act on the premise that the held opinion is correct, the greater the consequences to that individual in discarding the opinion.

The presence and accumulation of facts that undermine one's opinion cause cognitive dissonance: To accept these facts as facts, the opinion holder must acknowledge that he or she was mistaken (and therefore unwise) in holding the opinion in the first place. The alternative to this naturally unappealing outcome is to discount the facts and deny their veracity. Given the choice, most individuals will indeed do exactly that. And this is so, even when the opinion holder is presented with overwhelming evidence to the contrary.

The Rule of Immutable Opinion, therefore, teaches two corollaries: The best opportunity to present fiction as fact is the first opportunity; and, the longer the fiction is accepted, the easier it will be to maintain (in the face of conflicting evidence).

What does this mean in business? It means that you should be skeptical of long-held views which have not been independently and recently tested. It means that simply because many analysts, investors, and bankers hold a belief about a company, there is no reason to act upon that belief.

How does a publicly traded company, the information about which is supposedly in the public domain, go from $120 a share to $20? How does a publicly traded company ship inventory to distributors and book it as sales without a single analyst noting the practice? It does so by pretense. It does so by suggesting that its story is so well known and documented that it need not be verified or confirmed.

So do not be afraid to be the party pooper, the skeptic, the child who asks to actually see the emperor's clothes, if that's not too much trouble, please. Because oftentimes, you will be the only one who has ever asked those questions.

We sat back down around the table. I was sand-wiched in between Maria Trastevere and Luigi Francesi. Hallad addressed the group in English, explaining that I was a dottore in the Italian Civil Air Command on a "special" visit to Libya. He effected an exaggerated wink and nod and everyone at the table laughed.

"Bene." I slapped my hand on the table. *"Cameriere, una bottiglia di champagne, per favore."* I just blew another 20 percent of my vocabulary. But, again, early investments yield the greatest returns.

"Splendid idea, old boy, splendid idea," Hallad said. "You see, Salvatore, another good Italian."

"Rafaelo, e' la prima volta che viene? Cosa pensa del paese? Della gente?"

The ambassador was making small talk, but at the same time he was fishing. Who was I? Why was I here? Why, perhaps most important, was he not informed of my arrival? Although I understood his questions, I would not be able to answer them. At least not without one of the three Etruscans detecting a distinctly non-Italian accent. I still had one good phrase that I had been keep-ing for the opportune moment and this moment was as opportune as they come.

"Ambassadore, io sono qui in viaggio d'affari. Mi scusi."

("Ambassador, I am here on business matters. Excuse me.")

A polite but firm "mind your own business" delivered with the right amount of false humility conveyed the message that for all his ambassadorship I outranked him (otherwise, how dare I tell him to mind his own busi-ness?) and that if he doesn't make a fuss about me and my mission, I will pretend that he outranks me.

"But, please," I continued in my best Spaghetti Eng-lish accent, "let us speak in English for our host, Signor Hallad. No?" I dared anyone to object.

"Va bene, Rafaelo, va bene. E' molto gentile da parte sua." ("Good, Rafaelo, good. It is very thoughtful of you.")

Mrs. Trastevere came to the rescue. She was probably more quick-witted than Salvatore and did not want to see him in a facedown with me. At least not until she knew more about me. Fortunately, given the time lags in official diplomatic communications and in liaison between the ministry and the diplomatic corps, my secret would probably be safe for several months. And I needed only tomorrow.

Thanks to Maria's intercession, we moved back to English, and that's where we stayed through the meal. Every now and then, I would toss one or two of my dwindling phrases to Salvatore, his wife, and Luigi, but I kept the pickings slim. I managed complimenting Maria once every fifteen minutes on one thing or another just to keep her in my good graces and off the scent. And since Salvatore and Luigi seemed genuinely more interested in Hallad's business stories and their alcohol than in me, I started to feel better and better.

We enjoyed a wonderful dinner with excellent wines. Salvatore let me understand that this by far was not a typical meal in Tripoli, which was becoming increasingly wrapped up in Islamic purity. Of course, he could still arrange a thing or two. . . .

"E'stato un pasto delizioso. Tante grazie" ("That was a delicious meal. Thank you"), I said to Salvatore as we departed. He seemed genuinely pleased with my public display of gratitude.

Hallad and I waited with the Italian cohort as their driver picked them up and then we boarded Hallad's limousine. I was pleased and relaxed. I passed the test, I proved my mettle, I took the hardest blow a spy can take and I came away standing.

The next morning, nursing a hangover the size of Sicily, I pulled my Italian Civil Aviator's uniform out of the carry-on. You've got to hand it to the Italians, they may not be much in the fighting department, but boy, could they design a uniform. The uniform was a beautiful blue suit, the blue being not unlike that of Italy's national soccer team. Adorning that was a yellow silk aviator's scarf that went around my neck. A true "*cravatta*." Considering what I had been through, I thought I looked pretty good.

I was ready to face Hallad.

I walked down the corridor to the dining room. The table was set with wonderful fresh fruit, dates, nuts, pita bread, cheese, and thick dark coffee. Hallad was at the table reading the paper. He stood to salute me as I walked in. I laughed and gestured for him to sit down. We shared a convivial breakfast, and then his driver arrived to take me to the air show.

After a bit of Tripoli's traffic, we drove on to Umm Aitiqah, a rather old and unattractive airfield. We arrived just as most of the other dignitaries did. The chauffeur stopped at the entrance to the base and asked for my passport. I gave it to him, and he gave it to the armed soldier checking the guests' credentials. The soldier said something to the chauffeur, who turned around and asked me for my invitation.

"Tell him we already gave our invitation to another soldier," I said to the chauffeur.

The chauffeur and the soldier exchanged words, but it was clear that the soldier was not going to be persuaded by my driver. I got out of the car, pulled myself up to my full height, and let loose with a barrage of every wicked Italian phrase I had.

"*Fa schifo. Se veramente vuole morire, la accontento. Sulla tombe de sua madre. OK, ecco cinquecento lire. Allora lasciaci in pace . . .* " All to no avail. Fortunately, a small queue had formed. The occupant of the car behind mine, a chubby jovial Romanian fellow, walked up to the guard. He said a few words in Arabic and shoved some money into his hand. The soldier muttered to himself and lifted the barrier. I invited the Romanian to join me in my car, which he did.

The Romanian, Andrei Kochalsciu, was the military attaché to Libya. He knew some Italian, although he preferred English (whew), and loved my "argument." I told him that his "argument" seemed to work better.

"Ah, they are all idiots."

We were waved through the gate and the driver proceeded to the review stand. Our door was opened by a polished Libyan soldier with spit-shined shoes, not a small feat in the desert. He took Andre's invitation and walked us to our seats, which were in the diplomatic section. It was populated for the most part by other military attachés of the Eastern Bloc countries and of North Africa.

The review stand was placed at an angle to the landing field and the President's review stand. We would be able to see the planes land and Colonel Ghaddafi salute them. These seats would be hard to beat. The airstrip ran south to north ending in a marsh that extended into the sea.

The event began with the playing of the Libyan national anthem: a god-awful tune played by a lousy military band or vice versa. Immediately after that, there were "fly-bys" of two formations of jets. The first were MiG-21s, the mainstay of Libya's air force, and the second was of Tupolev bombers. After the fly-bys there was a march of Libyan air force cadets and a drive-by of air corps officers on Jeeps. Ghaddafi, attired in a military uniform, looked much better than he did in his faux Islamic robes, which, as of late, he had been favoring; the "Man of the People" shtick. I was almost relieved to see him back in khaki again.

There was an interlude of military music played by a marching band and then, finally, two MiG-29s flew by overhead. They were larger and more menacing than the MiGs we had seen before. Whether that was also true on an operational level, I didn't know.

After two fly-bys, the MiGs were coming in for a landing. This was the moment we had all been waiting for. The dignitaries in the stand in which we were seated all rose to their feet. We did so out of anticipation but also because the Great Leader rose to his feet. To do less would be an insult.

The first MiG roared onto the runway. I knew from my briefings that the plane had tremendous thrust and required both a long runway and a "braking" parachute, which was a parachute that came out of the plane's tail section, billowed up with air, and, thus, helped brake the plane. Hearing the plane's engines and seeing the strength with which it came down, I wasn't surprised.

The MiG screamed down past the reviewing stands toward the north. It didn't seem to be slowing down. I was waiting for the braking parachute to billow out and yank the plane to a stop. But it didn't. There was no parachute. The plane didn't stop. It kept on running forward until a huge sound of metal and mud filled the air. The plane was in the marsh.

The stunned silence lasted for a moment. It was broken by the wailing of a siren as rescue Jeeps and vehicles sped north to the plane. I took Andre's binoculars and focused on the plane. I could see the pilot, no doubt a Libyan, climbing out of the cockpit. The plane was essentially bent or broken in two with the cockpit and nose of the plane angled toward the sky and the body and tail angled down into the mangroves.

No one dared to laugh, although it was a very funny scene, especially given that no one, at least then, was physically hurt. I wouldn't want to be that pilot later on in the day.

We braced ourselves for the second landing. I'm sure that Ghaddafi did not want that plane to land in front of us gawking spectators. But he really had no choice. What goes up, must come down. And so moments later it did.

MiG number two hit the runway as hard as MiG number one had. One had to assume that the second pilot knew what happened to his colleague and that he was praying with all his might for his plane's parachute to open—that was assuming that his plane had a parachute. It did.

The second MiG's parachute, silky white, billowed with all its glory on the runway. The plane continued to run north toward the marsh and the grounded first plane. But strangely, the parachute was fully filled and the plane was not slowing down. The parachute in fact just continued to blow further and further northward. *Sacre bleu.* The parachute was not attached to the plane.

The parachute was now fully extended and obviously not attached to anything, continued to blow south. The plane, unstopped and apparently now unstoppable, continued to rush north until, moments later, it landed with an ear-shattering metal-screeching thud on the first MiG plane. The second pilot, however, wasn't doing any climbing. He must have hit his ejection seat button before impact because he was airborne just as his plane and the plane below his plane burst into flames. Seconds later a huge explosion rocked the field, and clouds as dark as night covered it.

Sic transit gloria.

The Limits of Pretense

You *can* fool all the people some of the time. But only *some* of the time. Therefore, in employing pretense, don't push it. It is a tool, not a substitute engine.

Use the time gained through pretense to acquire the substance you lack. If you had to bluff your way through a financial presentation, make sure that until the next time, you understand everything presented (by you or others) at the presentation. If you do, your pretense shall be forever fortified. If you do not, sooner or later your edifice will crumble and restoring it will be nigh impossible.

I grabbed Andre's hand and pulled him behind me. The stands were emptying onto the field for a closer look. There would be chaos in a moment. I was concerned that Ghaddafi's police would not allow anyone to leave the base utnil the government put out its own story, and I certainly didn't want to have any part of that. Andre followed me like a good puppy, and we were the first to reach the gate. It was closed. This is where Andre and I parted company. I jumped over the fence and ran to find Hallad's limousine. Fortunately, Hallad's chauffeur must have been trained in quick escapes because he was already in the car prepared to drive away. I jumped in and he whisked me straight to the airport as I requested.

If I hustled I could be in Paris by nightfall.

Fighting Terror with Terror

HOW TO PREPARE THE GROUNDWORK FOR SUCCESS

▊PREPARING THE GROUNDWORK

> *"Avnei Gazit . . . UBarzel . . . Ve Nehoshet . . . Veatzei Arazim . . .*
> *VeYakhin David LaRov."*
>
> "Wrought Stones . . . Iron . . . Brass . . . Cedar Trees . . . David
> Prepared Abundantly."

Avnei Gazit . . . King David is on his deathbed. His son, Solomon, will soon be king of Israel. And God has decreed that it is Solomon—not David—who will build God's temple.

But the construction of the temple has been David's lifelong obsession. He, perhaps even more than Solomon, desires that the temple be built and that it be built properly, expeditiously, and impressively. He, therefore, does not rely upon his son Solomon to prepare that which requires preparation. Even though Solomon's wisdom is already renowned. Rather, David himself prepares for the temple's construction. And he continues to prepare until death, until he is no longer able to.

Over the course of the past several months, there had been a spate of terrorist attacks against Israel, Israeli installations, and Israeli intelligence officers carried out by Black September, the PLO offshoot, but inspired and many times directed by Fatah, the main military arm of the PLO. The government of Israel decided it was time to strike back at the heart of the PLO's body politic, as it was, Beirut.

Until 1973, my career had not taken me to Lebanon. But early in the year, Studio registered an opportunity through an ad in *The Economist* magazine. An international monetary organization was seeking a senior financial analyst to support credit operations in Lebanon and several other peripheral countries. Through a series of manipulations, I became that analyst.

A Task's End Is in Forethought

In every culture and in every language there is a folk saying espousing planning as the way to success. This is not mere anthropological coincidence. Success and preparation are directly correlated. The more you plan, the more you succeed. The less you plan, the more you fail.

Consider the story of King David and the temple. King David is planning the temple's construction and preparing for it because the construction of the temple was of great importance to him. His planning and preparation are the embodiment of that desire. He wants the temple built as expeditiously as possible. He wants to use the best building materials for it. Yet he knows that without preparation, without the ordering of "long-lead-time items," the temple's construction will be delayed. And delay is oftentimes death.

David does not cease his preparations even though he is on his deathbed. There can never be too much preparation. David's preparation of God's house while the Angel of Death waits is the strongest metaphor of that reality.

What do you prepare for? Everything. How do you prepare? By careful analysis of the objective, the alternative to the objective, the way to the objective, and the alternatives to the way.

As a general rule, the Office did not like to keep Combatants unnecessarily "exposed to the elements." In Office jargon this meant that Combatants were not allowed to spend too much time on operational duty in any one country, nor were Combatants allowed back into countries where they had previously "littered." Of course, life isn't perfect, and in dire circumstances exceptions were made.

Since I had not been to Beirut prior to 1973, I was ripe for a Lebanese assignment.

The Objective

The objective is the "tactical" goal; it is a step or one in a series of steps that advances you to a strategic goal. They are concrete, quantifiable, and identifiable milestones toward a larger target.

By definition, objectives are usually clear: increase sales, lower costs, build a better product. But never accept an objective at face value. Because underlying every objective is a business rationale. Understand the rationale for the objective before preparing for the objective.

If the stated objective is to increase your sales, what is its underlying rationale? Is it to increase revenue? Or to increase profit? If the stated objective is to lower costs, what is the underlying rationale? Is it to increase margins? Or to reduce commitments? Understanding the objective, truly grasping why its attainment is important, is an essential tool in preparing for it.

In most cases, those seeking to attain an objective have not fully considered it. Therefore, in planning on how to attain it, they will be more prone to choose the wrong path toward accomplishing it. Understanding the objective is the first step in preparing for its accomplishment.

A good way to consider an objective is to analyze its alternatives. For example, if the stated objective is to increase your sales with an underlying rationale that to do so will increase revenues, then one might consider other ways of increasing revenues as an alternative objective. Similarly, if the objective is to lower costs with an underlying rationale that to do so will increase margins, then one might consider other ways to increase margins as an alternative objective.

This does not mean that you should challenge objectives and always *substitute* alternatives. It merely suggests that you should understand objectives in order to prepare for them. And that one way to understand them is to consider the alternatives.

> **My business appointment allowed me broad leeway in my travels to and in Lebanon with very little day-to-day responsibility. This freedom combined with the fact that I was a fresh face in the country encouraged Samson to task me to "Spring of Youth," an operation in planning about which I knew very little.**

The Rule of the Maze

In preparation, you begin from the end. Where do you want to be? When do you want to be there? How much will it cost to get there? Place your pin at any point on the map and work your route backwards from there. It is easiest to find the right path to a maze's end point by starting your search *at* the maze's end point.

Imagine that you are at the apex of a stairway with more than one staircase leading to it. From the top of the stairs, you can see all of the staircases and see which of them lead where. You can see how long it will take to climb them, which have more stairs, which have no banisters. Your perspective when you commence your planning from the end backward is all-encompassing. There is little that you shall miss by starting your analysis at the end point.

Descend that staircase one step at a time until the complete staircase has revealed itself. By the time you are at the bottom, you will know how many stairs there are, how long it will take to climb them, how difficult it will be to climb them, which among the stairs may be shaky. You will be able to ask: Which among them may be prone to slip or break? What alternatives are available if one or more should break? What will I need to take advantage of those alternatives? How will the necessity to utilize alternatives impact my resources? My time? My money? My stamina? How much should I prepare my body before I embark upon the climb? How much time do I have to prepare my body? Will I need teammates? What should be their skill? How should they be selected? What if one of them is not available? What if one fails the climb? What will it require to recruit a team member?

As you can see, from the top of the stairs the questions will suggest themselves. The answer to the questions is your preparation.

Any operation named "Spring of Youth" was undoubtedly a military operation. One could tell because military operations, in contrast to Office operations, are named by AMAN's computer, which has a peculiar way of turning a phrase. Usually, the more bucolic an operation's code name, the more bloody the operation. Spring of Youth, or SOY, as the Office referred to it, was no doubt going to be a doozy.

Much later, after the operation itself, I would learn that SOY was Israel's continued vendetta against the perpetrators of the Munich Olympic massacre. This vendetta, ordered by Israel's government, was usurping more and more of the Office's time and resources. So these types of operations, which were initially fairly popular in the Office, were becoming less and less so.

There was also the question of purpose. Revenge without more meaning, revenge without strategic value, seemed to me and to some of my colleagues a waste of effort. After all, misery breeds misery. We killed a terrorist and two more popped up to fill his place. They then killed some more of us and so on and onward. I did not see the strategic value in such operations. Sure, it made the masses feel good for a day or too, but were we risking our lives to entertain the masses?

And finally, there was the question of territory, turf: Who gets to do what, where. Assassinations, and SOY was assassination top to bottom, belonged to "Bayonet," the most secret cadre within the most secret of organizations, the Mossad.

Bayonet is the ultimate executive branch. It is also the Office "Holy of Holies." Bayonet receives its orders, little eight-by-five pink slips, directly (and only) from the occupant of the prime minister's office himself, the prime minister. The pink slip always reads the same way: It has a date on top and the prime minister's name on the bottom. Centered in the middle of the pink slip is a name and its known aliases. The pink slip contains nothing else.

The pink slip is a death sentence. It is a direct order from the prime minister of Israel to Bayonet. Since the early 1970s, Bayonet has been employed by prime ministers from both of Israel's political parties: Likud and Labor. The prime minister's order is nonappealable. It commands Bayonet to track down and execute the named party by any means available. To issue an order, the PM must have clear and persuasive evidence that the accused himself (not through intermediaries), with the intention of taking innocent Israeli or Jewish civilian life, either committed or caused to be committed two or more acts against Israeli or Jewish civilians in which both of such acts Israeli lives were lost. The shorthand elocution of this principle is "OBH^2," or, for the uninitiated, "Our Blood, His Hands."

Once the prime minister executes a pink slip, the accused's only chance is for Bayonet to fail. To date, that has happened only once, in Bayonet's 1997 botched attempt on a Hamas operative in Amman, Jordan. (Some commentators mistakenly refer to Bayonet's botched assassination attempt in Lillehammer, Norway, as a failed Bayonet mission. While it is certainly true that Bayonet assassinated the wrong person in Lillehammer, an act for which the entire team was jailed and later cashiered out of Bayonet and the Office, it is also true that the person who was the target of their attempt, Ali Hassan Salameh, was ultimately done in by a new Bayonet team five years later.)

Yet despite the tradition that assassination is Bayonet's territory, in this instance, Bayonet and the Office were being assigned a backseat role. Instead of AMAN handing Bayonet the intelligence and allowing it to plan and perform the mission as it saw fit, the government reversed roles: The Office would prepare the mission, but the IDF, through its special combat units like the Naval Commandos (SEALs) and Sayeret (Ranger) outfits, would perform the "kisses" (Bayonet slang for assassination).

SOY was by far the largest combined Ranger, SEAL, Combatant operation ever performed. Its objective was to assassinate three kingpins of Black September and Fatah in Lebanon, in Beirut, in their homes, in their bedrooms.

Target A was Abou Yousef, the head of what the Office called Fatah World: the Fatah directorate for international terrorism. Target A also held some unknown but unmistakable role in Black September. Target B was Kamal Adwan, the chief of all Fatah operations and a veteran of numerous terrorist operations in which numerous children had been killed. And Target C was Kamel Nasser, the PLO's information minister and a former terrorist himself.

To enable the combined SEAL/Sayeret team to assassinate the three, the IDF decided to conduct four diversionary raids, all to commence at exactly the same time.

The four diversionary targets were strung up and down the Lebanese coast with three of the four clustered around Beirut. From north to south, the targets were:

Target 1, a PLO mine factory; Target 2, the headquarters of the Popular Front for the Liberation of Palestine (PFLP) and a letter-bomb factory; Target 3, an RPG projectile factory; and Target 4, a petrol reservoir and garage.

Calling these targets "diversionary" does not mean that they were in and of themselves unimportant. Rather, it was just that on their own they would not have been worth the risk or the effort required for such an elaborate plan of attack. As part of a bigger picture, they qualified as "alpha" targets.

My job was to prepare the reconnaissance file, referred to in Office jargon as "IFO," or Information for Operation, on Target 2, PFLP headquarters and letter-bomb factory. This for an operation the details of which I knew nothing about and which I would know nothing about until after it was executed, no pun intended. But one did not need to know the exact nature of the operation in order to gather IFO. Rather, preparation meant that I would gather all relevant information about a target using my experience and my common sense. If the Office wanted anything beyond the obvious, it would let me know.

To some, preparation is an unglamorous chore. It is a task to be performed as one might do housework. Something to get over and done with before moving on to the main course, the task itself. To those individuals it is as though there is a clear dividing line between preparation and performance. To those of us who know better, there is not.

If It Hasn't Been Recorded, It Hasn't Been Done

This simple rule, more honored in its breach than in its observance, is the foundation of preparation. Committing something to writing requires a very different mental effort than thinking about something or verbalizing it. It accomplishes two purposes: First, it forces you to be coherent; and second, it commits it to your memory.

Thinking about a matter must be, of course, the starting point for any planning effort. But thinking about a matter itself is not enough to qualify as preparation. For most people, thinking about a matter is like writing on water: As soon as you do it, it disappears.

Verbalizing a matter engages more of our mental capacities than just thinking about it. It is an additional level of concentration, an additional layer of cement on the foundation. Verbalizing your thoughts will force a coherent structure on them. If you cannot verbalize what you are thinking, what you are thinking is probably incorrect. But verbalization without doing more is like writing on soft clay; it will be preserved, but just for a while. Unless hardened, it will sooner or later disappear.

Writing something down has the strongest impact on our mind. On the one hand, it quickly reveals whether thoughts are coherent, logical, consistent, and compatible. The written word will not tolerate the "fuzziness" that one can get away with in speech. The written word, fixed as it is against shifting tides, memory lapses, and subtle changes in restatements, must rise and fall on its own, as written. It must do so as it is, not as it may later be interpreted and supplemented, not as it may later be restated or edited. Either it makes sense as written or the thought itself is suspect.

Moreover, committing words to paper etches them indelibly in your own mind. Most of us are "visual," meaning that we are far better remembering something that we have seen than something that we have only spoken about, let alone only thought about. In this regard, one need think only about one's dreams.

If you wake up from a dream and do nothing more than think about it, you will most likely forget that dream by the time you've brushed your teeth. If you tell the dream to someone, two things happen. The first is that you suddenly realize that either the dream had gaping holes in it or you simply cannot remember it all. And second, you are far more likely to remember it. But if you write your dream down as soon as you wake up from it, you will very likely remember it for weeks without ever having to refer to your writing.

There is more that writing does.

Writing allows you to chart your preparation against time, effort, and funds. In this way, a chart forces you to note long-leadtime items, costly items, items that require reevaluation. A writing allows you, in fact, almost requires you to enumerate and list equipment and accessories, which will then allow you to track their arrival. It keeps a live record of what has been done, what needs to be done, and how much time is left to do it. It requires you to determine how you will respond to the matters that you have already put to paper and, in so doing, forces you to consider other issues and unknown factors.

A writing blends planning into preparation and, ultimately, into performance. There is no dividing line. It is a continuum toward the objective. And that is why King David, near death as he is, does not stop his preparations.

My first act would be to visit the target. There is no substitute for seeing. You can read descriptions of a target from morning to night and you can read reports from here to there, but unless you see something with your own eyes, you'll never feel as though you know all you need to know about it.

Target 2, the PFLP headquarters in Beirut, was close to my hotel. I had a miniaturized Dictaphone in my shirt, which received an infrared beam from a "bone microphone," a thin cellophane-type strip, glued to my jaw and covered by my beard. Unless I shaved, no one would detect it. Using my bone microphone, which picked up my jawbone vibrations and translated them into words, I could talk to myself as I observed and collected the operational information the IDF would require.

The PFLP building was a modest seven-story building in a bad part of town. It was surrounded by other PLO and PFLP installations and was therefore swarming with armed Palestinians. An unaccompanied European did not have much reason to be there. Fortunately, Banc du Liban had a branch office not far from the building. As international credit advisor to the bank, I could walk into any branch in any part of town.

Perhaps not surprisingly, the local Banc du Liban branch was the PFLP's bank. I introduced myself to the branch manager, Ibrahim Geaga, a grandfatherly, Paris-educated banker. Ibrahim was at the sunset of his life and his career. He, therefore, offered more than the usu-

ally generous hallmark Lebanese hospitality. Refusing to accept my polite declinations, he took me to his home for lunch, where he regaled me with bankers' stories. He told me of international jet-setters, sheiks, and gamblers, of money-laundering schemes, CIA funds, and the naïfs and innocents at the American University only several blocks away. He bemoaned the recent drop in civility in the country, pointing an accusing finger at King Hussein of Jordan.

"King Hussein?" I asked with some bemusement.

"Oui, oui, ze petite monarch. If not for ze king to chase away ze Palestinian, no Palestinian arrive in Beirut. Would be quiet, tranquil, like before . . ." Ibrahim's voice tailed off, and at the time I wondered whether these were the insights of an astute political scientist or the rantings of an old man facing change.

We left Ibrahim's house to walk the several blocks back to the bank. The streets were filled with machine-gun-toting Arabs, most of whom were Palestinians of one exile organization or another: the Palestine Liberation Organization, the Popular Front for the Liberation of Palestine, the General Command, the Fatah, the Democratic Front for the Liberation of Palestine, and Lord knew how many others. Ibrahim was right to court their business.

When we returned to the bank, instead of entering at the main level, Ibrahim took me by my hand and asked me to follow him. I did and we entered the building's hallway. We climbed the stairs to the fourth and top floor in the building. Ibrahim took a key from his pocket and nodded to me as though sharing a tremendous inside joke.

"Zis is my 'working apartment,'" Ibrahim said, barely stifling his giggles.

We entered into a very nice and modern two-room apartment. Ibrahim explained that he used to use the apartment quite a bit, nudge nudge, wink wink. Nowadays, Ibrahim explained, he used the apartment rather intermittently, if that, for the occasional nap. Ibrahim stuffed the keys into the palm of my hand.

"What is this?" I asked.

"*Pour vous, mon ami*. For ze women, oui?"

Ibrahim was rather pleased with himself, as was I. I pocketed the key and thanked him. I gave him a bear hug and kissed him on both cheeks. I sensed that his acquaintance with me, a "real" banker, gave his tired ego a nice boost of spirit. I liked that. That was good. Capitalizing on our newly forged kinship, I walked out of the bank with hard copies of PFLP account numbers, correspondent bank accounts, transfer ledgers, and payroll activities.

Target 2 was mine. I would use Ibrahim's apartment to register whatever activities took place at the PFLP. Long before SOY, I would know the routine and lifestyle of every comer and goer on the block. I would know what happened at every minute of every day outside of the PFLP building, and I would know who could saunter by the building unimpeded and who was stopped by the PFLP sentries for questioning.

I spent several weeks collecting additional IFO. This meant long and boring observations of Target 2 from Ibrahim's apartment. Of course, the Office wasn't relying upon me alone. It had tasked several other Combatants with the same target. It was a wonder we did not stumble over one another.

Belts, Suspenders, and More Belts

If it's important, secure it. If it's important enough to secure, secure it again. And if it's important enough to secure again, make sure you have a substitute.

Take no chances with your business needs. If information is required, assign two individuals, working separately, without knowledge of one another to obtain it. Two, because one may fail. Working separately, so that you receive two reports (which will probably not be identical). And without knowledge of the other, because if one knows of the other, each is less likely to do all it takes to get the information sought.

When it absolutely, positively has to be there overnight, take it yourself. Failing that, send duplicate originals with two different courier companies. Belts and suspenders.

In the early-morning hours of April 19, 1973, the IDF attacked Targets 1, 2, 3, and 4 and Targets A, B, and C at exactly the same time. By daybreak, the PFLP bomb factory was in ruins and Abou Yousef, Kamal Adwan, and Kamel Nasser lay dead in their apartments.

Money and Politics

WHY BLEND IN WITH YOUR BUSINESS COLLEAGUES

ADAPT

"Im Tehiyu Kamonu . . . VeNatanu Et Benuteinu Lakhem."
"If Ye Will Be As We Be . . . Then Will We Give Our Daughters unto You."

Im Tehiyu Kamonu . . . The Canaanites wish to forge a commercial relationship with the sons of Jacob by having one of their own, Shechem, wed Jacob's daughter, Dinah. Although Jacob's sons have no intention of allowing this union because Shechem had defiled Dinah, they wish to stall for time while plotting their revenge.

Simeon and Levi, Jacob's sons, tell the Canaanites to become like Jews, adopt their customs, become circumcised, and follow their traditions. If you do, say the brothers, then and only then can there be a union of the two peoples.

This request is well received by Shechem and his father, Hamor. After all, it was even then already widely acknowledged that to be accepted, one must blend into the community.

Acceptance depends upon the party seeking acceptance demonstrating "acceptability." And that usually hinges upon similarity.

I t was a lot of money. A lot of money indeed. Fourteen million six hundred thousand United States dollars, to be exact. In hard currency. One-hundred-dollar bills. With untraceable serial numbers. A money launderer's dream. Only one problem: It was in Syria. In Damascus. In a condemned building. Slated for demolishment. Any day.

Large sums of money in a Combatant's hand made the political echelon nervous. Perhaps they were projecting their own proclivities on us. Nonetheless, when the political echelon was nervous, Pinnacle had to be psychiatrist and exorcist rolled up into one.

We would have to get the money out and we would have to account for every penny lost or missing.

The Rule of Likes

People prefer like people. That is the rule. Simple, concise, elegant, and true. Note again: People prefer people who in as many ways and in as many customs and habits as possible are like themselves. The rule is ironclad. It is watertight. It is airtight and hermetically sealed. You can bank on it. You can wager your last dollar on it. You can act as though it were as immutable as the law of gravity. For it is.

The rule has its operation on many levels and in many walks of life. One of the more institutionalized areas where it is found is in the workings of the "Old Boy Network."

The proverbial Old Boy Network (OBN), in which an individual is accorded preferential status by virtue of an affiliation with a certain group, has nothing to do with old boys and little to do with networks. Rather it is a abstruse way of stating the Rule of Likes.

What is an Old Boy Network? It is often described as a web of individuals who share something in common: a club, a school, a fraternity. But in fact that is only part of the story, and the uninteresting part at that. In fact, an OBN is simply a reliable "marker" for sameness. In other words, if you are admitted to an OBN, it is because you are perceived by the OBN to share its physical traits, its values, its mannerisms, etc. . . . .

Entry into the OBN is regulated by the Rule of Likes: If you are "like" the rest of the OBN, you will be admitted to the OBN.

Why, you might ask, does it matter whether the privileges to an individual OBN member accrue by reason of actual membership in the OBN or by reason of being so alike to the other OBN members that the individual is assumed to be part of the network?

Because it matters to you, the perennial arriviste.

If the OBN worked because of an individual's membership in one club or another, there would be no way to acquire OBN benefits without being a member of that club—a requirement that, for you, would be rather impractical and impossible. But if, on the other hand, the benefits of the OBN could be had by virtue of some other factor— "likeness," for example—then OBN benefits could be had by anyone aware of the true OBN indicator and capable of simulating it.

If you walk like a duck and talk like a duck, you will be treated like a duck whether or not you are called a duck.

Importantly, the OBN is but an example of the operation of the rule. The Rule of Likes also works where there are no formal OBNs. It works on a business level. It works on an individual, one-on-one level. It works virtually everywhere. And it works well.

Say you do not walk like a duck. You do not talk like a duck. And you are not called a duck. Yet the party with whom you wish to do business is, in fact, a duck. What should you do? Become a decoy: Walk like a duck and talk like a duck and hope that the duck with whom you are interacting thinks that you too are a duck. If it does, you will benefit from duck-to-duck treatment. If it doesn't, it's going to be a duck-eat-dog world.

The point is this: If you can appear to be similar to the party with whom you wish to do business, that party is more likely to accommodate you and your interests. The less alike you appear, the easier it shall be for the other party to deny you your interests and objectives. If the other party can see himself in you, he is likely to want you to succeed. The more obscure that vision becomes, the less kinship that party will feel with you and, therefore, the easier it shall be for him to see you fail.

Listen, Look, Like

You wish to become one with another. You wish to become the person sitting across from you. You wish to become, in a sense, a chameleon. So, like a chameleon, quietly, unobtrusively observe the surroundings, notice their detail, and methodically adopt them.

If your first encounter with your antagonist is a telephonic one, listen. Allow the other party to do most of the talking. Aside from the fact that this is good business practice anyway, doing so will enable you to hear the speaker's style, intonation pattern, rhythm, inflection, tone, mannerisms, accent, jargon, and attitude. As you hear them, you should begin to make them yours, incorporate them into your speech so that it becomes indistinguishable from the speaker's speech.

If your first encounter with your antagonist is a face-to-face meeting and you know nothing about your antagonist's appearance, don't go. Cancel it. Reschedule it. Try not to hold the meeting until you have had an opportunity to know something, anything, about the antagonist.

Assuming that you have learned something about the person you are attempting to harmonize with, do so in a subtle fashion. The point is to harmonize with, not mimic, the person. You don't want the person to think that you are, perhaps, making fun of them, or, in a different vein, trying to steal their style. But you do want harmonic convergence. If the individual favors Italian designer suits, you would be best advised not to wear the same designer's suit but to wear another Italian designer's suit. If the person frequently wipes his brow, you need not wipe your brow. But you might want to comment about the heat.

If you cannot postpone your meeting or if you have no way of learning something about the person with whom you shall be meeting, focus on features that you can quickly adapt rather than on dress and external style, which you cannot. If the person speaks slowly, speak slowly—but do not exaggerate. If the person speaks fast, speak fast too. Allow the antagonist subconsciously to feel that he has found a kindred spirit.

These efforts hold twice true for attitudes and opinions. Remember, your objective in meeting this individual is to hopefully conclude a business agreement with him. You are not there as a brimstone-and-fire preacher. You are not there as a friend. You are not there on a social interaction. You are there as a businessman, on the other side of the deal, with a predetermined agenda.

If the person likes coffee, you like coffee. If the person hates sugar, you hate sugar. If the person smokes, you smoke. If the person likes steak, you like steak. If the person is a socialist, you are a socialist. If the person dislikes the IMF, you dislike the IMF. You follow him to the line. But you do not cross it.

What is the line?

It is the law as it is modified by the prevailing morality—not your own but the society within which you are, as further modified by the role within that society that you and he are playing.

What if the antagonist smokes not cigarettes but hashish? Do you join in? Well, that depends on where you are and who you are.

If you are in Switzerland and you are a banker, then clearly not. Swiss law says no and the local morality says no and a person in your position would and should say no. If you are in Yemen, and you are a smuggler dealing in rhino horn, then clearly yes. The Yemeni law may or may not prohibit it (depending upon which revolution has just taken place), the local morality says yes, and a person in your position would and should say yes. If you are in Greece, on Corfu, and you are a banker on vacation, then clearly the answer is not clear.

In all events, do not engage in criminality or a breach of local ethics if it will place you in an inferior position vis-à-vis your antagonist. Do not allow yourself to be jeopardized by a criminal act even if done by your antagonist who is urging you to partake in it.

What if the antagonist is a bigot? What if you are in Marseilles and the antagonist has been mouthing off about the bloody Arabs this and the bloody Arabs that? No law against it. Morality? Not in Marseilles. Let him proceed and rely upon creative silence to get you by.

But what if it is England, at a City business meeting, and someone mouths off about the "damn niggers"? Don't take the bait. Respectfully ignore the comment and, if you cannot, then make it politely understood that you will not play by those rules. As always, use common sense, allow one leeway, and don't launch into a morality lecture. At the same time, however, don't allow yourself to be sold out cheaply.

There may come a time when a shared secret, a conspiracy, is beneficial. But by that stage it should be you, not the other side, calling the shots in the relationship.

Remember, if you will, we are now talking about business, not undercover work. When you are out in the field, undercover, with no contact, no communication, and no way out, circumstances change. You do what you must.

A cautionary note: Remember how Shechem, Hamor, and the people of their village ultimately wound up. They were massacred by the Israelites. Don't assume that wearing the right tie will convincingly transform an outcast into a socialite. Don't start believing your own pretense. You are not in the OBN, you are only pretending to be. Don't drop your guard.

As the Combatant with the best "banker" cover available, I was considered a natural to take on the challenge. While I didn't quite see the connection, Gray Cell claimed to have worked the whole thing out.

Gray Cell wanted me to enter Syria, find the stash in the abandoned building, and leave the country with the money safely hidden in a double-bottomed suitcase. This was not one of Gray Cell's shining moments.

First of all, no one enters Syria without an invitation. Henry Bloody Kissinger doesn't enter Syria without an invitation. So there was a bit more work to be done on that front. Second, one does not simply roam around Damascus in condemned buildings. So there was more work to do on that front, too. And lastly, no one gets by the Syrian authorities with a double-bottomed suitcase no matter how well made it is. I mean you might as well try and sneak the pope into Mecca, for Christ's sake.

Sure, I wanted the operation, but not on those terms. Samson and I would have to work on Gray Cell for some leeway for me to improvise, even if that meant

elevating the panic level to hysteria, which it did. For-tunately, all parties wanted the money out before it was too late, and frankly, I was the only real shot they had.

No one wanted to tell me how the money got there in the first place. But there were ways to find out what the Office did not want you to know, and the Office taught me most of them.

Untouchables in the know told me that the money had been brought into the country over an extended period of time in order to bribe Hafiz al Assad's son, Basil. The "fix" apparently was an agreement between Basil and a Combatant, known among the Untouchables by his nom de guerre Puzzle, who had befriended Basil and become very close to him.

Puzzle had told Basil that he, Puzzle, could get several million dollars in cash from Edgar Bronfman, the wealthy Jewish philanthropist businessman, for the release of Syria's Jews. (Today, they are essentially trapped, though not harmed, inside the Jewish ghettos of Damascus and Haleb.) Puzzle offered to broker the deal with Bronfman for a modest "broker's fee." Basil had only to lean on Dad (President for Life Hafiz al Assad) to obtain his con-sent for the great, magnanimous gesture. Puzzle was careful to not suggest any motive for the release other than greed, and greed was Basil's mother tongue.

Basil took to the plan like a fish to water. He was very pleased to show Dad that he was his own thinker, and he also liked the idea of making money that was not directly tied to his standard government kickbacks.

Of course, Bronfman had nothing to do with this. His name was just bandied about as the money's source and the interested party. But given Bronfman's very public generosity and his engagement in humanitarian efforts, the story was more than plausible. In fact the money came from Israel's "black" budget, and the plan had been all Gray Cell.

Unfortunately, life got in the way of the plan. After a

night of ribaldry, Puzzle and Basil were driving to the airport. Basil was driving his trademark Mercedes Benz, and Puzzle was driving another of Basil's cars. They were headed to Stuttgart, Germany, where they were going to pick up yet another custom-made Mercedes for Basil. Basil, hung over from too much good booze and with a young woman, head down, in his lap, was not quite focused on his driving. Before he knew it, the car careened off the road onto an embankment. Basil's Mercedes flipped over several times, instantly killing Basil. Puzzle, who miraculously survived uncut, pulled the shaken and injured girl from the wreckage. Then he calmly continued to the airport.

Puzzle now had to leave Syria immediately. No packing, no luggage, no accident report. Because regardless of blame, Assad would have strung him up by the balls.

And that is why the cash was still there.

Several years before this incident, I was at a London cocktail party where I met Kamal Adham, at the time a Saudi government intelligence liaison who was known in intelligence circles as a man worth knowing. As I was still in my financial advisor guise, Kamal insisted that I meet his colleague and business partner Dr. Malek. While waiting for Dr. Malek to tear himself away from the Bank of America's representative who was button-holing him, Kamal told me Malek's family story. The story was a typical one from *The Thousand and One Nights,* which, ironically, would soon pale in comparison to Kamal's story as a shareholder in what was then the hottest financial institution in the world—the Bank of Credit and Commerce International, or as it became better known, BCCI.

Kamal told me that Dr. Malek's father had been a prominent Syrian physician. As the story went, and in the Middle East stories always go, Dr. Malek Senior was minding his own business in Syria when the then king of Saudi Arabia arrived on a state visit to Damascus.

During his stay, the king came down with a bad attack of the flu. Dr. Malek was called in and with his gracious bedside manner, must have told the king very nicely to take two aspirin and call him in the morning.

Well, the aspirin must have worked just fine because the next morning, the king summoned the physician and requested that he return with him to Saudi Arabia to be the king's personal physician. Since one does not refuse the king of Saudi Arabia anything, least of all one's services, and since one certainly does not do so when one's own country is an economic dependency of the Saudis in the first place, Dr. Malek packed his black bag and his family and departed to Saudi Arabia to be the king's personal physician.

After several months of service, the king asked the doctor what the doctor's wages were to be. The doctor, smart fellow that he was, told the king that his wages were the privilege of serving the king. No more was needed.

But the king insisted, as kings will do. And after several consistent refusals from Dr. Malek, the king urged the doctor to accept something, perhaps a concession, for the sake of his young son, Fayed. The doctor yielded to the king and agreed to take the Saudi cement "concession." In a layperson's words, the concession meant that Dr. Malek and family received a percentage of every bag of cement used in the kingdom. The year was 1960. The oil boom was yet to happen. The cities of Jedda, and Riyadh, not to mention others, were mere tents in the sand. Twenty-five years later, the Malek family could not be richer unless they printed money. Which, in a way, was what the bank that Fayed invested part of his inheritance in decided to do.

The annals of BCCI are now public record. The details can be gleaned from numerous indictments and other sources of information filed against the bank all over the world. Suffice it to say that Fayed upstaged even his father's knack for business.

When Fayed and I met, I knew nothing of BCCI's shady affairs. Nonetheless, there was something about Malek that led me to believe that he played by his own set of rules. Rules that he wrote himself and rewrote when necessary. We exchanged pleasantries, and I quickly attempted to discern what made him run. Well, there was money, but I could hardly play in his league. And there was Paris, where he had an office and where I had an office, and then, deus ex machina, there was diving. Fayed was an avid diver and Jedda, where he lived while he was not traveling, was a diver's Mecca, or so he said. Malek suggested that I come see him in Jedda "sometime," where he had access to a private reef ordinarily reserved for the Saudi royal family.

Now, five years later and after the collapse of BCCI, I was following up on Malek's offer.

Almost OBN

You will not always be able to chameleon-like transform yourself into the other. You will not always be able to become a member of the Old Boy Network by proxy. You will not always be able to lay claim to all of those traits that set apart the OBN from its surrounding. What do you do then? You adopt parallel traits.

It would serve little purpose when traveling in the Gulf to pretend to be a Muslim. The religion is far too complex, its habits far too esoteric, and the likelihood of a European businessman or -woman being Muslim is so small that any assertion of Islam would raise far too many inquiries. There would, however, be nothing wrong if you emphasized and adhered a bit more closely to your own religion when in the presence of a religious counterpart. Your respect for your own religion, however different from the target of your attention, shall make you closer to him than a nonreligious businessman would be.

It would serve little purpose when encountering a Manchester United football (soccer) fan to pretend to be a devoted fan, too. First of all, you are not likely to persuade the fan that you truly know anything at all about United, let alone the game. But there would, however, be nothing wrong if you were to adopt the pose of a sports fanatic—generic but useful. It would then not be out of the ordinary for you to have (and to express) an interest in all sports, including football, and in all sports teams, including United.

"Almost OBN" is a characteristic not to be lightly dismissed. In the heat of a business disagreement, in the challenge of a missed deadline, in the harsh environment of lost opportunity, a kinship, however remote, may be the only thing that holds you together with your business partner. When business sparring partners fight, coming together again on another deal is the challenge. The OBN as a common denominator between them allows them to do so. The "almost OBN" is the functional equivalent to that. It is "three-ninths" to someone else's "two-sixths."

I am quite sure that Dr. Fayed Malek had not the slightest clue who I was when I called him. But Saudis are hospitable and Fayed especially so. Since I was in Riyadh anyway, of course I should come see him. He would send a driver to meet me at the airport.

Aside from that chance meeting with Fayed in London, I knew nothing more about him. I would therefore have to play this encounter by ear. I did know that being from a once-prominent Syrian family, Fayed could get me an invitation to Syria. I also knew that such an invitation would probably allow me relatively free movement in Damascus and that it would "harden" my cover against failure. I did not know how the fall of BCCI impacted Fayed's standing in Saudi Arabia or Syria, but since as best as one could ascertain at the time, neither country was heavily damaged by the bank's collapse, I hoped that the repercussions, if any, would be minor.

Arriving in Jedda, I was taken to a mansion, a palace really, in what had to be Jedda's most coveted neighborhood. The building was the size of a city block and was covered with white Italian marble. Fayed waited for me at the doorway in a traditional galabiya. He embraced me

the Arab way, kissing me on both cheeks. I embraced him back in the same fashion, firm but not too familiar.

Fayed said that he was happy to see me, pretending to remember who I was.

I, too, said that I was happy to see him, although I wasn't about to remind him exactly where we met and how he knew me because I did not know what he truly thought of his former business partners at the bank. Fayed took me by my hand into the expansive living room, where we engaged in chitchat. Then, after a few minutes:

"Would you care for a drink, my friend?"

This was tricky. I was in Saudi Arabia, a country controlled by Sharia, Islamic law, in which alcohol is prohibited. Local customs prohibited it as well. Moreover, there was nowhere to legally buy the stuff anyway. And, although Fayed seemed to be holding a highball, it was a clear liquid in a clear glass. It could have been gin, vodka, araq, or water.

"I'll have what you're having. Thank you."

"My pleasure." Fayed proceeded to the wet bar in the living room and turned his back on me as he prepared my drink. His broad dimensions blocked the ingredients from view. He turned around moments later with my drink in his outstretched hand. "Tfadal," he said.

I took the drink from his hand, made the expected upward gesture with my glass, and took the drink to my lips. I didn't know what to expect. I would have preferred to take a sip before committing myself to the drink, but Fayed was not a man with whom one sipped drinks. I opened my mouth and took a hearty drink. It was water. I was disappointed.

Fayed and I engaged in small pleasantries: Jedda, the recent Saudi economic troubles, and the weather, which in the desert is always a rather brief conversation. I then commented on a photograph on the wall, which showed a huge white tent in what looked to me like the pilgrimage site at Arafat, one of the three objects of Islam's holy "Haj," or pilgrimage. (The Haj is the pilgrimage to Islam's three holy sites: Mecca, Medina, and Arafat, following in the footsteps of the Prophet. Each devout Muslim is supposed to make the Haj at least once in his lifetime. Although I had never been to Arafat—or to Mecca, which is of course closed to infidels—I was very familiar with the way it looked, having studied Islam and its holy places during my Combatant training.)

"Yes, quite good, my friend. That is Arafat. That is our family tent. You see, every five years, I gather all of our friends and family and we make the pilgrimage together. Look, let me show you."

With that, Fayed pulled out two very large leather-bound photograph albums and beckoned for me to join him on the couch.

"You see, many people in the West have a misconception about Islam. They think it is a harsh, fanatic religion. But it is not. It is a social religion. It is a family religion. It allows us to spend time together, on pilgrimage, on Ramadan. Yes, there are fanatic offshoots, late-comers to Islam, like the Shia of Iran and parts of Iraq. But they are not true Muslims. That is not the true, Wahabi, religion. We Sunnis, we observe these rules and customs devoutly, for us, for our family."

"Yes. I understand. I agree. You know, I too am an observant, traditional man. We are Catholic, like you, the true religion, not a later offshoot. Catholicism is, in fact, Fayed, quite similar in many regards to Islam. You have Ramadan, we have Lent. You have the Mecca pilgrimage, we have our pilgrimages to Lourdes, to Bethlehem. And, of course, the family plays an important part of our rituals, too."

"Quite, quite. Here, let me show you." Fayed opened the album to show me his personal "family pictures." Inside were photographs of tents the size of those of the

Ringling Brothers Circus sporting open flaps with truck-sized air conditioners alongside. There were about ten or fifteen Range Rovers parked around the tents. There were at least one hundred or more people in the photos. They were all part of Fayed's small immediate "family."

"It must be very nice to have the family and friends together like that every now and again. We do so every year at Christmas when we bring the entire family to our Provence home for a small gathering, no more than twenty or so families, not larger than yours. The children love it."

"The children must indeed love it. So where are your children, now?"

I looked up at the coffee table where there was a photo of Fayed with a young man who in appearance at least looked like his son.

"Oh, they're grown and out on their own."

"Yes, mine too. In college, here." And with that, Fayed reached over to the photo that I had espied and gave it to me. "That is my son. In business school already."

"Mine too. Where does yours attend?"

"California, USC."

"Excellent, mine is at Fontainebleau, near Paris."

"Come." Fayed got up from the sofa. "Let us have dinner."

Fayed and I were bonding.

We passed through Fayed's study on the way to the dining room. The study walls were covered floor to ceiling with the most impressive series of "power photos" that I have seen this side of the Potomac: Fayed with Jimmy Carter, Fayed with Andrew Young, Fayed with Bert Lance, Fayed with George Bush, Fayed with Robert Altman. If there was a Washington power broker worth hanging on the wall, Fayed had him.

I was impressed and, to tell the truth, a bit concerned. Here I had made the pilgrimage to Jedda hoping to find someone I could do "business" with and all

I find was an upstanding, respected, well-connected, and observant servant of Islam. I needed a drink.

Fayed, putting his large beefy arm around me, steered me toward the dining room. We entered a comfortably sized semicircular dining room. Off to one side was a table covered with chafing dishes and plates laden with exotic foods. Next to it was a rolling wet bar laden, top to bottom, with bottles of gin, vodka, bourbon, whiskey, and wine.

Hallelujah.

At Fayed's request, I sat catty-corner to him and our wineglasses were immediately filled. I, of course, said nothing to Fayed, as though this rich display and variety of alcohol was a commonplace matter in Saudi Arabia, and Fayed acted as if it were. I suppose the rich are different.

Dinner was served by four waiters and a wine steward. The doctor had concluded, for reasons known only to him, that I was "OK," and after several glasses of an excellent Bordeaux, he decided to get down to business, which was fine with me. If Fayed was ready for business, so was I.

"So what does bring you to Jedda, my dear friend?" he asked.

"Oh, the usual. It is boring, I'm afraid. Money problems, actually. Too much money, too few options."

"And what precisely does that mean?"

"Only that my clients have, shall we say, made some unwise investments in the so-called emerging countries only to learn that they were emerging not quite as quickly as they had hoped. So, as I'm sure you've seen time enough before, they have large sums of money tied up in assets which can't be liquidated or even if liquidated cannot be repatriated. They are stuck with cold cash in some very inconvenient places. Saudi Arabia is merely a way station for me between Yemen and Syria, where, most unfortunately, one of my clients has a rather large amount of hard currency with very few good options. But, why am I boring you with these matters?"

"No, not at all. Not at all. This is what I do, after all. Well, of course, not me, not now, but we have relations, from our bank. We address problems like this every day. And you say you have these problems frequently?"

"All the time, Fayed, all the time."

"And what are, if I may ask, without offending, of course, what are 'large sums'?"

"Ten, fifteen million dollars at a time. Not quite in the national league but large enough to be an irritant to my clients. You know, for many it isn't even the money, but the principle of salvaging at least something."

"Yes, yes, I quite agree. So you're on your way to Syria, you say? Do you know that that is our family's home? That is our ancestral home. Damascenes, all of the Maleks."

"No, I didn't. But I am quite charmed by the city. Quite beautiful too. Unfortunately, I am there to, I suppose, write off several million dollars. We shall have to forfeit it to the government, to the Alawites, such a shame, when you think of it. Good money, bad investment." (Assad, the president of Syria, is an Alawite, a minority sect in Syria. Most Muslims scorn the Alawites, who are not considered to be true Muslims. Nonetheless, because of Assad's iron rule, Alawites rule the country.)

"But no, no. You shall go to our family bank there. Here, one minute."

Fayed got up from the table and disappeared into his study. He came back with a handwritten note, in Arabic, on his own stationery and, on a separate piece of paper, the name and address of the general manager of what used to be BCCI's Damascus correspondent bank.

"You call this gentleman. He will solve your problems for you whatever they are. Tell him that I promised you so. And if this transaction goes to your satisfaction, you shall return to me and we shall do more business together. Here, there, money knows no boundaries."

Fayed handed me the papers and raised his wineglass. I was tempted to say L'Chaim.

PART 3

PERSISTENCE

Money and Politics

HOW AND WHEN TO PLAY A ROLE

▓ ROLES

"Natati Kesef HaSade, Kach Memeni . . ."

"I Will Give the Money for the Field, Take from Me . . ."

Natati Kesef HaSade . . . Ephron, the son of Zohar of the children of Heth, the inhabitants of Hebron, offers Abraham a familial burial site free of charge. "Take it, it's yours," he says. But Abraham will not do so. He insists, indeed demands, to pay for it. Otherwise, if he may not pay for it, he tells Ephron, he will not accept it. Ephron agrees and Abraham acquires the cave of Machpelah, where eventually Abraham and Sarah, his wife, are buried.

Why did Abraham insist on acquiring the cave? Why did he not simply accept the good graces of his host and accept the site as a gift?

Abraham refused the gift because of the "Tyranny of Roles." Abraham did not wish to be thrust into the role of a recipient, a dependent, one who took from others. Abraham did not want someone, someone about whom he knew very little, to be able to say: "I made Abraham what he was . . . Abraham took from me." Abraham knew that one's role will eventually and ultimately determine the dynamics of present and future relationships. And Abraham had no reason to settle upon a dependent status, knowing, as he did, that status determines outcome.

Damascus always gives me the chills. Here I felt more "in the cold" than anywhere else in Arabia. While the Arab world was (and, unfortunately, continues to be) characterized by regimes that had little solicitude for human rights of their own citizens let alone others, there was no place in the Arab world, Iraq included, where the rulers summarily executed the entire population of one of its towns and wiped it from the face of the earth. Yet that was precisely what Syria's president for life, Hafiz al Assad, did in the town of Hamah: In the early 1980s, twenty to thirty thousand people were slaughtered by Assad's military regime in less than a week.

What was the life of one spy in the balance?

The Tyranny of Roles

All human commerce resides in status; there are but two roles in business and they alone determine action. There is the "buyer" and there is the "seller." The buyer wants to buy and the seller wants to sell. Knowing which you are is elementary, obvious, and hardly a difficult task. Knowing, however, how to act in each of the two roles can be the key to success or failure.

The Tyranny of Roles dictates that, knowingly or not, those with a greater stake in the outcome of a transaction will behave like the seller and those with a lesser stake in a transaction's outcome will adopt the stereotypical role of buyer.

In the common illustration, the seller (the proverbial "salesman," with all of its connotations and baggage) is the eager, persistent, dogged, and ever-cheery side of the equation. The buyer occupies and balances the equation's other side: skeptical, cautious, elusive, and remote.

In the typical business setting, for example, the entrepreneur is the seller; the bank, the buyer. The public company, the seller; the stock market the buyer. The vice president, the seller; the CEO, the buyer. In romance, for example, the male is the proverbial seller while the female is still, virtually always, the buyer—

even, you will note, when the buyer is actually more interested in the seller's wares than the seller is to sell those wares.

In other words (and quite ironically), the Tyranny dictates that even when the real buyer wants to buy more than the real seller wants to sell, the parties will nonetheless conform to their stereotypical roles and thus defeat the true purpose each is aiming for.

But should you?

No, regardless what role you occupy and regardless whether you wish to buy or sell, in general, one should always be a seller, not a buyer.

First of all, if you do wish to sell (or if you simply desire the fruition of the transaction more than the other side), you must be the "seller." Otherwise, if you are not, you are quite unlikely to conclude the transaction. You must be nice, cheery, eager, open, persistent, responsive, attentive, determined, flexible, and reasonable in order to see the transaction through. The buyer will expect it of you, and somewhere along the timeline of the transaction, as the party more interested in the transaction, it will fall to you to exhibit each and every one of these traits. You will be far more likely to succeed in the endeavor if you embrace these characteristics than if you do not.

But you should also embrace and exhibit these traits if you are the "buyer," the party who is less driven to conclude the transaction than the seller, because doing so will throw the seller off kilter and out of intellectual equilibrium. By breaking the Tyranny of the Roles, you are placing the other party into an unfamiliar landscape. You are creating a cognitive dissonance in the other side: "If I want the transaction so much, why is the other party working harder than I?"

By shattering the Tyranny of Roles you will gain points with the other side by being "nice" when, according to the Tyranny, it was not your responsibility to be "nice." More important, you will be grabbing the dynamics of the relationship away from the other party along with the situational, sociological confines into a realm all your own.

It was for that reason that Abraham, the needy outsider, refused to accept the gift. By declining hospitality, he transformed from a known quantity into an intangible force. That was where he wanted to be, and that is where you must be.

Arriving in Damascus, one immediately noticed the all-pervasiveness of Assad's Mukhabarat (secret police). The airport was surveyed by so many police and so many different military and paramilitary police that one wondered who was watching those police who themselves were watching the police? Passports, not only mine, were carefully scrutinized, and the border police demanded to know not only how long one intended to stay but where and to what end. By the time I left the airport, I felt as though I had already been through a hostile cross-examination.

As anyone who has ever had a police car pull out from the road's shoulder to follow them with flashing lights and siren, only to then pass them to pursue another, one need not be guilty to feel guilty and pursued. Consider, if you will, the feeling when one, in fact, is guilty and that police car pulls out. . . .

As a matter of caution and convenience, I had contacted the Damascus Sheraton Hotel ahead of my arrival and arranged for them to send a car to the airport to collect me. It added a measure of legitimacy to my presence, and every bit helped.

I spent my first afternoon and evening in Damascus, for the most part, in my hotel room. I was hoping to get my anxiety back to a manageable level. I roamed the lobby and had several glasses of the Damascus trademark bland lemonade in the bar. I returned to my room at about 10:00 P.M., popped a few Zanax, and fell into a deep sleep. I had dreams of running around Hamah wrapped in an Israeli flag. In my dream, hundreds of Assad-driven tanks fired unmarked dollar bills toward me. It could have been worse.

In the morning, I awoke calm and refreshed. Chemicals. Without them undercover work itself would be impossible. I showered, put on my asbestos-treated suit, and went down to the restaurant, where I had several thick and muddy cups of coffee and a traditional Syrian breakfast of pita, labna, olives, and tomatoes. By nine, I was in the lobby, near the reception area, awaiting Dr. George Hawran, a prominent member of Syria's landed gentry and a real estate and sometime hotel broker.

Hawran was here to broker a deal for a hotel development in the city. He represented the property's owners and I, well, I represented Hilton Hotels.

Operationally, there was little risk associated with a broad and bland claim of representing as large and as amorphous an institution as Hilton Hotels. First of all, Hilton had recently split into several companies with an ongoing feud persisting between its various claimants to be the true Hilton. Second, no one in an organization as large and as diverse as Hilton would ever be able to categorically state that John Harrington, my pseudonym of the moment, did not represent Hilton. And last, but certainly not least, the hotel business was notorious for people claiming to represent international hotel chains in the hope of brokering a deal.

Most hotel chains, and Hilton is no exception, are either franchises or "operators" operating the hotel for a cut of the revenue and profit. So hotel companies always had their sharks, commissioned agents, snooping around for new opportunities.

A portion of the Damascus property in question was Puzzle's former residence. It was part of a city block that the government had condemned in order to widen a main thoroughfare and convert the area into a "business" development zone. Assad still didn't seem to understand that the reason Syria was a commercial backwater had little to do with the availability (or lack thereof) of another conference center.

Hawran, an educated, rather quiet wisp of a man, seemed ill suited for the role of broker and real estate agent. Perhaps his were the ingredients that allowed for success in the Syrian climate. Hawran was in his "seller" mode; he was smiling so much that I began to wonder if the sides of his mouth were attached to his nostrils. Hawran wanted to take me to lunch, dinner, and another breakfast if it would make me happy. Clearly, Hawran perceived that the transaction was more important to him than it was to me, which in ordinary circumstances would have been a correct perception. But these were not ordinary circumstances.

Hawran was taken aback by my "seller" mode. He had planned and prepared for a hard sell. Yet here was I, the buyer, so to speak, welcoming his overtures. Why, he must have been asking himself, was I being so nice and eager to please? That was his role. As he mulled over that, I suggested that we visit the sites.

Hawran's driver drove us around the block, pointing out which properties were condemned. The driver then parked the car, and Hawran and I walked the grounds. Our first stop was Puzzle's house.

Hawran walked up the open stairs to the door and pulled out a key ring. After trying one or two keys, he found the right one and opened the bottom lock. I was leaning against the door with all my weight. As the door swung open, I stumbled onto Hawran, throwing him forward. Hawran took the brunt of my weight and dropped the folder he was holding, scattering papers and city maps all over the dusty hallway.

It took a few minutes for Hawran to catch his breath, but when he did, he apologized to me even though I was the perpetrator of the fall. I in turn apologized to him and helped him up. Hawran turned quickly to gathering up his papers while I took the keys from the door. Quickly, I "impressed" the door key into the soft wax mold that was hidden in the tobacco can that I had kept in my blazer. A second or two later, I closed the can and returned it to my pocket. Hawran was still collecting his papers. When he was through, I handed the keys to Hawran.

Hawran was still flustered and shaken. I came down very hard on him in the fall, and for all I know, I may have cracked one of his ribs. He was in pain and needed a few moments to catch his breath. Would I mind very much if he took a moment to recover?

"Hawran, I insist. Let's go get a lemonade, cool off, catch our breath, and then come back here. I am in no hurry. And you need to rest a bit. After all, I want to see everything."

"Fine, fine. Very good. Let us go to a café. Follow me, please."

Hawran walked us two blocks down the road to an open-air café. He chose a table in the shade. I excused myself and went to the bathroom. In the bathroom, with the door safely closed behind me, I lowered my trousers and underpants, sat down on the toilet, and took the locksmith implements out of my blazer's pockets.

First, I opened the tobacco can and blew the tobacco off of the wax mold. Then I screwed the top off the liquid zinc tube that Illusions had kindly enclosed in an eyedrop tube. I poured the liquid zinc into the mold and let it sit on my lap for a moment while I unscrewed the nose-drop dispenser, again, provided courtesy of Illusions. I placed three drops of the nose drops into the liquid zinc. The nose drops were some sort of hardening agent that hardened the liquid zinc. Illusions had warned me about it: "Put a drop in your nose and you'll be sneezing cement" was the way, if I recall correctly, that they put it.

Lastly, I broke the wax out of the tobacco can, broke it up into the toilet, and removed the now hard silver-looking key from the wax. I flushed the toilet and joined Hawran. The entire procedure took less than five minutes.

Hawran was calm and visibly enjoying the cup of coffee he was sipping. There was a glass of lemonade on the table for me. I sat down next to him and took a sip of my lemonade: warm, sweet, and sickly, just as I liked it.

"Great lemonade." I smiled at Hawran. He smiled back.

We finished our drinks, I made the motion to my wallet but allowed Hawran to pay, and we walked back to the development site. Hawran proposed that we reenter Puzzle's house.

"I don't think so, Hawran. Maybe we need to build ourselves up for this one. Let's start instead with one of the other buildings and work our way back here."

Hawran agreed and we walked one house past Puzzle's to a large stone house encircling a courtyard. Hawran fiddled with his key chain again while I waited behind him. He opened the door into a dark, dusty, large home. Its furniture and draperies were still intact, suggesting that whoever left this place was not given a lot of time to pack. I closed the door behind me. The electricity had long ago been turned off, so Hawran walked ahead of me with a flashlight. The walk-through was perfunctory, just to give me a sense of the space occupied by the building since all of it was coming down anyway.

In the darkness, as we approached what looked like the living area, I reached into my pocket and took out a slightly oversized roll of Mentos, a mint candy. Illusions' instructions were to throw each candy down onto a hard surface. I took a handful of them out of the wrapper and let them drop to the floor.

The Mentos hit the floor with a large crackling noise and immediately burst into flames. Some of them bounced to other areas on the floor where there, too, each of them went up in flames. Hawran, startled, dropped the flashlight, which, to my good fortune, came apart and stopped working. We were now shrouded in darkness save for the small flames reaching up from the floor. I tossed the rest of the Mentos to the floor, and the

entire living room was now alight. I pretended not to see
Hawran as he stumbled around the room. He called to
me but I did not answer. I waited a few minutes for the
smoke to intensify. I had my Illusions-treated handkerchief, which made the smoke a lot easier to tolerate.

With the smoke now filling the house, I quickly let
myself out of the front door, leaving it slightly ajar. The
fire and smoke were now visible from the outside of the
house. In a few minutes the area would be surrounded
by fire trucks and police. Fortunately, the fire was
spreading quickly, and with all of the homes in close
proximity to one another, the fire could be expected to
spread to the other condemned buildings as well. I made
a beeline for Puzzle's house.

I dashed up the stairs and slid my key into the key-
hole. It didn't work. I tried again. This time the key
broke in the door. I took a step back and kicked the door
open. Taking my own halogen flashlight out, I quickly
climbed the stairs of the building. Having studied the
house plans for hours in preparation for this mission, I
could have walked through this building in my sleep.

In the master bedroom, along the southeastern wall,
was a prayer alcove. I tapped the inside curve of the
alcove with my pocketknife until I heard the deep
empty thud that distinguished empty plaster from the
otherwise thick concrete blocks that made up the rest
of the house. Finding the thin plaster, I scratched at it
furiously with both hands, literally pulling the wall out
of place. In the background I could hear the sounds of
sirens. I glanced out the window. The fire was now raging through the rooftop and was spreading rapidly.

After pulling more of the plaster off the wall, I came
to a cardboard layer. I yanked it out too. Behind it was a
black canvas bag. Inside the bag was the money. Hur-
riedly, almost frantically, I dropped the cash bundles
into my double-lined jacket. Would it fit? Illusions said
it would, but at this point I could only guess. I was get-

ting hot and I noticed that I was soaking wet. The room I was in was quickly filling up with smoke. I looked out the window and saw that I was in the midst of a smoke cloud with fires burning everywhere. As best I could tell, they had already reached the house.

I stuffed the remainder of the cash wads into my jacket, and whatever didn't fit I kept in the bag. I ran down the smoke-filled stairs. Instead of leaving through the front, I ran to the back of the house, where the kitchen opened up onto a courtyard. The entire area was blanketed with dense black smoke. I took the Illusions handkerchief out again but it was far less effective now than before. Through the courtyard, I was able to identify and reenter the building Hawran and I first entered. It was now an inferno. I could only hope that the asbestos-impregnated garments I was wearing would do the job. After all, even Armani himself could not afford the suit I was now wearing.

The building was filled with the hubbub of the fire-fighters. I shouted for help, and one of them quickly came to my side, showing me out the door. I had already rolled up the black money bag and stuffed it into my shirt. I stepped outside, doubled up, coughing and wheezing. Hawran was right there, nervously waiting for me to reappear.

He tried to hug me, but I pushed him away.

"Hotel," I mumbled.

"Hospital?" he offered.

"Hotel," I sternly replied.

Hawran helped me into the waiting car and drove me to the hotel. I coughed so as to avoid talking. As soon as we arrived, I bolted for the elevators. I was a mess and Hawran, to my good fortune, stepped out of the car and explained to the bewildered guards and tourist police about our misfortune or good fortune, however one viewed these things.

Safely in my room, I tore my clothes off and stuffed

them into my suitcase, which I then locked. I collapsed into the bathtub more out of exhaustion from anxiety than true fatigue.

Another day, another dollar.

I must have spent the better part of the afternoon in the bathtub. I ignored the phone calls and the knocking on the door. I dozed off at least once, awakening only when my head fell over into the water. When I finally gathered the strength to get out of the tub, I was as wrinkled as a little old man. The phone was ringing.

Listening to Roles

Every player "speaks" a role. And every listener can determine whether any given player is a "seller" or a "buyer." Doing so requires no special talent or sensitivity. It is simply a matter of practice and attention. There will always be one party more eager than the other to advance the relationship, conclude a transaction. That party is the "seller." You have power over that party.

In light of the above, it is essential for you, the business player, to develop the antenna that will enable you to make that distinction, to identify the seller. It is information that you cannot glean from any source other than the player himself, and it is information that overpowers many other so-called objective criteria such as financial need, business necessity, or personal gain.

It is difficult to say why one is a "seller" or a "buyer" in any given transaction. It may take a psychologist years to determine a player's motivating forces. Some people need to be loved, others need to be liked. But you don't really care about that. What you care about is how to read the role and use it to your advantage.

In dealing with a seller, you can afford to push harder than you otherwise would. Ultimately, even in a crashed negotiation, the seller will not allow discussions to break off. Therefore, know your opponent's role and use it to your advantage.

In contrast, in dealing with a "buyer" you must be cautious. A buyer will by nature be skeptical; if you push too hard you will simply raise his suspicions about you and about your motives. In dealing with a buyer you must be conservative. A buyer will be waiting for a hard sell; if you fulfill that expectation, you will be playing the role he is prepared to see you play. By being conservative and guarded, by allowing that you might not care if he "buys," you will pull the rug out from under him and cause a complete turnaround in his expectations.

Do not, however, push your position with a buyer. A buyer is not one to salvage a broken-down negotiation or to repair a botched presentation.

"Hello?"

"Hawran here. I am so happy to hear you. What an adventure. I did not want to leave the building without you, my friend. The fireman, they forced me, I couldn't control it. But I sent them back in for you. But good news, you save the demolition costs now."

Hawran was in his seller's mode. It was time to cool him off.

"Sorry, old boy. I really can't proceed with this right now. It was very dangerous to have entered that building. I was quite shaken, you know. Perhaps in a month or so. We'll have to see. Stay in touch, if you will."

"But, no, this is a very good opportunity. . . ."

I hung up. I had more important things to do now than scouting out hotel sites for dubious investors. I ordered room service and crawled into bed. Tomorrow I would meet Mr. Ahmed El Azzem, the scion of an ancient political family dating back to Syria's seventeenth century, the former director of the Syrian branch of BCCI and today a Malek family banker.

The next morning, I phoned the bank. I waited for ten or more minutes while someone went to fetch Mr. El Azzem. When he finally answered the phone, I assumed that I was speaking to him and to every police and security detail in the greater Damascus region.

"Welcome, welcome, welcome, my dear sir. A pleasure, a pleasure, truly. Dr. Malek speaks most highly of

you, most highly. Might I entertain you here at the bank?
Anytime, anytime."

"Well, thank you, Mr. El Azzam. I promised Dr.
Malek that I would entertain you, not vice versa. I therefore insist, if I may, that you come here so that we may
lunch together. Today. Perhaps now?"

El Azzam wasn't stupid. What matter if I was asking
him to a 10:00 A.M. lunch? I was Malek's man. He'd be
there.

I waited for Mr. El Azzam in the lobby. I made sure
that the tourist police missed none of our warm embrace.
I wanted El Azzam's political standing in Damascus to
reflect well upon me. I took El Azzam by the arm, turned
him around, and walked back to his limousine, which
was still standing in the entrance to the hotel. El Azzam
did not object. We got into the car and I told the driver to
drive away. The driver looked at El Azzam, who nodded
approval. El Azzam told the driver to head to the New
Bab (New Gate) of the city of Damashq, the old city of
Damascus. I looked out the back to see how many cars
were following us. None. Either my quick maneuver had
worked or El Azzam was beyond regime surveillance.

El Azzam and I walked the distance from the city gate
to an indoor café. Inside, El Azzam was all business and
no pleasantries.

Changing Roles

In an ideal world, the buyer's stance is preferable to that of the seller.
As the buyer, you control the situation's dynamics and you can, quite
subtly, dictate the relationship with the seller. After all, the seller
wants what the buyer has, sometimes money, sometimes something
else of value to the seller, whereas the buyer may or may not want
what the seller has and certainly does not need to let the seller know
even if he does.

But not always.

What happens when the seller has something that the buyer wants and both the seller and the buyer know that. Role reversal. The seller becomes in a sense the buyer and the buyer becomes the seller. The seller shall now control, or at least be on equal footing with, the buyer and the buyer shall have to accommodate the seller, sometimes to the point of buying the seller's wares even if he does not want them.

Consider the roles of a policy-setting government official and a lobbyist. The lobbyist is the seller; he wants the government official to change government policy to suit the lobbyist's industry. The government official, the buyer, has no particular reason to accommodate the seller. Unless he wants a job with the seller. Unless he needs a campaign contribution from the seller. Unless he seeks the seller's support in changing a different policy, which in order to effect, he shall need the lobbyist's support. Some call it politics, others bribery. The important lesson is the role reversal effected by the lobbyist.

There is an old Arab proverb that states: The cow wishes to give milk more than the calf desires it (the milk). What is this proverb than another way of suggesting that role reversal is possible? Most observers would suspect that the calf is beholden to the cow—without the cow's milk the calf cannot grow. On the surface a seemingly classic buyer-seller relationship. But the cow, as any farmer knows, must unload its milk or suffer excruciating pain and illness. So the cow needs the calf as much as, if not more than, the calf needs it. Role reversal.

In a business setting, on or off the farm, be aware of the opportunities to effect role reversal. When you are a seller, seek the occasion to make the buyer a coseller. Discern what the buyer's interests are. Where can you fill one of the buyer's needs? When you are a buyer, be alert to attempts to compromise your position. Has a new job been suggested? A kickback possibility bandied about?

"Dr. Malek mentioned a problem. . . ."
"A problem of riches, if you will."
"Perhaps we can help."

"We have a client, perhaps here in Damascus, hypo-
thetically, of course."

"Of course."

"The client, well, the client has a large sum of money,
small unmarked bills, hard currency, which the client,
you know how clients can be, finds rather difficult to use
here."

"I understand."

"The client, shall we say, would like to know whether
he might make a loan of the money to you here in
exchange for an unsecured borrowing abroad. Some perfectly legitimate transaction, of course, because my
client, as Dr. Malek may have mentioned, is quite prominent."

"We have arranged some such transactions for the
doctor's associates before."

"Of course, there would have to be no names."

"Of course."

"And if it proceeded well, there could be many more
such transactions."

"Proceed well it shall."

"What, my client might wish to know, what would the
standard commission be on something like this?"

"How much is at question?"

"Millions."

"Yes, one would assume that. How many millions?"

"Fourteen and change."

"Seventy cents to the dollar. Quite like BCCI. I
assume it is dollars?"

"Yes, it is."

"Then seventy cents it is."

"Is that the Malek rate?"

"That is the only rate."

"Then that is the rate. Would you care to join me in
my room?"

"It would be my pleasure."

El Azzam took the money without even counting it.

He handled it as one who did this sort of thing daily, and for all I knew he did. One week later El Azzam transferred $10,220,000 from Damascus to my own numbered account at Bank Indo-Suez. From there it was wired through two Panamanian banks, onto the Office and, from there, back to the government's Black Budget to be used for another day.

Service with a smile, the good old BCCI way.

Fighting for Air

THE POSITIVE NO

"Halm BeAvour Hamishim Ve Lo . . . ?"
"Peradventure There Shall Lack Five of the Fifty Righteous . . . ?"

Halm BeAvour Hamishim . . . ? God said to Abraham that he would save the city of Sodom if there could be found fifty righteous men in the city. Fifty—no more, no less. This is the direct word of the Lord. God. Not an angel, not a messenger, but God.

Does Abraham take this announcement to heart? Does Abraham take his leave to begin a search for the needed fifty men? Does Abraham accept the Lord's "bottom line"? No, he does not. He proceeds to negotiate with God. To bargain with God. To ignore and disregard God's position, clearly stated.

And Abraham does not stop until the Lord accedes to an 80 percent discount: ten righteous men. Only ten.

Libya was stockpiling chemicals, and there was more than just bullshit involved.

For months now, the Office was aware of Libya's intentions in chemical/biological warfare, and for years Israel voiced its frustration with Libya's main supplier, Germany. Unfortunately, Israel's protestations were to no avail. The German authorities persistently and with righteous indignation denied that any German company would, indeed could, be engaged in the sale of banned chemicals to the terrorist state of Libya.

The Germans were right to be indignant. After all, how would it look if Germany, stopped from exterminating Jews with Zyklon-B in World War II, were to be found to be supplying Libya, one of Israel's most rabid enemies, with the chemical weapons to do the same?

My mission was to provide Israel with the hard evidence of Germany's actions.

Avoid the No

It is easier to preserve than to fix. It is also easier to avoid a no than to reverse one once it is given. Listen. Pay close attention to body language, sounds, tone of voice, direction of the head, eyes. If you do, you will spot a no coming from afar. When you do, avoid it. Promptly change the question, alter the landscape of the conversation so that the no is no longer required. Do not persist in face of a certain no expecting to contest it. Avoid it entirely and regroup to refashion your strategy.

Children follow this rule intuitively. They do not have to be taught to avoid a no. Children will preface a request with: "Please don't say no until you've heard me out. . . ." They do so because they have experienced the difficulties of trying to reverse their parent's no once it is uttered.

Learn from the children: Better a yes to an unwanted request than a no to a sought-after objective.

To obtain the evidence I required, I would have to some-how obtain hard shipping documents. I would need doc-uments showing the name of the manufacturer, the name of the shipping agent, and the country of destination. There would be only one way to do that: I would have to order the chemicals myself.

In most civilized countries, getting a permit to import the kinds of chemicals I am referring to, chemicals that allowed you to manufacture weapons for warfare, was virtually impossible. In Libya, it would be a question of pushing the right buttons.

I had Studio do some research for me on what possi-ble Libyan business covers might provide me with an excuse to request the authorities for chemicals, any chemicals. My guess was that with the offer of some busi-ness opportunity, my chances were greater to interest the type of high-level bureaucrat I would need to carry out this caper. I knew that finding such cover would be a challenge anywhere. Finding one for Libya would be well nigh impossible.

But, of course, Studio was quite comfortable with the impossible. It accomplished the impossible for its Com-batants daily. Worldwide. And indeed, it did not take long for Studio to provide me with the blueprint I required.

"Goats."

"Goats?"

"Goats."

I was talking with Zoe, one of Studio's ace scriptwrit-ers, about the Libya cover I was seeking. I was a bit sur-prised to hear her talking about goats, but while Zoe had surprised me before, she never let me down. If she wanted to talk goats, I would talk goats.

"OK, listen carefully because this is how you do it: Libya has goats. Goats have skin. Skins can be turned into leather. Leather can be exported to Europe for hard currency. Libya wants hard currency. Voilà, there's your cover."

"Bear with me here, Zoe, because I'm missing something. How do I get from goats to chemicals?"

"Tanneries, Simon, tanneries. Tanneries are where you turn goatskins into leather. Goatskin in, leather—or at least something that is much closer to leather than a goatskin is—out. To do so, however, you need chemicals. To get chemicals, you have to buy them. The only place to buy such chemicals—logically for a Libyan tannery, that is—is Italy or Germany. That, Mr. Simon, is how you get your chemicals."

"Great. Now how do I get a tannery?"

"You don't, silly. That's the beauty of this. You simply tell the Libyan authorities that you wish to buy or build, you'll figure that one out, a tannery in Libya. Then you tell them that as part of your tannery infrastructure you need tannery chemicals. The Libyans make all of their chemical purchases centrally from their Department of Agriculture. We know that they regularly insert into their innocent requests purchase orders for banned chemicals. In listing the chemicals you require, we will provide you with names of one or two compounds that cannot possibly be used for anything other than binary chemical weapons. The Germans fill your order and the Office has its proof."

I liked it. But I would have to get permits and licenses to do business in Libya, and that would be no small matter.

"No" Is Often Not the Final Word

A no, any no, as indeed any child will tell you, is no reason to stop asking for the desired result.

There are many reasons why people say no. Few of them have anything to do with a sincere, heartfelt desire to deny you the thing that you want. Think of it. When you last said no, why did you? Was it to gain time? To spare yourself an immediate commitment? To avoid a momentary inconvenience? Would your answer have been different under different circumstances? How difficult would it have been to change those circumstances?

In negotiations, as in life, a no is merely an opening position. Admittedly, a useful opening position, but only an opening position. If you are able to process a no as code for "This is a position which will require more, and perhaps more subtle, negotiation," you will accurately interpret the message being sent. If you are able to process a no as code for "This is a request which I shall have to rephrase," you will accurately process the message being sent. Otherwise, you will lose an important element of the negotiation: determining what is and what is not negotiable.

Emerging from a six-week crash course in the finer points of goatskin selection and tanning from some cooperative tanners in the Italian village of Santa Croce, I arrived in Libya with strong references and several names in the Libyan Ministry of Agriculture. I was quite confident in Studio's suggested business cover, and I could toss around business jargon like "wet-blue" and "pickled" with the best of them. My challenge now was to get the ministry officials to approve my request for a chemical import license—no small feat given that I had no tannery yet.

My first meeting was with Dr. Ahmad Awady, a low-level functionary at the Libyan ministry. My only goal in this meeting was to get on Awady's good side and to recruit him as an advocate for my efforts. I had little doubt that although Awady himself had no power to approve my request, his objection to my request would be enough to deep-six it.

All I knew about Awady was that he had received a Ph.D. in agriculture from Texas A&M in the early 1960s, before Ghaddafi had nationalized Libya's oil. Back then, a degree, any degree, from a Texas institution of higher learning was a guarantee of upward mobility in Libya's civil service. Post-revolution, it was a kiss of death. My guess was that Awady had the misfortune of being in the

wrong place at the wrong time. Given his age, he must have graduated from A&M just as the previous Libyan regime was packing its bags to leave the country. After it was gone, his Texas Ph.D. barely qualified him to make coffee for a Lumumba Community College undergrad.

So I counted on finding a bitter, petty, and unhappy bureaucrat who would want nothing more than to make my life miserable. And I was not mistaken.

After I had been cooling my heels in the ministry's large lobby, chain-drinking cups of sweet tea, for about an hour, an old man in a galabiya gestured for me to follow him. I felt like I was being led by Igor to Dr. Frankenstein's office. He led me through a wide and cobwebbed corridor to a small waiting room. He knocked on the door and opened it. He waved at me to enter. The office was a nasty place: small, dusty, and cluttered. Light streamed in from a small window off to one side and a dark lightbulb hung from the ceiling. Awady was paying heavily for whatever fun he had had in College Station.

Dr. Awady, dressed in a suit that had seen better days, months, and years, welcomed me to his office and to Libya. He told the old man to bring us tea. He offered me the only seat in his office, and he went into the hall to get another. When we were both seated he began.

"I have read your letter, Mr. Simon, and it is quite an interesting proposal. Yes, we should very much expand our leather production. *Aiwa*, good, good. But with Italy, you know our relations are strained, colonial, I cannot recommend a return of Italians to one of our important industries."

"I understand. And, in fact, I think your point on that matter is well taken."

"You do?"

"Absolutely, I do. And that is precisely why I would like to see the underminister for development. Because I think the former policy, as you have said, was quite a

good one for its time and, of course, we cannot change policy on our own. But, if you could simply arrange for me to speak with the underminister, perhaps he can reconsider the government's policy. . . ."

The Appealable No

There is no point in arguing with one who cannot make decisions, change policy, or modify existing practices. A no from such a person, usually a lower-level employee, is really not a no at all. Rather it is a plea from such a person to leave him alone and a request that you appeal his decision to a higher echelon.

If you pleasantly and understandingly accept this no, you should be able to recruit the lower-level decision maker into your camp and learn to whom the negative decision should be appealed and how.

Do not, under any circumstances, waste your time, effort, and emotion arguing an appealable no with such a person. First of all, you will look bad. You will appear as one who cannot read the social pecking order. You will project to onlookers a high degree of obtuseness; how do you not understand that you are wasting your time arguing with one without authority?

Second, you create an enemy where you need an ally. The person with whom you are arguing did not set the policy, indeed he probably doesn't even understand the policy. But by arguing with him, you are forcing him to effect a commitment to the policy that he may not have had before. Now, once he has made such commitment, he will not lightly see it altered, especially by or for the likes of you.

Third, you are wasting precious energy, time, and emotion on the wrong person. And time, energy, and emotion are important resources. At times, they will be the only resources available to you. Therefore, conserve them for effective use. Getting angry is a luxury. Don't indulge yourself.

Dr. Awady became a valuable ally. As could be expected, he was only too happy to create trouble, that is,

work, for his bosses, those arrogant, unqualified bas-
tards who were, after all, not nearly as qualified as he
was for their jobs. Under the guise of impartial
research, and at times, after hours, Awady collected for
me a folder of the Libyan rules and regulations pertain-
ing to the tannery business, including statistics showing
the steady decline of revenues received by Libya for the
export of its "raw," that is untanned, skins. Armed with
this information, I had a real shot at altering government policy. Had I wasted my time in arguing with
Awady, he would have been my enemy. By accepting his
no and recruiting him as an ally, I gained an invaluable
tool in my venture.

Awady was able to get me an audience with the
underminister much sooner than I had expected. All the
same, I was prepared and ready. Awady, having witnessed other foreigners attempt to talk their way into the
Libyan skin trade, knew exactly what issues and questions would arise, and I therefore knew the correct
responses to them all. The underminister, a professional
government bureaucrat, was actually quite knowledge-
able and reasonable. He trotted out all of the usual
arguments against foreign intervention in Libya's
industry, and I, rather than then and there trot out all of
Awady's responses to those arguments, requested time to
consider those points. We scheduled another meeting for
later in the week.

"No": An Invitation to Proselytize

You have been turned down. You have been denied. The surefire,
"no-doubt-about-it" plan you conceived has been destroyed without
even a discussion. Your reasonable, measured request has been jettisoned. Good for you. Your plan (or request) stands a very good
chance of adoption.

Sound absurd? It isn't. A "clean" denial of a request is better than a denial that is based upon careful analysis because the latter tells the request's author that the request has been seriously considered and found to be wanting. It demonstrates that the analysis and consideration due the request have already been afforded the request.

To bring about the adoption of a request that has been analyzed and rejected requires a counteranalysis of the analysis and a dismembering of it. The proponent of the request is now arguing on someone else's terms and is compelled to adopt and attempt to impart a negative point of view regarding that analysis. That fact alone places the likelihood of success at the margins.

Moreover, a reasoned rejection has an author, a parent, a responsible adult who has had to step forward and publicly disparage your request. Once that occurs, your request is taken outside of reason and into the realm of politics. For your request to be approved now, after a reasoned rejection, someone else's reasoning must be rejected. And that may not be possible for reasons entirely extraneous to the request. For example, the party arguing against the request may be more important in toto than you. Therefore, regardless of the request's merits, no one will rock his boat. Or the person arguing against the request may have taken a very strong antirequest stance which when contrasted with your stance (and stature) may warrant rejecting the request even though on balance it would have otherwise been approved.

In short, a reasoned rejection leaves very little room for a comeback. A laconic rejection, in contrast, may mean one of several things, all of which provide you with an excellent starting point for persuasion. A short no may mean that your proposal was misunderstood; or that no time was available to analyze it; or that no one person wanted to bear the ownership of its rejection. It may mean anything, everything, or, most likely, nothing at all.

A rejection of this nature is an invitation to its author to proselytize on its behalf. The naysayers can accept your request regardless of their previous no because none of them have put their intellect at risk by individually studying and then rejecting your plan. They haven't (at least to your knowledge, and from their vantage point that is what counts) analyzed it, dissected it, studied it, and found it wanting. Rather, at this stage, they have really said only the equivalent of "No, not until you tell us more about it."

At my next meeting with the underminister, I came armed with a full-blown "show and tell." I hired a Tripoli artist to transform Awady's statistics and rules into an appealing visual presentation. I also restated my goal from that of wanting to own a tannery to simply wanting to have the right to acquire all of the tannery's output.

The underminister did not stand a chance. He agreed to my requests and invited me to deal directly with him on all tannery matters. No doubt he was seeking a payoff and had no doubt that sooner or later I would give him one. But until I had my chemicals, I would keep him waiting. When it comes to rewards, one's imagination tends to be better than reality.

So, even though I still had no investment in a tannery and no legally binding documents with a tannery, when I submitted my request for chemicals, including those chemicals banned by international treaty, to the ministry, no one blinked an eyelid. And exactly six weeks later, I had my written evidence of Germany's sale of banned chemicals to Libya.

Bad in Brussels

HOW AND WHEN TO ACT BOLDLY

THE BOLD ARSENAL

> "Yatzu Benei Yisrael BeYad Rama LeEynei Kol Mitzrayim."
> "The Sons of Israel Started Out Boldly in the Sight of All the Egyptians."

Yatzu Benei Yisrael . . . The "Sons of Israel," notwithstanding the plagues visited upon Egypt, were nothing more than a raggedy band of slaves; wretched, poor, weak, and downtrodden slaves. Yet they leave Egypt "boldly." And they leave "in plain sight of all of the Egyptians." Why do these slaves leave "boldly"? And why do no Egyptians take action to stop them?

The first question answers the second. The Israelites surprise their oppressors and immobilize them by taking bold action: a surprising move executed in an unexpected fashion. Boldness transforms the very act of leaving into the device that enables the leaving.

Brussels is spy heaven.
Brussels is today what Berlin or Vienna used to be in the bad old days of the cold war. As the seat of NATO, the European Community, and a horde of other national, international, multinational, and nongovernmental organizations, Brussels is home to professionals and other

career-minded individuals of every nationality in every occupation that any spy anywhere might aspire to get close to.

Brussels is to espionage what Paris is to epicures: a place to feast.

Because of its obvious charms, Brussels attracts a lot of spy "pretenders," a motley assortment of men and women who always claim to be acting on behalf of "people in very high places."

Occasionally, these "clandestinites," as we called them, are, in fact, telling the truth. Sometimes they truly are representing outside interests. And when they are, it invariably turns out that they are milking some African chieftain who is seeking either soldiers of fortune or a place to store his ill-gotten gains. My colleagues and I made it a rule to steer clear of these types, although rumor had it that KGB agents used to make a pretty penny in this lucrative sideshow.

The rumor was that KGB agents would regularly sell their equipment and custom-made devices to the clandestinites in exchange for hard currency and lots of it. The agents would then hang out in Brussels for the time period in which they were to have performed their operation, report to Moscow that the operation had been carried out, and then head back to Mother Russia with a pretty penny in their pocket.

The clandestinites used the equipment to bolster their standing with their clients and to generally show off around town. One could see the newest Russian satellite communication technology in the bars of Brussels sooner than one might see it in the CIA's stockpile.

Brussels also attracts a lot of self-made and self-employed "logistical support agents," or, as we called them, McQs, with wry reference to Ian Fleming's "Q," Her Majesty's Mastermind of Gadgets. These enterprising souls parlayed a special skill, whether forgery, lock-smithing, currency laundering, or some other gift, into a not-so-cottage industry. These men and women were usually to be found on the second and third floors of commercial buildings under cover of art galleries, doctor's offices (psychiatrists and psychologists, for some Freudian reason), and the occasional travel agency. One gained access to this secret world by invitation or recommendation only.

The McQs could provide you with anything on a moment's notice. Need a second passport? McQ had it. Want an electronic hotel key for room 344 at the Grand Hotel? McQ gets it. These talents made one a believer in unplanned economies and in the theory of supply rising to meet demand.

Ordinarily, Combatants never acquired goods from McQs. After all, we had a well-oiled machine to provide us with whatever tools we required. But every now and then, we did. When, for example, one of us had a "brilliant" idea, the gist of which we thought—for the moment—it best not to share with the Office, we opened our own pocketbooks and approached the McQs.

The McQs were quick, effective, and for the most part, discreet. The McQs didn't care what we wanted or why we wanted it. They cared only about whether they could get it and how much they could make on it.

Was going to the McQs stupid? Without a doubt; a McQ had loyalties only to his or her pocketbook. Was it necessary? Probably not. After all, if Gray Cell and Illusions nixed an idea or refused to allocate tools to support it, it was probably for good reason. Did we do it anyway? Of course we did.

When you teach someone how to break another's rules and you authorize that someone to break another's rules, then sooner or later that someone will break everyone's rules, including your own.

Boldness Is the Weapon

We inhabit a meek world. Observe it. Who among its inhabitants effects bold action? Bold thought? Bold choices? The truth is that most individuals will follow the trodden path. Most individuals will make the choices that have been made before. Most individuals will think what others have taught them to think. Most individuals will therefore not stand up to a bold thought, a bold plan, or a bold execution of an idea.

The Meek shall inherit what the Bold leave behind.

Bold action, because it is rare, becomes a commodity unto itself. The action carried out takes second place to the method in which it is carried out. The departure of the slaves was effected without opposition because the focus of the oppressors was the method of departure—"boldly"—rather than the departure itself.

Oftentimes you will agonize over the best plan of action to accomplish a goal. Oftentimes, however, there simply is *no* good plan of action to accomplish a goal. The Bible tells us to let boldness be your plan.

There was no "good way" for the slaves to leave Egypt. The slaves were too numerous to leave by stealth. Yet they were too weak to leave by war. Indeed, any course chosen would likely raise the ire of the slaves' masters, or that of the pharaoh, the government ministers, or the army.

So the slaves left "boldly," "in the sight of all the Egyptians" without shame or apology or care of attack. And in so doing they stunned the Egyptians.

Their boldness *was* their plan. Their boldness *was* their weapon. And their boldness *was* their victory.

Boldness in thought and action will enable you to carry forth many tasks without regard for another's interference or obstruction. But what is boldness? It is not arrogance. Nor is it confidence. It is the *projection* of confidence. It is the ability to persuade others that you are confident in the act you are taking, regardless whether you are or not.

If you are bold—that is to say, if those around you perceive you as bold—they will usually provide their own rationale for the basis of your confidence. And that is good because any justification they come up with will be uniquely styled to satisfy themselves.

In other words, your audience will consider the following: He is bold, in other words, I perceive him to be confident; therefore, he must have a reason to be bold. That reason must be because . . . And here the party perceiving your action will supply that rationale which explains most convincingly to that party why you would be acting in so bold a fashion.

Can you be bold if you yourself are not confident?

You *must* be bold if you yourself are not confident. After all, if you feel compelled to undertake action even though you are lacking in confidence in that action, lacking in confidence in yourself, or lacking in confidence in your ability to carry out that action, then you must be embarking upon that action because you have little choice but to embark upon that action. And in that case, boldness is the only weapon that can boost your chances for success.

The slaves were not confident. Moses was not confident. Aaron was not confident. Yet leave Egypt they must. Therefore, they would leave boldly. Let the Egyptians make their own explanations as to the source of the slaves' confidence. Perhaps they said to themselves that the God of the Hebrews truly is the best and only God. Perhaps not. It does not matter. What mattered is only that they dared not challenge an action carried off boldly.

The plan, as it was, was relatively simple: I would enter NATO headquarters, I would walk into "my" office, I would receive the phone call on "my" private line, and then I would leave through the front entrance. The only problems with the plan were that: (1) There was no way for me to enter NATO; (2) I did not have an office in NATO; (3) I did not have a private line at NATO; and (4) I would not be allowed out of NATO without showing how I entered in the first place.

Unfortunately, there was little alternative. I had to get into NATO if we were to obtain the documents we were promised. And the documents we were promised were the blueprints for the Syrian chemical warfare

laboratories at CERN, the center of Syria's atomic/bio-logical/chemical warfare effort, on the outskirts of Damascus.

I was girl-watching at the Petite Café in Brussels's Grand Palace (Grote Mart). The café, which was a popular hangout for NATO and EC Berlaymont secretaries, was therefore a popular hangout for the clandestinites, the McQs and the "MacGyvers," which was how some Belgians referred to members of the Western intelligence agencies. The café was actually more a bar than a café, but I never expect things to be what they advertise themselves to be anyway.

The girl I was keeping tabs on was Analis, a pretty German-speaking NATO secretary. She was my object for the one reason that she could get me into NATO. A drinking buddy (more accurately, someone whose drinks I paid for) told me that she was among the café's regulars and that she rarely left the place with the same guy twice.

Analis came to Belgium seeking eternal love, adventure, and sex, not necessarily in that order. At the moment she was the object of a Dutch army officer's advances. Ordinarily, I wouldn't try and muscle in on a fellow buck in courting. Nasty things can happen and I was in no mood for nasty things. But Analis kept looking over the fellow's shoulders as he spoke as if to signal to the café at large, "Hey, I'm not really with this loser."

I was almost old enough to be Analis's father and decided to play that to my advantage. I walked up to her and put my arm over her shoulders while quickly pulling her near me.

"Analis, your father told me that I would find you here." I gave her a kiss on both cheeks.

"Excuse me, sir," I said as I maneuvered Analis through the crowded café, around the bend from the Dutchman. Analis looked up at me, still stunned and very much out of control.

"My father, sir, is dead. And who are you?" She made a halfhearted gesture at squirming out of my hold, which actually succeeded in getting her more tightly wedged into my arms.

"I know, my dear. And I was very sorry to hear about it. You have my deepest sympathies."

"He died fifteen years ago, when I was a child."

"Has it been that long already? Come, we must talk." And with that I pulled her after me out of the café and into the square. She now pushed herself away to take my full measure. She must have been pleased because she did not run away.

"Who are you?"

"No, my young lady, who are you?"

"Inshuldingunze? Who am I?"

"Precisely, I wish to hear all about it."

"Is this about Grisha? Because I swear I did not know that he was KGB. Only afterwards, did I think that that might be the case. I told him nothing. You are security, yes? Oh, no, will I lose my job?"

Analis assumed that I was with NATO Internal Security.

I took Analis to dinner. Over a bottle of wine and a warm continental meal, I calmed her down. No, if she cooperated, she would not lose her job. But it was important that she tell me everything, who else she had slept with, what she was doing at NATO at the time of these liaisons, what she was doing now. She must not omit a thing, and she didn't.

We spent close to four hours on Analis's eight months with NATO. The girl was certainly active. Analis explained that she was a "floating" secretary at the Air Command, Control and Sensors Division (Air C2 & Sensors) within NATO headquarters. Because of her lack of experience—of clerical experience, that is—she was a "floater" not assigned to any one department.

Ironically, conceived as a way to ease someone into

NATO with minimal exposure before the organization
has had adequate time to determine her trustworthiness,
her posting as a floater allowed her much greater leeway
in where she went and what she did. It also meant that
she had not completed her security clearance procedures.

Her presence at Air C2 & Sensors was perfect because
of the broad swath it covered. Not only did it house the
Surveillance Branch but it also worked for SHAPE
(Supreme Headquarters Allied Powers Europe), NATO
Air Command and Control Systems (ACCS), NATO Air-
borne Early Warning and Control Program Management
Agency, and the NATO Maintenance and Supply Agency.
In other words, Analis was just where I had hoped she
would be. And that would put me just where I would be
expected to be.

Analis understood that she must cooperate with "our"
internal investigation and, of course, not to discuss it
with anyone else. If she cooperated with us fully, then we
would be inclined to drop the "Brisha" affair as though
it never happened.

"Grisha," she corrected.

"Of course."

To be on the safe side and because, as my mentors
advised, one should always combine business with pleasure, I instructed Analis to spend the night with me in
my hotel room. I told her that if she preferred, she could
spend the night on the couch. She was scared and shak-
en, so she preferred otherwise.

The Methodology of Bold

You have only poor choices available. Nonetheless, you are obliged
to perform the task required. You determine to assume a bold
course of action because you have to; there is no other choice. Fine.
But beware, bold action knows no compromise. There is no, nor
can there be, semibold action. There is no, nor can there be, some-

times bold, sometimes not-so-bold action. And above all, there can never be a retreat, a successful retreat, from boldness.

When you come in as a lion, you must act like a lion and leave like a lion. To be a lamb is to be lamb chops.

The commitment to bold action is like that of a swimmer on the edge of a pier. The swimmer can dive into the water headfirst, however cold, and get on with it. That is what is required for bold action. Alternatively, the swimmer can put a toe in, then a foot, slowly easing into the water. That may be prudent action. In fact, it may even be more convenient action. Moreover, it too will get the swimmer into the water just as the irreversible dive did, but it will not provide the swimmer with the bold entry required.

Embarking upon the bold carries its own hazards. Bold has very few "getting-off" spots. That swimmer cannot turn back midair should he see a shark below him awaiting his entry. He must be prepared before his jump to handle and address every contingency because having chosen the bold course of action, he must continue on it.

Having left boldly, the slaves could not turn back. Upon reaching the Red Sea, they had to address the Red Sea as they addressed their departure, boldly and without hesitation.

A retreat from bold action is worse than never having taken the action at all. It is a sign of weakness, confusion, and desperation. It is the scent of blood to the waiting sharks.

In boldly. Out boldly.

WorldCom acquired MCI because it showed no weakness: Once it decided on an acquisition, it would pay any price and litigate in any court to achieve its goal. British Telecom and GTE wavered, fussed, and moaned. AT&T couldn't even decide if it was in the game. They never stood a chance.

Starwood Lodgings acquired ITT Sheraton because it moved swiftly and boldly and broadcast its determination with cash and more cash. When Hilton raised, it raised. It was certain not to be deterred and it broadcast loud and clear that it was in the fight until one side was no longer standing. Hilton was sluggish and cautious. It never stood a chance.

Ali Dimashq Yasin was the Syrian-born son of a prominent Syrian political family. His father was among the
founders of the Ba'ath Party, the Arab Nationalist
Socialist party, which had controlled Syria for decades.
Sorbonne-educated, Yasin shunned his political legacy,
earning a Ph.D. in chemistry. He had spent his entire
professional career in Syria's state university system.
But his true occupation, one that you would find
nowhere in his résumé, was deputy director of the "C"
in Syria's ABC (atomic, biological, chemical) warfare
program.

Yasin was the lead scientist on the "3rd Generation
Project": a modern toxic gas that killed on contact.

Yasin lived the charmed life of one born to privilege.
International travel, professional conferences, a secure
and prestigious job at a secretive, powerful institution—
in short, everything that an academic in a totalitarian
state could hope for. There was but one fly in Yasin's
ointment: While living in France, he was married in a
Catholic church to a Catholic woman. As far as the Syrian
regime was concerned (and, for that matter, the Catholic
Church) Yasin had converted to Catholicism. And, in
Alawite-run Syria, a country already fanatically
obsessed with an individual's affiliation to sect and religion, being a Sunni or Shia (non-Alawite) Muslim was
bad enough. Being a Catholic, married to a foreigner,
was a deathblow to promotion.

Yasin would always be an Indian, never a chief.

At first, Yasin pretended not to care when people of
lesser talent were advanced to director of "C" and from
there, on more than one occasion, to director of ABC
itself. Yasin persuaded himself that at the level of director true science stopped and politics began. And Yasin
was a scientist, not a politician.

The first time Yasin was passed over for a younger,
less experienced scientist, he told his wife that he
wouldn't have wanted the director's job anyway. His

work, he explained to his French wife, was too important to leave in the hands of others.

But the second time and the third time less talented Alawites and then even mere Sunnis leapfrogged into positions over him, Yasin was harder pressed to accept them with sanguinity. His wife was angry. She had left her motherland believing that she had married into the Syrian establishment. Instead, she had married a social cripple; not quite an outcast, not quite a leper, but one who would never attain full integration into the ruling elite. She was unhappy, and she made sure that Yasin knew her feelings.

Yasin was ripe for the picking. His was the classic profile of the defector: bright, educated, high regard for himself, and resentful. Very resentful. As the psychologist's tract read: a narcissistic personality.

The Office had been following Ali Dimashq Yasin's career ever since he began his studies at the Sorbonne and before he was married. The flagging of Yasin at so early a stage bore all of the Office's hallmarks: the ability to detect a defector before the defector himself had even contemplated defecting. It was for this insight, and others like it, that the Office's reputation was well earned.

On a recent trip to Germany, one of the few European countries that despite its unsavory recent history continued to be a major chemical supplier to the outlaw governments of Syria, Libya, and Iraq, Yasin was "encountered" by an Untouchable. The usual method for an Untouchable to begin a dialogue with a potential Retailer is through a seemingly chance encounter. And Helmut, a German-speaking Untouchable who was assigned to recruit Yasin, was reputedly among the best in the business.

Several years before my Belgian escapade, Yasin was in a taxi en route from Frankfurt's airport to downtown Frankfurt. As Yasin's taxi left the airport ramps and was entering the autobahn, Helmut, in a sleek new BMW 7 Series sedan, sideswiped the taxi and forced it off the road. Helmut immediately pulled his BMW over and approached the taxi, apologizing profusely to Yasin while sticking several hundred deutsche marks into the driver's hands.

Helmut would not be deterred; he would drive Yasin the rest of the way into town. And after all, since, coincidence of coincidence, they were both staying at the Steinberger Hotel, Helmut would not have it any other way.

Office folklore has it that an Untouchable needs only one opportunity to create a bond of trust with his "object." Helmut now had that opportunity.

Over dinner, which Helmut insisted that Yasin allow him to buy, Yasin confessed his life worries to Helmut. The long and short of it was that Yasin wanted to "come back" to his beloved France. But, now being a family man, with mouths to feed and a status-conscious wife to consider, he had to have an appropriate and suitable position before he would break his ties with Syria. If Helmut, who Yasin now believed to be a senior German defense department official, could arrange for the right situation for a man of Yasin's position, Yasin would provide Helmut with the documentation and information Helmut requested.

But Yasin had conditions. He was a Francophile and his wife was French. Germany held no attraction for him or for her at all. Therefore, if he were to defect, it must be to France, not Germany. If Helmut could arrange that, then Yasin, directly and not through intermediaries, would deliver the requested documents to a senior French military officer and only to a French military officer. And he would do so only at the headquarters of the French army in Paris.

As much as the Office wanted Syria's chemical warfare plans, given its shaky relationship with France and the quirky nature of French foreign policy, it could not risk approaching the French regarding Yasin. A Frenchman could perceive a greater French national interest in delivering Dr. Yasin and his papers directly to the Syrian authorities instead of to Yasin's beloved Sorbonne. Unfortunately, without the French authorities' approval, this operation was a nonstarter.

Turning to the Germans was rather impractical too in that foreign policy begins at home. Israel was in this mess, the chemical warfare mess, precisely because German politicians turned a blind eye to the export of German chemicals by German companies to Israel's enemies. They did so because the German companies made a lot of money from these exports and the memory of Zyklon-B was far enough removed from these "New Generation Germans" to allow them to pursue this dangerous policy with ethical impunity.

Samson thought that a Combatant might have a chance of making Yasin believe that he, the Combatant, was in fact a French intelligence officer. But given that an operation in France was taboo, Studio would have to stage the French officer outside France. Studio suggested Brussels, which in one way made sense given its centrality in European matters. But on the other hand, why would a French officer choose to meet Yasin, a Syrian national seeking French asylum, in Belgium?

Studio suggested that we tie it to NATO. Although France was not a member, it did have observer status and its officers did come and go at NATO's Brussels headquarters. Samson suggested that Helmut arrange for Yasin to meet his "French officer" in a Brussels hotel.

The only problem was that Yasin would have nothing to do with this plan.

Helmut had been able to persuade Yasin that the transfer of documents had to be done in Brussels, where the German defense ministry would be able to immediately obtain the documents from the French. Because, after all, as Helmut explained and Yasin understood, the Germans were the linchpin in this transaction. But Yasin would not accept a meeting in a hotel with an unidentified French officer. If there were to be a meeting at all, Yasin would meet the Frenchman at NATO or not at all.

Yasin was no fool. As a Syrian civilian with extensive travel privileges, he was continuously briefed by Syrian intelligence. And Syrian intelligence cautioned him to be on the lookout for unsubstantiated promises. The irony in this case was that Yasin was seeking to be recruited—he was seeking to defect. He simply wanted to make sure that he was defecting to the right people.

At this point Pinnacle was ready to wash its hands of the matter. Pinnacle would not, indeed it could not, allow this show to go forward. Imagine the transgressions, the international ramifications, of a Combatant impersonating a French military officer in Belgium in order to meet a Syrian defector at NATO headquarters under the pretense of turning secret documents over to the German Ministry of Defense. If the smallest thing went wrong, it would implicate Israel in a scandal of astronomical proportion. The operation would be a flagrant violation of French, Belgian, and German law, let alone the issues surrounding NATO. And yet, on the other side of the equation was chemical war. And that is nothing to sneeze at.

The Bold Action: No Survivors

Bold actors do not survive. Their very existence is a threat to the established order. Neither private nor public institutions can long tolerate the maverick who takes it upon himself to save the day. And while it is a truism that the bold often save the day, for the continued preservation of the institution and the meek within it, the bold player must be sacrificed. The irony in most cases is that the sacrifice may be even swifter in the case of the successful bold actor than in the case of the failed one because the failed bold actor ultimately vindicates the institution's meekness while the successful one challenges its very foundation.

The point is this: A choice to be bold, a decision to take bold action, requires more than contemplation of the outcome of that action. Rather, it requires the bold actor to consider what happens to him after the bold action is effected.

If you, as that individual, seek a long and safe career, success is not the appropriate yardstick with which to measure your chances to achieve that career; longevity is. If you, as that individual, seek a productive and successful career, then longevity is not the appropriate yardstick with which to measure your chances to achieve that career; boldness is.

The bold actor should never expect the accolades of his group as his reward for bold action. It may sometimes come, but it should not be expected. Rather, the bold actor should be prepared to be sacrificed for the continued existence of the organization on behalf of whom he has acted. The bold actor is a necessity to the group. Without him, it will perish. Without him, it will not achieve success. But it is also a threat to the group because the bold actor perforce breaks the group's rules in order to save it. Therefore, at the first opportune moment the bold actor will be sacrificed.

Neither the institution nor the institutional memory can tolerate the existence of the successful iconoclast. And the bold actor is, by definition, an iconoclast.

The turnaround president who saves the company is the first fired by the reinvigorated company's board. The innovator who changes the established order while blazing a trail through uncharted territory is often the first to be trampled by the following herds.

There is no value judgment here. You should simply understand the consequences of your choice. Organization man or entrepreneur. Leader or follower. Institutionally meek or institutionally bold. The choice is yours.

On the one hand, the institutionally meek can enjoy a long and fulfilling career, most often ascending the corporate ladder through the avoidance of responsibility more than through its assumption. Examples abound of senior corporate management who lack any particularly distinguishing career milestones. More often than not, the most distinguishing aspect of such a career is the avoidance of error, which in itself is no small feat over a lifetime of responsibility.

On the other, the institutionally bold will have a short but memorable career at a number of institutions or on his own, each component of which will be marked by one or more bold actions, innovative or tradition-breaking decisions that yielded positive results. In the long run, however, the organization cherished its institutional ways more than the possibility of greater success in changing those ways.

On a global scale, you can look to the relative demise of conservative England against the relative ascendancy of less tradition-bound corporations and business entities in Europe and certainly the United States.

On a corporate scale, you can compare the tradition-bound banking industry to the relative freewheeling investment banking industry. Whose employees turn over faster? Whose shareholders fared better? Where do you fit in?

We all understood that Pinnacle, being a political appointment, could not be in the command chain for this operation. Yet, all the same, we were not about to let the likes of Yasin just slip away. The stakes were too high. We, after all, were the silent forces upon which the very existence of Israel depended. We, who gladly risk our lives for the state, could not refuse to risk our jobs in exchange for the reduction (if not elimination) of the chemical nightmare from our country's horizon.

We would take the bold action.

Helmut told Studio that Yasin had agreed to the hotel transfer. He lied. Yasin was as steadfast as ever. But Helmut and I had worked out a plan of operation. I would get myself into NATO headquarters and meet Yasin there. Helmut and I would keep everyone else in the Office on a need-to-know basis, and until we got those documents, as far as Helmut and I were concerned, no one else needed to know.

Initially, Helmut suggested that we hold the meeting

at SACEUR (Supreme Allied Commander Europe), arguing that since that was where ACE (Allied Supreme Command Europe) was located, that would be where Yasin would expect to meet me. But Helmut was being far too esoteric.

First of all, Yasin asked for a NATO meeting place; he would, therefore, expect NATO headquarters, Belgium.

Second, SACEUR was in Mons, a much smaller town southwest of Brussels. I hated small towns. Over a decade before, Bayonet was tripped up in Lillehammer, Norway, a quintessential small town, precisely because it was a small town. People notice things in small towns. I preferred to stay in the larger city, where people stepped over the street drunks without a second glance. More important, I knew my way around Brussels and I already knew about Analis. I had no comparable link into SACEUR.

Helmut instructed Yasin to have his wife and daughter fly to Lyons, home to Mrs. Yasin, to visit her parents and obtain medical treatment for her fertility problems. For a Syrian man to have over the course of a ten-year marriage only one child, and a daughter at that, surely raised the reasonable inference of infertility. This was not a matter of small importance. Syrian exit visas are painstakingly reviewed and considered. It is virtually impossible for a person of Yasin's standing to obtain an exit visa from Syria while his wife and daughter are out of the country, too.

But "medical visas" were handled by Syria's health department. And in an amazing lapse of security and an incredible piece of good fortune to the Office, it had no cross-reference function with the Ministry for Internal Security. So when Yasin applied to Internal Security for his travel visa to visit a Munich factory, no one there knew that his entire family had already left the country.

Meanwhile, shopping at the McQs, I purchased a French Intelligence Army lieutenant colonel's uniform. Apparently on "special" this week, it came with all the appropriate insignias and ribbons. I also acquired a NATO building pass, Air C2 & Sensors attaché case, along with an authentic, but "doctored," picture ID. The uniform would get me into the building and Analis would do the rest.

Analis left the hotel early the next morning. She would go to work as usual. Today, however, she would "float" less than normal. She would reserve a conference room for a closed subcommittee meeting of the Surveillance Branch (one of Air C2 & Sensor's five branches). She would be discreet and answer questions, if any arose, as vaguely as possible. She would not be afraid of acting stupid if confronted with too many questions. She had a message from a Lieutenant Colonel Marchais to reserve the room. That's all she would know. And, of course, if things got messy with her boss, I would be there to bail her out.

Did I like lying to her? No. Did I enjoy setting Yasin up for a fall? No. But I believe that the end sometimes does justify the means. It is a balancing act, never an absolute. In our case, the means were lying and deceit. The end was allowing Israel to understand the extent of Syria's chemical warfare threat and thereby quite possibly save hundreds of thousands if not millions of innocent lives.

Did the end justify the means? I thought so.

I dressed slowly. Until I've had several cups of coffee I am a very slow mover, and this morning I had yet to have one. I called down for room service and ordered three double espressos. That should hold me for a while. I retrieved my army black shoes from the hallway and put the finishing touches on my outfit. Fortunately, it was an unseasonably sunny day in Brussels. So the decision not to purchase the full-length coat turned out to be the right one. I hoped it was an omen.

I was not a novice to bold action or, for that matter, to risk taking. But today would be different. First of all, I was working out of channels with an Untouchable. I had never before worked out of channels, and Combatants never work directly with Untouchables. Untouchables know too much. They are, after all, an integral part of the Office. They are the Office body. We, its Combatants, are merely its long arm.

If I get caught, all I can reveal are tools of the trade, gadgets, gizmos, toys, which in the final analysis are probably no different from those of every other clandestine service. The "Q"s of the world are actually very unimaginative. After all, there are only so many ways to conceal a gun. But if an Untouchable falls, he can lay out the Office's entire structure from A to Z, including its array of operations, its operatives, agents, missions, and objectives.[1] It made me uncomfortable to even think about it.

But I was also edgy about what I was about to do. It was not every day that I faked my way into NATO, a military installation, impersonating an officer of a country that was not even a member of the organization. Yet today I would do all that and more.

Fear is a Combatant's friend because it makes us hypersensitive to everything and anything that is "off." It compels an awareness that one does not ordinarily have. Today I would need every bit of fear I could muster.

I approached the imposing NATO HQ main building. By now, Analis would be waiting for me at the telephone number she gave me. I had no way of knowing whether, in the light of day, my story still made sense to her. I prayed that it did.

---

[1]*Imperfect Spies* and *Every Spy a Prince,* both by Dan Raviv and Yossi Melman (Ma'ariv Library and Houghton Mifflin, respectively), mention a failed con man, Victor Ostrovsky, who briefly entered Mossad field officer training. According to Raviv and Melman, he was unceremoniously cashiered soon thereafter. The con man then determined to use whatever he gleaned and wrongfully appropriated during his short stay at Mossad in order to harm Mossad, its "Untouchables," its Combatants, and, ultimately, the state of Israel. One newspaper called him a failed man in a failed life, and I doubt that many would quarrel with that assessment.

I joined a cadre of German officers chatting easily as they entered the HQ building. Each of them took out his magnetic card and swiped it through the turnstile. I took my card out and swiped it by my mouth first to kiss it and then put it through the magnetic card device at the turnstile. The turnstile yielded against my pressure. Lord, thank the McQs.

As Analis promised, there was an internal phone bank opposite the security guards. I dialed her extension. It rang several times. While I was waiting for her to answer I was hoping that whatever she did with Grisha was sufficiently naughty that she would feel obliged to follow through on this escapade. At the fourth ring she answered.

"Analis Richter, *bitte*."

All right, Grisha.

"Analis, I am here."

"I will be right there."

I turned to my right where a junior United States Army officer too had just hung up the phone.

"Warm day, quite nice, *non*?"

"Yes, yes. It is. I'm Lieutenant Green, pleased to meet you."

The young officer saluted me, but I waved him off. I offered him my hand instead and we shook. I had no interest in anything he had to say and I certainly did not intend to answer his questions, but, as a general proposition, whenever one is somewhere where one should not be, one is best advised to appear as though one is not loitering. For nothing draws the attention of security guards or of onlookers as someone with no sense of purpose. My instant association with this NATO officer would also bolster my standing with Analis, who, given the stress she must be going through, would no doubt require some bolstering.

Analis showed up a few minutes later. "Colonel Marchais, *s'il vous plait*."

I said good-bye to Green, tapping him on his shoulder and shaking his hand with both of mine, attempting to convey to Analis that Green and I were old NATO buddies. I followed Analis down the long corridors to Air C2 & Sensors. She showed me into a small circular conference room, no windows, one door. I poured myself a cup of coffee and sat down. Analis returned to her station.

I waited the few minutes until 10:00 A.M. At exactly 10:03 the conference room phone rang.

"You have a call, Colonel." It was Analis.

"Put it through, please. *Oui. Ici* Colonel Marchais."

"Yes, Colonel. Our package is ready."

"*D'accorde.* By all means, bring it by. We shall be waiting."

"In five minutes."

"*Cinq minutes.*"

I dialed Analis's extension. "Do you have the pass?"

"Yes."

"Then now."

I hung up the phone. I did not want to provide Analis with an opportunity to renegotiate this deal.

Analis walked back to HQ's main entrance with the visitor pass that she had used until her regular pass had arrived. If she followed my instructions, Yasin would have no problem entering the building. By the time she arrived at the entry, Yasin was already standing to one side, next to the guards. She walked by the first guard, stopping at the second. She matter-of-factly told him that the gentleman at the door was attending a conference at Air C2 & Sensors.

At the guard's request, Yasin signed in and somewhat reluctantly showed his passport to the guards. Analis waved the visitor pass by the guard and swiped it through the turnstile. She pulled Yasin through the turnstile and, without stopping, appended the visitor pass to his lapel and pulled him behind her. The guard had started to rise to request to see the pass itself but, halfway on his way to an upright position, thought the better of it and sat back down. Yasin was in.

As we agreed, Analis took Yasin the long way to the conference room. She pointedly made him aware of how deep into the beast he was being allowed to come. At about 10:20 she knocked on the conference room door and opened it. I was face-to-face with Yasin.

I spent six hours interrogating Yasin. I relied upon the AMAN checklist that Helmut had swiped from the Office. It addressed issues that even Yasin did not know he knew. There was little doubt that Yasin was thoroughly impressed with the comprehensiveness of his interrogation and it pleased him. He was glad to be taken seriously. He was glad that someone had gone to the trouble of sending a well-prepared officer to meet him. He was satisfied that France obviously understood not only what his expertise was but also how great it was. I'm sure that as far as he was concerned, he was already at the Sorbonne.

At one point a Dutch officer poked his head through the door, but I angrily waved him off. Analis, as instructed, showed up with lunch and sandwiches and at one point was even able to improvise a blackboard for Yasin's use.

At 4:30 P.M., after covering most all of AMAN's requests, I stood up, straightened my uniform, collected all of Yasin's documents, computer disks, and photographs, placed them in my attaché case, and saluted Yasin. Helmut had prepared him for this sequence of events.

"I wish to say only good luck."

"Thank you."

I opened the door and without a further adieu, walked to the building's front entrance. I did not stop at the gate to sign out, nor did I swipe my card through the turnstile. I just fixed my gaze straight ahead and kept walking. The guards shouted something in my direction, but I just waved at them with a distinctly Gallic gesture of contempt. My uniform was wet through and through. My knees were rubber. I prayed that my legs would carry me into the waiting taxi.

At 5:15 P.M. Helmut had my bag. At 6:15 it was in Israel's diplomatic pouch on its way to Tel Aviv. At 7:00 P.M. I was on a Swiss Air flight bound for Lugano. At 10:00 P.M. I was in a car across the Swiss Italian border on my way to Milan, new name, new passport, new clothes.

I don't know what happened to Yasin. I can only guess that when he was finally found in the conference room, it would have been very difficult for anyone to believe his story. I do know that neither he nor any of his nuclear family ever returned to Syria. I also know that he is not teaching at the Sorbonne.

Analis left NATO HQ only several minutes after I did. She was smart enough, Grisha or no Grisha, to not be there when Yasin began asking for his professorship.

Today, Analis is a Combatant.

Countdown in Beirut

◼ LEADING

"Be Amood Ashan Lanchotam HaDerech . . ."
"In a Pillar of Cloud to Lead the Way . . ."

Be Amood Ashan . . . The Lord is not a passive bystander in the Exodus. He directs Moses in his negotiations with the pharaoh. He smites the Egyptians with plagues. He determines the Israelites' path out of Egypt. He assumes a physical presence at the head of the camp. He is Smoke by day. He is Fire by night. He is present and active. All of the time. He is the leader. And the people follow.

His appearance inspires awe. His ongoing presence inspires confidence. He is leadership.

Mike was a member of Bayonet: a unit that does not exist on any organizational chart, does not appear in any budget, and does not take credit for any of its actions. It is the ultimate nonentity in an organization, the Mossad, which itself has no formal existence.

Leadership Is a Verb

Perhaps no other topic commands as much attention as leadership. The number of books, articles, and seminars on the qualities of leadership is staggering. From the sheer quantity of material on the subject, you would expect to find that everything there is to know about leadership is already known and that therefore effecting leadership is merely a matter of painting by numbers.

You would be mistaken.

Leadership is not a descriptive narrative. Rather, leadership, true leadership, is a verb; it is action. This is not to say that leadership cannot be exerted in static situations or through passive existence. But if it has been so exerted, we have yet to see it.

Leadership is an ongoing story of work and effort, which can only be accomplished by total, zealous commitment to the cause it seeks. It is the commanding performance of a continuing task in devotion to a cause.

To lead you must have a clear vision of where you want to go and a strong desire to bring this vision into being. Many people at all stages of life have desires, goals they believe are worthy of pursuit. But few of them have the drive or the desire to devote the effort and time required to bring them into existence. Few of them are willing to make the sacrifices required to change the course of events. Fewer still are willing to undertake extraordinary efforts over a continuous period of time. But that is what leadership requires and that is why leadership is a scarce commodity.

Leadership: a visible commitment to a cause over an extended period of time.

Mike was not yet born when his father was killed in action during Israel's War of Independence. Reared an only child by an overprotective, single mother, Mike was not "one of the guys." As a child, while his classmates were outside playing soccer, his mother kept him home to "avoid the heat" and other dangers of the Middle East. He spent most of his free time reading the very popular British children's books of the time, like *The Secret Seven* and the Hardy Boys, along with their best-known and most popular Hebrew imitator: *Hasamba,* in which brave little Israeli boys and girls did battle with the evil colonial British Empire in Palestine.

After high school, Mike faced the mandatory service of the Israeli Defense Forces (IDF), the same army that took his father's life. As a single child and an orphan to a war widow, Mike could not serve in a combat unit without his mother's express written approval, an approval that she was most unlikely to grant. Mike spent a year as a desk clerk, pushing papers in a Tel Aviv office. On his first anniversary in the military, Mike forged his mother's signature on the required release form, and within several days he was posted to an elite Southern Command Ranger Unit, Sayeret Shaked.

Mike rose rapidly through the ranks, and in two years' time, he attained the rank of captain and Sayeret commander. He completed his tour of duty after the 1967 Six Day War, during which Sayeret Shaked broke through the Egyptian lines so rapidly that the regular IDF troops had a hard time keeping up. Mike was one of the handful of IDF soldiers to be decorated for bravery, a rare recognition in an army widely recognized for its brave men and women.

After a brief stint studying computers, Mike decided that he had yet more to offer the country's security. At the ripe old age of twenty-seven he volunteered to reenlist in Israel's air force pilot training. After much concern and debate, the Israeli air force agreed to accept the old-timer on the condition that he strip himself of his rank and that he pass each and every examination, course, and training exercise with a grade no less than ten full points over and above his class's mean passing score. Two years later, Mike graduated first in his air force class.

After his distinguished stint in the air force, Mike joined the most secret enclave within the Office, itself one of the most secret of the secret services. Mike was assigned to "Bayonet."

Leadership Must Be Seen

A leader does not do his work "behind the scenes." Leadership does not emanate from backroom deals. Such action does not suit the profile of one who intends to inspire others. Behind-the-scenes action may allow you to accomplish much, but it also suggests a distrust in the public process, a fear of exposing your beliefs to the scrutiny of the open market. This is not what leadership constitutes.

Leadership is the public taking of risks for a cause you believe in. When the public applauds a high-wire act, it does so because the acrobat's success and failure are both in full view. When the troops rally behind a leader, they do so because of their leader's willingness to pursue an uncertain goal because it is right, not because it is easily attainable or risk-free.

Coca-Cola's Roberto Goizueta, a business leader of impeccable credentials, was raked over the coals in the press for his aborted attempt to change Coca-Cola's formula. Goizueta's thinking was to align Coke's taste more with that of the sweeter Pepsi. The attempt was an immediate failure. A leader of lesser stature or confidence would have sacrificed a subordinate, wrung his hands of responsibility, or worse yet, persisted in a disastrous course simply because it was preset. But not Mr. Goizueta. He took full blame. He repositioned the brand. He restored the traditional formula. He was a leader and he led.

Both before and after the Classic Coke incident, Roberto Goizueta could have hopscotched across corporate America like no other CEO before him. He, too, could have amassed great fortune bouncing from one corporate corner office to the next. After all, here was a man who was always on the "short list" of the Fortune 100. But Goizueta grew up in Coca-Cola, he came to term at Coca-Cola, and he would stay with Coca-Cola until his death.

Leadership over time.

In life, leaders create their own space. The notion that a vacuum sucks in a leader or that time or place make the leader is just that, a notion. Time can no more make a leader than "place" can make geography. When historians ask whether History Makes the Man or Man Makes History, it is largely because they have not seen leaders in their lifetime. Time or place may allow leadership qualities to be expressed in a unique fashion, but they certainly do not create such qualities.

In business, leadership is no different. One who takes the reins of leadership will create his own space. Most businesspeople will move aside in the presence of one who asserts himself. Why? Because organizational behavior is such that most businesspeople wish to avoid error rather than claim success.

Therefore, do not hesitate to assert yourself with your colleagues. Take charge of that meeting. More likely than not, you shall become by sheer force of personality the leader of your cohort.

Do not wait to be anointed. Kings are anointed. Leadership is taken.

In early 1978, the prime minister issued a pink slip on Ayad Ahwad, a known terrorist who had murdered eighteen schoolchildren in the border town of Ma'alot, a low-income housing community in northern Israel, and photographer Jill Rubin in the coastal Ma'agan Mikhael kibbutz.

Most of Bayonet's ground rules, the "where" and "when" of an operation, are dictated by outside forces. A target is where he or she is, and there is little that Bayonet can do about that. The timing of Bayonet's "kiss" (Bayonet's euphemism for assassination) is always "as soon as possible" because the targets are deemed to be (and most often are) "armed and loaded."

Every day that a target is left alive increases the probability that he or she will kill again. So the only thing left to Bayonet's imagination and planning is the

"how." The Bayonet "how" has no limitations. It can dispose of its target any way it sees fit. It must follow only three rules. Rule Number One: No North American activity; Rule Number Two: Only the target gets hurt; and Rule Number Three: The team must get away.

Bayonet begins its plan from the end—the escape. Before any discussion of methods and mechanisms, the team begins by discussing, debating, and analyzing how it can get away after the kiss. Once that is resolved, the plan itself seems to flow naturally. All kisses had to end successfully, and as far as the Office was concerned, a successful kiss was one in which none of Bayonet were apprehended. Successfully performing the kiss came second to that.

Because of the demand for perfection and the rigorous procedures attendant to the issuance of a "pink slip," an average Bayonet team member could go through an entire career (usually three to four years) without ever being part of a kiss. So when the time finally did come for action, one could rest assured that if there was an escape route to be had, Bayonet would find it.

Discretion

Leadership is more than just leading the charge up the mountain. Leadership is the ability to know *when* to lead the charge up the mountain. Leadership is the ability to know *when not* to lead the charge up the mountain. And most of all, leadership is the ability to command one's troops to heed that knowledge.

God does not strike Egypt with the plague of death until all other plagues have failed to move the pharaoh. Discretion.

When all your competitors are going public to raise more funds to effect more acquisitions, should you follow suit? The privately held Hyatt Hotel chain, immensely profitable year after nonpublic year, certainly puts the lie to that notion. Its owners, the Pritzker family, demonstrate their business leadership during each day of those privately held years. Discretion.

When all your competitors are cutting spending to cut costs, should you join the bandwagon? Not if you're Donald Trump and your success depends as much on the image of Donald Trump, the high-rolling, unapologetic, undaunted mogul, as it does on Donald Trump's bank account itself. Discretion.

Ahwad was living by himself, in Lebanon, in a mountainous suburb of Beirut. His apartment was in a complex of several high-rise towers at the end of a cul-de-sac. The drive time from the apartment to the international airport was about forty minutes, and the drive time from the apartment to the sea was about an hour and ten minutes. Even though the Beirut airport is as porous as a sieve, Bayonet chose the sea as the safer escape route.

The plan was quite straightforward: Bayonet would observe Ahwad's movements to learn a habit, any habit, that was performed with sufficient regularity to be relied upon. The kiss would center around that habit, as kisses always are. In the case of Ahwad it was his punctual departure from his apartment to downtown Beirut where he worked in the (unofficial) offices of the Popular Front for the Liberation of Palestine (the General Command) planning Lord knows what.

Ahwad drove a Fiat 124, which was parked in an outdoors parking space located under his apartment building. He lived alone and, as far as Bayonet could tell, had no regular girlfriend, boyfriend, or pet. Every morning at 7:00 A.M. sharp, Ahwad was downstairs, in his car. He was either an early riser or an irrepressible optimist who thought that by getting an early start he might avoid the Lebanese traffic nightmare.

Bayonet decided that Ahwad's parked car, when in the parking lot, was the best site for the kiss. Ordinarily, Bayonet would have kissed Ahwad by motorcycle. A motorcycling pair would roll up to Ahwad's car in traffic and the motorcycle's backseat rider would hit Ahwad

with a barrage from a snub-nosed AK-47, a unique Bayonet design. Ahwad would disappear in a hail of bullets.

But in this case a motorcycle drive-by shooting was
out of the question. In Beirut, with its narrow streets and
its winding alleys, there was simply no way to drive by.
The traffic downtown and in most of the periphery was
far too congested to realistically plan and coordinate
arrival times and kiss times, let alone plan for timely
escape routes.

No, the kiss would have to be out of town and away
from congestion. And the best place for that, perhaps the
only place for that, was in Ahwad's car lot, in his apartment building. There would be no way to kiss Ahwad
while he was walking to his car or while he was driving
away in his car because the parking lot garage was too
confined. The lot was squarely under the building, which
was supported by columns that ran both around the
building and in the middle of the lot. There were too
many obstructions for a motorcycle to maneuver.

So Bayonet decided to rig a bomb to the car. But here,
too, the plan was fraught with challenges. First of all,
there was the problem of activation; an automatic
"timer" device was out of the question because although
Ahwad was reliable, he was not the Big Ben and he didn't
live on Greenwich Mean Time. Bayonet would not waste
an explosion on an empty car. Therefore, Ahwad would
have to be verifiably inside the car before the detonation
took place.

Moreover, a remote control device, one in which you
detonate the bomb by way of radio signal upon eye contact with the victim, would not work because the car was
in a narrowly defined space at the end of a cul-de-sac.
Operating the bomb that way would require that the
team stay behind in the cul-de-sac in order to see Ahwad
get in the car. But if it were to do so, it could find itself
trapped in the cul-de-sac if, on the off chance, someone,
or thing, blocked it after the explosion.

Temperate risk taking required that the bomb be detonated automatically, only upon Ahwad's physical presence in the vehicle. Bayonet, therefore, decided that its sapper would attach a weight-triggered detonator to a bomb. The bomb itself, which would have to be small enough so as not to bring down the apartment building yet large enough to break Ahwad up into several smaller, less dangerous pieces, would be fastened to the bottom of the car, just under the driver's seat. The detonator would be primed to detonate the bomb ten seconds after Ahwad was sitting in the driver's seat. This would be enough time to allow him to start the car but not enough time to drive the car in harm's way. The explosives would be Czech-made "plastique," a pliable, Play-Doh-like material that was very stable under most circumstances.

Bayonet guessed Ahwad's weight at about 180 pounds, and so the bomb's detonator was set to trigger the explosives at any weight between 150 and 200 pounds.

The Bayonet team comprised six Combatants. The team leader, Coby, a veteran of several successful kisses; Fia, a crack explosives expert and sapper who had been the highest-ranking woman officer in the IDF's demolition corps before she was recruited to Bayonet; Yoel, chief mechanic; Neta, a former police detective and an expert in "tailing" (following suspects), eavesdropping (phone tapping), and locksmithing (although with her killer looks and deep blue eyes, she did not look the part); Ellie, a sophisticated and suave international lawyer who had turned in her wig for the adventure and challenge of Bayonet, was the team Beirut expert and the only team member proficient in the Arabic dialect spoken in Beirut; and then there was Mike, "operations coordinator," which was a polite way of saying that he was to watch the way things were done and not get in anyone else's way.

In Beirut, Coby assigned Mike to "tracking." Mike would be Bayonet's last watch point on Ahwad. Safely positioned in a secure vantage point, Mike would visually follow Ahwad as he exited his apartment building, walked to the parking lot, and entered his car. Mike would watch Ahwad and his car detonate. After that, he would follow a pathway between several of the other apartment buildings in order to meet up with Ellie and Coby with whom he would drive to the rendezvous point along the waterfront. By then, the rest of the team members should be long gone.

The plan called for Neta, Ellie, and Mike, in a motorcycle and a car, to "pick up" Ahwad at his downtown office and tail him home. They would continue their watch on his apartment until they were joined by the other team members later that night. The other team members would meet at Café Olympia later that night, for a traditional Lebanese "mezze" (open table). From there, they would drive on two motorcycles to the general vicinity of the apartment houses. Not far from the apartments was a "lovers' leap" where young Christian Lebanese drove their cars for some real kissing. Yoel and Fia would wait there while Coby continued to the lookout team.

Once Coby confirmed with Neta that Ahwad was safely in bed and his car parked where it was expected to be parked, Coby alerted Fia. Coby brought Fia and Yoel to the parking lot while sending Ellie and Mike to rest at the lovers' leap.

Fia and Yoel under the watchful eyes of Coby and Ellie attached the explosives to the Fiat. Neta had picked the car's locks before she left, so for Fia and Yoel it was just a matter of adhering the plastique under the driver's seat and setting the weights on the detonator. They were in and out of the parking lot in minutes.

The team's escape vehicle was a yacht in the Jounieh (North Beirut) marina on which there would be two other

Bayonet members, both former seamen. The yacht would take the entire team out to sea, where soon thereafter they would be picked off the deck by an unmarked civilian helicopter. The helicopter would ferry them on to the Cyprus coastline, from where they would take separate cars to Nicosia. In Nicosia, each of them would board a commercial airline to a different European destination. They would all be back in Tel Aviv three days after the kiss.

As 7:00 A.M. approached and the sky turned bright, Ellie and Fia left Mike and adjourned to their waiting point. Mike was now alone. He could hear his heart beat and he felt his pulse racing. He had fought in three wars as an infantryman, Ranger, officer, and pilot. He had devoted his life to the security and well-being of Israel. He had done it all. But nothing had prepared him for the experience of manhunting.

Just before 7:00 A.M., like clockwork, Ahwad exited his building and began to walk toward his car. Mike could feel the sweat roll down his nose. Ahwad was jiggling the keys in his hand as he walked toward his car as he did every morning. He turned to his car to open the door. Mike readied the little phonac button in his hand, ready to tell the girls that it was time to go. Before Ahwad opened the car's door, however, someone called his name. Ahwad looked around and Mike looked around. A little girl, a ten- or twelve-year-old with dark red hair and a slim build, was running out of the elevator column toward Ahwad.

Rule Number Two: Only the target gets hurt.

Mike had to move quickly and think even faster than he moved. He revved up his motorcycle and drove it out of his hidden cove into the parking lot and over to Ahwad. Ahwad was turning toward the girl while looking back over his shoulder at Mike's approaching motorcycle, all the while still juggling his car keys.

Mike rammed his bike in between Ahwad and his

car, knocking Ahwad and his keys to the ground. Then, still on his motorcycle, Mike grabbed Ahwad's keys off the ground and the girl off the floor and with a feat of mind over matter slung the girl between himself and his handlebars, over the motorcycle's gas tank. Mike turned the bike around and zoomed out of the parking lot on his way down the hill.

As he drove he could see that this little girl was a Lolita of sorts, as she had on heavy makeup and had been wearing a wig that flew off in this bout of acrobatics. Mike looked back over his shoulder and saw Ahwad chasing him on foot. He "phonacked" Fia to tell her to drive back up the mountain and pull the plastique off the Fiat. The kiss was off.

The Lolita was now fighting Mike and struggling to get off his bike. He dumped her halfway down the mountain. On their way up the mountain, Fia and Ellie passed Mike, the Lolita, and Ahwad, who was chasing Mike down the mountain and shouting at the top of his voice. A minute later, now in the parking lot, Fia looped under the car and pulled out the plastique. The detonator could stay behind and no one would know the difference. Job done, Fia and Ellie took off to the rendezvous, where less than an hour later they met up with Mike and the rest of Bayonet.

How and why the team missed the arrival of the girl would remain open questions. The lookout's attention may have been diverted for a moment; the girl may have been in the apartment before they arrived; the girl may have lived in the building. They would never be able to know for sure. But surprises happen, and, therefore, in a sense, they should not be surprises at all.

The mood on board the boat was glum. No one likes a botched mission even if no one is hurt, no one is caught, and the rules are preserved. Mike was not popular but he was respected. He acted quickly to avoid innocent bloodshed, and that is a paramount value. Killing one person for spilling innocent blood while, in the process, spilling innocent blood yourself was unacceptable.

Later that year, Mike received Israel's highest civilian honor, the Israel Prize for Defense. Shortly thereafter, he became Bayonet's new leader. The year after that, Bayonet kissed Ahwad. Discretion.

Waterlogged in Beirut

HOW TO MAKE THE BEST OF BAD SITUATIONS

▉MAKING THE BEST

> *"Hisagta Merube Lo Hisagta."*
> "Having Attained Much You Have Attained Nothing."

Hisagta Merube . . . Is this passage a non sequitur? Or is there a message in this contradiction? The Sages advise that attaining much is attaining nothing. What do they mean?

Attain only what you can cope with.

"Much" in the words of the Sages is not the equivalent of a great quantity but rather of too much. Too much, that is, for one person to digest and process. The consequence of attaining too much is that you are left with nothing. Thus, by attempting to attain much you attain nothing at all.

Full hands cannot grasp firmly any one object; a full mouth cannot properly chew any one portion of food; an attempt to do everything results in doing nothing at all.

I was at the bottom of a dark and murky harbor searching for a telephone cable. Visibility was nil and a flashlight was out of the question. It was the second day of the Yom Kippur War and most of Mossad was sitting this war out on the sidelines.

As a general rule, in an all-out war, a Combatant is a liability rather than an asset. There is little that a Combatant can do that a tank or a jet fighter can't do better. Moreover, this war started so suddenly, so abruptly, at least from Israel's vantage point, that none of its Combatants had been tasked or briefed for it.

But mine was a different story. I had served as a SEAL (Naval Commando) during my tour of military duty, and since I was still relatively fit enough, I was the natural choice for this operation. After all, it was difficult enough to get Navy SEALs into Beirut Harbor during peacetime. During war it would be virtually impossible.

Let Your Reach Exceed Your Grasp— but Grasp What You Can

Reaching for the stars is a much-praised and time-honored pursuit. You should always aspire to the best. But you should also grasp what you can attain. Do not allow the pursuit of perfection to affect the performance of the possible.

In October of 1973, I was stationed in Beirut, still keeping tabs on the PLO and the Black September organizations. As it happened, though, on the day before the war broke out, I was summoned to Israel by a very nervous Samson whose "nose" turned out to be better than her superiors' and better than the noses of the Israeli political echelon—all of whom discounted the possibility of war with Egypt and Syria.

Samson wanted me in Tel Aviv in anticipation of the war. Since my Beirut cover was ironclad, Samson knew that I would be able to return to Beirut at will. I was, after all, an international credit advisor to Banc du Liban, a subject I actually knew something about, having had international banking experience in a prior life.

Returning to Lebanon, a noncombatant country, during a war among Israel, Egypt, and Syria, would display just the right sort of naïveté that could be expected from an international financier.

Up until the war, my undercover mission was to monitor the international terrorist activity and actors in and around Beirut and Sidon. Only several months before the war, Bayonet and elite units of the Israeli army had assassinated several members of the Palestinian leadership in the "SOY" (Aviv Neurim) raid. My continued presence in the area was by way of a prolonged postmortem on that event. The Office wanted to know how the organizations reacted to the assassinations, who moved up in each group and why, who was blamed, and why and whether the organizations were recovering as quickly as AMAN feared.

Samson called it the "trinity of coincidence": Here I was, a Combatant, a SEAL, and a Lebanese banker in Israel's hour of need. Unfortunately, that trinity seemed to be about the only thing going well for Israel during those fateful October days.

My task was to force the Egyptians and Syrians, the two countries actively fighting Israel, to divert their telephone communications from the underwater telephone cable to the airwaves, to radio or satellite, where they could be intercepted by Israeli intelligence. "Hard links" (cable and telephone lines) present a challenge to intelligence-gathering operations. In order to tap into such calls, one must physically hook up to the lines carrying those calls. The airwaves, in contrast, were an eavesdropper's dream. Anyone with the right equipment could listen in on anything that was being carried up there, however jumbled, coded, or otherwise mixed up.

Therefore, once the war was raging, it became a matter of utmost importance to divert the Syrian–Egyptian communications link from the ground to the air. And the only realistic way of doing that would be to sever the ground line somewhere along the way.

Severing the link in Egypt or Syria was impractical because any damage to the cable could and would be repaired immediately. Attempting to sever the cable off the coasts of Egypt or Syria would not work because their respective navies would be carefully patrolling their shores looking for enemy naval activity. And attacking the cable at sea was a nonstarter because of the great diving depths involved and the amount of time that would be required to find the cable. Moreover, searching the seas for the cable would be impractical because it would tie up the much-needed Israeli navy and its SEALs.

That left Beirut.

Because of Lebanon's strategic location between Syria and Israel and because of the large number of militant Palestinians and other international terrorist organizations in Lebanon, Beirut, Lebanon's capital, was a very important target of Israeli intelligence. Israel made it its business to know everything there was to know about Beirut: its geography, topography, harbor, you name it. If it was relevant, Israel either had it or could get it. In fact AMAN referred to Beirut jokingly as "Haifa North." (Haifa is Israel's northern harbor, located about a hundred miles south of Beirut.)

As it turns out, the Pan Arab Telephone Cable (PATC, pronounced "patsy"), which was dedicated several years ago at one of the never-ending string of "unification" ceremonies between Egypt and Syria, ran through the very heart of Beirut's harbor. Although at first blush PATC's layout made no sense given that Alexandria (the Egyptian starting point for PATC) and Latakia (the Syrian end point for PATC) were a straight line from one another, it was not. PATC curved off the straight Alexandria–Latakia line and ran through Beirut in order to

allow the Lebanese to service the cable and to allow
for an eventual Lebanese hookup to it. Perhaps, if
there ever was peace, PATC would stop in the real
Haifa, too.

The ideal frogman combat operation is carried out
with a closed-circuit breathing apparatus, an
"Oxygers" (commercial name), an oxygen diving lung
that does not release bubbles to the surface. But the
Oxygers is a "military only" device. There was no
excuse for a civilian to be caught with one because it
had no civilian purpose. Its sole function was to help
conceal a diver in enemy waters. Anyone caught with
the device would be recognized for what he was—a spy.
Moreover, the Oxygers, because it used pure oxygen, is
restricted to a depth of about twenty feet. Diving below
that for any duration of more than several minutes
would prove fatal due to oxygen poisoning. Since PATC
was estimated to be at about sixty to ninety feet below
the surface, the Oxygers was out.

Scuba, which uses compressed air, would raise different problems. First there was the matter of all those
bubbles. The Lebanese would be on the lookout for
SEAL harbor activity because even though Lebanon
was a noncombatant, it was technically still at war
with Israel. And scuba bubbles are quite noticeable on
a quiet night in calm waters over a light-swept harbor.

Equally important was the fact that this would be
nobody's walk in the woods. It would take even the
most skilled diver diving at sixty to ninety feet an hour
or more to find the cable, attach explosives to it, and
get away from it. In other words, it would take more
time than the compressed air in one, two, or even three
tanks would provide. And that doesn't account for
decompression time on the way up.

Given that switching tanks in mid-job was out of
the question and given that there was no decompression chamber in Beirut that would accept me without

asking too many questions, it was clear that scuba too was not the answer.

There was a third choice. There was a civilian device, the DC-10, used by commercial divers. It released about one-fourth as many bubbles as conventional scuba yet allowed the diver to reach and stay at much greater depths without suffering the consequences of decompression. DC utilized mixtures of nitrogen and oxygen in various percentages in order to enable commercial divers to remain at greater working depths without having to go through lengthy decompression. It moderated the supply of nitrogen (which can cause air embolism and the "bends") with oxygen (which at greater depths can cause oxygen poisoning) to allow for a lengthy, deep dive. So, if oxygen barred you from sixty feet and compressed air would run out before you completed the task, DC would allow for over an hour's dive with no need for decompression and plenty of "mixture" left over for emergency use.

Better still, I could "borrow" a DC unit from the Beirut harbormaster's divers, a rowdy bunch of British and French ex-patriates who were Jounieh (the affluent Beirut, Christian suburb) drinking buddies of mine. I knew where they kept their gear, I knew how to fill the DC cylinders, and I knew their work schedule. On Sundays, they did not work. By raiding their equipment shed, I would also spare myself the major headache of smuggling in explosives. The harbor divers had explosives galore. I would be able to take what I wanted before they noticed anything at all. It was simply a matter of using the Old Boys Network.

The Office's plan was elegant in its simplicity: I would walk into the water at an empty Jounieh beach and swim southwards to Beirut Harbor, towing my gear behind me. Just outside the harbor, I would gear up, descend to the harbor's bottom, drag a weight along the harbor's silted "floor" from south to north until it snared on the cable, and then I would blow PATC up.

I assumed that reentering Beirut during the war would be easy. The city was not immediately affected by the hostilities, and its banks, as yet unaffected by the turmoil to affect them in later years, still attracted hordes of deal makers in all weather. As it turns out, I was right. Travel continued unabated into Beirut, and aside from routine questioning I waltzed right through border control.

Rather than return to my apartment in East Beirut, I checked into my favorite Jounieh hotel, where the Jounieh bay meets the Casino du Liban. I chose not to stay in my apartment because I wanted to avoid my doorman. I wanted him to think that I was still abroad. It would also have been too difficult getting from my apartment to the harbor and to the harbormaster's equipment room.

As soon as night fell, I drove to the harbor's periphery where the harbormaster divers' equipment and offices were. It was dark and, not unsurprisingly for a Sunday night, it was empty. I quickly picked the locks on the door and let myself into the wooden shed. Using a small flashlight, I found the gear I required and stuffed it all into a diver's bag. I chose a DC unit off the shelf, quickly filled its rubber lung with calcium (which serves as the cleansing agent for the CO_2 that accumulates in the rubber lung), attached two cylinders to the DC's body, one oxygen, one nitrogen (I could tell that they were full by their weight), and moved on to the explosives.

Here my years as a SEAL served me well. One cannot adequately explain to a Combatant, or to anyone else for that matter, the "what" and "how" of explosives in a short briefing, which is all I had. This holds especially true for the submarine use of explosives. But I knew exactly what I wanted, where to find it, and how to make it work. I completed my Christmas shopping and departed as I came, quietly and gratefully.

I threw the stuff in my car and drove back to Jounieh.

I stopped the car a bit north of the casino, at a quiet beach, where I geared up for operation: wet suit, mask, sneakers, fins, depth gauge, compass, watch, flares, revolver, deadweights, explosives, and a bundle of U.S. dollars, just in case of anything, in a watertight wallet. Under my wet suit I wore a lightweight, drip-dry, khaki shirt and slacks. If I was caught, I would claim to be a soldier. Under the Geneva Convention, spies die, whereas soldiers are prisoners of war. I also had with me a "Ruthie," a waterproof homing device Samson provided me with before I left Tel Aviv. When activated, it would allow friendly aircraft to hone in on its beam and find me wherever I was.

A few minutes later, with gamblers and drinkers huddled around roulette tables just a few yards away, I made my way into the sea. The casino lights glistened on the black water as I waded in.

It took only three or so hours to swim to the Beirut Harbor from Jounieh. It was a clear night, the water was not cold, and Beirut never looked more lovely. The pearl in the Middle Eastern pigsty. Who could imagine that all of this glory would be brought to rubble in less than a decade? I mourn the glory that was Beirut until this very day.

As I approached the harbor, I placed the DC's mouthpiece into my mouth and I gathered and reassembled the rest of my gear. I put the explosives on a stomach pack, the revolver in the upper leg of my wet suit, and wrapped the deadweight around my body and my weight belt. I took one last look at the city lights and prepared to descend to the harbor's depths. In one or two leg strokes, I would be an enemy frogman in a hostile harbor. During my four years as a SEAL, I had trained for this role day in and day out. Yet in all that time, I never had the honor of a "live performance."

Patience has its own rewards.

The Bad Situation

A bad situation, is just that, a situation: a temporary constellation of circumstances in which you are temporarily stranded. A bad situation, however, does not change who you are. It does not change the fundamental nature of your business. It does not limit your imagination. It should not limit your ability to think. While a bad situation may preclude you from attaining your original goal, it does not preclude you from attaining a worthy goal.

What is the essence of a "bad" situation? It is the coming together of circumstances that were unforeseeable or unforeseen or that were foreseen but for some reason ignored. How should you respond to this situation? First, by recognizing that the circumstances you planned for are not present and will not be present: You've dressed for basketball and the game is hockey.

Second, by understanding how your old plan impacts your ability to succeed under the new circumstances: You had planned on being the tallest and the fastest on the basketball court. But in hockey, height has little value and running up a court is not skating with a puck.

Third, through your willingness to abandon your meticulously crafted plan and—while grasping how your prior planning is now a hindrance—to adopt a new plan: Your height and speed have little value in hockey, but your reach (a function of your height) and your agility (a function of your speed) do.

- You're in the midst of a presentation when the overhead viewer burns out. Copy your transparencies and hand them out. Not the best of visual presentations but better than the alternative.

- You enter your boss's office seeking a pay raise, but he fires you before you can speak. Ask for a severance package that is not conditioned on other employment. Then get another job. Not exactly a pay raise, but a sight better than the alternative.

- You're committed to the delivery of one million widgets and your machinery breaks down. Buy the widgets from a competitor and make your delivery. Not exactly the deal you had in mind but no long-term damage from which there is no recovery.

• You've committed the company's resources to a market that's been hit by an economic downturn. Enter the market anyway. Sell your products at a substantially lower margin than planned but penetrate the market thoroughly. Not the quick returns you had expected, but better than wasting your resources altogether. The market will come back and so will you.

Do what you can—not what you plan.

When the Chrysler Corporation was facing bankruptcy, it certainly was not in the situation it had planned for. After all, Chrysler, primarily a car company, planned to sell cars. Its great fortune was that its chairman at the time, Lee Iacocca, understood that to survive and succeed, the company's annual plan of building and selling cars had to be trashed. Instead what was needed was a new plan that responded to the new reality.

The old reality was that Chrysler employed many workers in building cars. Chrysler's plan was, therefore, to have its workers build many quality cars that Chrysler's sales force could sell at high prices. When that didn't happen, Mr. Iacocca changed Chrysler's business plan. Chrysler would prosper not by building cars with its workers but by extracting money from the state and federal governments by holding its workers hostage to its survival.

Had Mr. Iacocca ignored the new reality, had he not changed his plan, had he pursued an attempt to do nothing more than continue to build cars and continue to try and sell them during that fateful year, Chrysler would have joined the ranks of American Motors, Studebaker, and others.

What in fact did Lee Iacocca do? First, he recognized that the circumstances he had planned for, Chrysler's continued economic viability, were not present and would not be present without a change of plan. Second, he understood how his old plan, continuing to support a large workforce that was not generating enough income to keep the company afloat, impacted his ability to succeed under the new circumstances. Third, he was willing to abandon his meticulously crafted old plan and—while grasping how that plan, business as usual, was now a hindrance—to adopt a new plan.

How did he adapt to the bad situation? By recognizing that the old plan's goal—success—would have to be jettisoned in favor of the new plan's goal—survival.

Contrast Iacocca's save from a bad situation to that of John DeLorean.

DeLorean's plan was to build a profitable, state-of-the-art, all-new sports car. To that end, he sought to raise enough money to sustain the company through its years of nonprofitability. And indeed, he began successfully. DeLorean raised funds for his company from both private and institutional investors and he found a hospitable climate, including government support in Ireland.

But when the circumstances changed for DeLorean, when the money he had raised was not enough to keep him going, when the market was not accepting his cars at the rate his plan said they would, DeLorean persisted in the plan: raise more money, build more cars. And that lead to the company's downfall and to his personal tragedy.

What DeLorean should have done was change his plan. He should have acknowledged the changed circumstances; he should have acknowledged that given those circumstances his plan was no longer viable; and he should have sold his company to an established manufacturer.

Better some accomplishment than no accomplishment.

My last act before descent was to pull my mask down over my face. Unfortunately, as I did so, I felt the mask's rubber strap snap. I was without a mask strap. Shit. In my haste, it had not occurred to me to bring any spare straps along. I was angry, very angry with myself. A rookie diver would not have made the mistake of going on a dive without a spare strap.

Well, I couldn't quite hold the mask over my face with

my hand. I would have to cannibalize a strap from somewhere. Given what I had with me, there was but one choice: I'd have to sacrifice a fin strap for the torn mask strap. That meant that I would be operating with only one fin, which would not only slow me down but would also make taking and keeping a compass course extremely difficult. There was no other choice.

Because my right leg was stronger, I thought it best to keep my left foot finned, at least initially, while I still was strong. So I pulled my right fin off and pulled the strap off of it and moved the strap to my mask. I then tried jamming the right fin back onto my foot, hoping that it might stay on my foot just because I needed it to. No such luck. No sooner had I taken half a stroke with my right leg than that fin was on its way to the murky depths of the harbor.

Well, as a SEAL I had been through one-finned activity numerous times in training. I knew that my mission was still doable, if somewhat more difficult. But I was not over all obstacles yet. First of all, as I descended, I couldn't see a thing. The visibility was zero. I couldn't see my hand in front of my mask, which I now regretted keeping. Whether it was silt, mud, or gunk, the harbor's waters were impenetrable. This job would be all touch or it simply wouldn't be at all.

There is a diver's adage that one's intelligence drops by 50 percent upon entering the water and another 50 percent upon going under the water. Let me add that when you lose your eyesight underwater, you might as well be diving without a brain.

I was disoriented, my legs were propelling me unevenly, I was breathing heavily and consuming too much mixture too fast, and, to add insult to injury, my mask was leaking water. Since I couldn't see anyway, I wasn't too concerned about my mask. But staying on course was important. I tried to focus my thoughts and concentrate in order to find a way that might make my predicament more manageable.

After a quick run-through of my options, I concluded that I was too heavy. I was, after all, carrying the dead-weight on a rope in addition to my regular weight belt. I thought that it might be best to unwrap the deadweight's rope from around my body, transfer its rope to my weight belt, and discard the extra weight. That way, I could just drag the rope tied to my weight belt on the bottom instead of the separate, heavy, and superfluous dead-weight. That was a mistake.

In trying to untie the rope from the deadweight, I dropped the rope and the deadweight. I was now left only with my weight belt, which meant that I would have nothing to drag behind me on the harbor's bottom except the length of the weight belt itself. But this would prove to be impossible because as I attempted to drag it with one arm, the other side of my body floated upward and lifted me off the bottom. And with only one fin, I was in no position to fight the lift. I would have to crawl along the bottom, feeling my way as I went.

The harbor bottom, as one might expect, was strewn with silt, garbage, and primeval goo. It was no place for a picnic. Crawling along the harbor's bottom looking for the cable while trying to keep an accurate course was like trying to read a map, while driving a car, at night, in a swamp. Only worse.

Just as I thought things couldn't get worse, they did. The sneaker on my right foot and my right foot itself, the one without a fin, snagged on a protruding piece of something sharp. I was somehow impaled on a sharp piece of metal or glass. Since I couldn't see anything and my mobility was limited, I turned back to try and release myself from the "sharp." As best I could tell, the sharp had run about halfway through the sole of my sneaker and my foot, which explained the sharp pain I felt. By the time I got my foot off the sharp, the sneaker was torn into shreds. To try and slow or stop the bleeding, I took off my left fin and my left sneaker in order to move the left sneaker, which was still in one piece, to my right foot. No sooner had I done that than I dropped the left fin into the silt and no matter that it had to be just inches from me, I couldn't find it.

So now I was tired, injured, without fins, with a leaky mask, no deadweight, and quickly running out of time and air. I was ready for a break and I got one, sort of.

Resolved to at least get across the harbor's bottom before dawn and before my mixture ran out, I dug both arms into the muddy bottom and pulled myself forward, dragging my legs as snares behind me. In what must have been only ten or fifteen minutes, but seemed like much more, I hit pay dirt. The cable. I was more relieved than happy.

I pulled the explosives off my back and immediately set about preparing the detonating device. As I moved around the cable, my hand brushed against another cir-cular tubelike object. It must have been less than a foot from the first cable. This was not good.

The Worst Is Behind You

In a bad situation, relax: The worst is behind you. If before you were in trouble your concern was that you might get into trouble, relax: You're in trouble.

When things go wrong and then go from bad to worse, staying calm is the only essential component of recovery. Only when calm can you assess the situation and determine how best to act. Panicky action, action without thought, is almost always going to be the wrong kind of action because it will almost always not account for all of the variables in the situation.

To stay calm you should understand that the status quo ante is gone, there is no way back. You should understand that the crisis must be resolved; if you don't resolve it, it will probably get worse.

Letting Go of the Status Quo

Like an old friend, for most, letting go of the status quo is difficult, if not impossible, to do. Most will continue to do what they have always done even when doing so no longer makes any sense. In a plentiful market, one who grew up in scarcity shall continue to horde. In a down market, one who grew up in a growth market will continue to buy. The acts take on a ritualistic, comforting pattern of their own, which is completely divorced from the new reality in which the individual player finds himself.

The reason there are no second acts for most businessmen and -women is that when circumstances change, they don't. Rather, they continue to do what they did under previous circumstances, and for that reason their success ends.

Most car companies did not survive the introduction of the production line. Most mainframe computer companies did not survive the onslaught of the PC. You may not survive the Information Economy.

Therefore, the most important element of survival in crisis is to recognize change and acknowledge it. You acknowledge it by divorcing your actions from what preceded it.

The Crisis Must Be Resolved

It won't go away. Even if you pretend it is not there, it is. Unless you come to grips with that fact, and the sooner the better, you cannot begin to succeed. No one else will solve the crisis for you because the crisis for you is not the same to others as it is to you.

The demise of Chrysler was accompanied by a weakness in the other U.S. car manufacturers, but it was not the same. If Iacocca was not going to solve Chrysler's crisis, no one was going to do it for him.

In Crisis, Opportunity

The most overlooked facet of crisis management is the opportunities present in a crisis situation. By remaining calm in the earthquake, by acknowledging the change of topography and looking afresh at the land, you should be able to identify the opportunities exposed by the shifting plates. By seeking opportunity in crisis, one has the field to oneself because most others will be panicked and will be seeking to minimize the effect of the crisis upon them.

When Chrysler was on the brink of bankruptcy, Iacocca did not try to stem his losses, he got someone else to assume them. When the markets fall, don't seek ways to sell your losers, seek ways to acquire bargain-priced winners. When unemployment strikes, seek to service the unemployed.

Stay calm. Think. Act.

In my Tel Aviv briefing, AMAN told me that Beirut had one and only one communications cable and that that cable was PATC. Find it, blow it up, and leave town, they said. But they were wrong. It now appeared—well, felt would be a better word for it—that AMAN's information was wrong. There were two separate cables. No mistake about it.

This was judgment time. I had entered Beirut, I had assembled the implements of destruction, I had reached the harbor, I had found the cable. In short, I had followed all of the instructions, directives, and orders that I had received and I had fulfilled them. But now I was in uncharted territory. No directive, no order, no rule book, no manual addressed the specifics of this situation: two cables instead of one. There was only the accumulated wisdom of my fellow Combatants over time: Attain the Attainable.

Here was the choice: I could detonate one cable, both cables, or no cables.

If I detonated one cable, as I was instructed to do, I would not know whether the cable I detonated was PATC until after I was long out of Beirut Harbor. By then it would be too late and quite impossible to return to explode the second cable.

If I detonated both cables, at least one of the cables was likely to be PATC, but I could only guess (and guess

poorly at that) as to what that second cable might be. It could be a gas line, an oil line, or even, for all I knew, a secret Israeli telecommunications line that had drifted from where AMAN thought it to be. Blowing either baby up entailed the risk of killing myself, creating an environmental nightmare, and/or pissing off some intelligence analyst at Mossad, AMAN, and perhaps even CIA.

If I detonated neither cable, well, then I quite obviously would not have performed my mission.

I did not have the luxury of a drawn-out analysis of my options. My foot was bleeding, I felt weak, I was probably underwater for too long already, and I was quickly running out of air. What was quite clear to me, even in the confused state I was in, was that choosing only one of the cables would have been stupid. To do so would run all the risks of blowing both cables up but with none of the benefits. So, as far as I was concerned, the option was between not blowing up any cables or blowing up both cables. There was no middle ground.

I would have preferred to perform the perfect. But reality interceded. There would be no perfection, just a choice between two imperfect outcomes: Do something and run the risk of doing harm, or do nothing and abort the mission. I could not do the perfect but I could do the nearly perfect. It was war. Israel's survival was at stake. If it was a gas line and I blew myself up with it, so be it. I was expendable. If it was oil and I created a mess in the harbor, so be it. There would be plenty of time for clean-up. If it was an intelligence line, so be it. There would be ways to rectify the damage.

I chose to perform the possible. Both cables would blow.

With whatever strength I had left in me, I tried to pull the second cable over to the first, but I couldn't really get it to budge. Fortunately, I had enough explosives to bridge the small distance between the two cables. With a bit of massaging and stretching, I was able to get enough explosives halfway around each cable and still have enough left over to run between the cables. Moreover, because water is so much more dense than air, the explosive force of my bomb would carry seven times the wallop it would have if exploded in the open air.

The timing device would give me three hours before explosion. Even given my sorry state, that would be plenty of time for me to get out of the harbor and make it to the helicopter rendezvous site, which was less than a mile south.

I pulled the detonator's wire and sensed that it had begun its slow waterproof "burn." I began a controlled ascent to see where I was relative to a harbor wall, any wall. It took me some effort to surface because I was still wearing my weight belt, and without fins the ascent was tough. I could have dropped the weight belt and attempted to carefully and slowly inflate my life vest, but I didn't do so for fear of popping out of the water like a flying fish.

When I was about a foot from the surface, I stopped my ascent and peered around me until I could orient myself and make out the harbor's general direction. I figured that I was about eight hundred yards from one side of the harbor and about another twelve hundred yards from the other.

I decided that either way was manageable. I took the DC's mouthpiece out of my mouth, and in violation of everything that I was ever taught as a SEAL and Combatant, I let the device drop to the harbor's depths. I tore off my wet suit and I tied my weight belt around it, my mask, backpack, and all of the other diving gear that I had on me, and let them, too, sink to the harbor bottom. I kept only my revolver, my Ruthie, and my dollars.

I surfaced to a dark, almost empty harbor. The brunt of the war must have affected the harbor's usually busy activity, which was good for me. Less chance of running into unfriendly tugboats and pilot boats. I turned over on my back and with my legs safely below water, quietly propelled myself toward a harbor wall. Once there, I climbed up the wall aided by the tires and floats tied to it. I took a few minutes in the shadows to regain my breath and my composure. I did what I could to comb my hair and wring the water out of my clothes and I was ready to go.

I walked out into the light on the main loading dock where several stevedores were manually unloading cement bags from a ship. They took no notice of me. I continued walking until I reached the harbor's main entrance. I could have tried to scale the wall, but frankly, I was too tired. I waited in the shadows just thirty or so yards from the gate. Soon enough a truck approached the gate. As it slowed down, I jumped into its back cargo area and slipped behind the canvas flaps. It was carrying some sort of fertilizer or other foul-smelling chemical. I felt like shit. Perfect match. I dug a hole into one of the large plastic bags and pushed whatever of myself I could fit into it. By now, the truck had come to a full stop at the gate. I heard some Arabic words being exchanged and I heard the truck roll on. Not even a perfunctory inspection.

I waited until the truck had traveled some distance from the gate. I then crawled out of the bag and went to the rear of the truck, opening the canvas flaps to see where I was. I was on the main road to my rendezvous. I jumped off the truck and almost ran the remaining distance to the rendezvous site, turning on the Ruthie while running. The helicopter must have been waiting just offshore because it seemed to me that they were down on the ground before the Ruthie was even working.

I half climbed, half was pulled into the Sikorsky helicopter, which was immediately airborne. It flew out to sea where it took a sharp left turn, south, toward Israel. I would be home in minutes. I drifted off into a deep and satisfying sleep.

When we arrived, I was taken in for a debriefing with

Gray Cell and the head of AMAN. I had accomplished the mission. An underwater explosion went off in Beirut Harbor at 0300 hours and 22 minutes. The entire Egyptian-Syrian communication system went airborne within minutes of 4:00 A.M. Realizing that their cable link was gone, Egypt's and Syria's commanders had no choice but to use airborne communication instead of no communication.

I also learned that as of 0300 hours and 22 minutes, all communication between Europe and the Middle East came to a halt. It turns out that someone blew up their phone cable.

Reach for the stars but grab what you can.

A Russian in Kurdistan

HOW AND WHEN TO CUT YOUR LOSSES

CUTTING LOSSES

"UBneichem Yehiyu Roim BaMidbar Arbaim Shana. . . ."
"And Your Children Shall Wander in the Wilderness Forty Years. . . ."

UBneichem Yehiyu . . . The Israelites, although now former slaves, continue to be ruled by a slave mentality. Instead of assuming the responsibilities of free men and women, they continue to mourn the loss of the Egyptian "Meat Bowl."

They cry and bemoan the difficulties of life as a free people.

God concludes that regardless of effort these individuals cannot be prepared for the lives of free men and women. The former slaves shall not be able to forge the nation of Israel God had envisaged. They cannot be prepared for freedom. Therefore, He stops preparing the slaves for the land of Israel. It is as though to say: "Better to start anew than to continue to prepare that which cannot be changed."

God decrees that an entire generation must perish to eradicate the slave mentality. Then and only then shall the Israelites be prepared to conquer the land and inherit it.

We had tried it all to no avail.

No matter what we did, we could not get Alex to learn the game. True, not everyone was cut out for undercover work, but we were hardly asking Alex to be James Bond. Our event horizon was rather more modest: We had to bring Alex to the point where he could articulate his cover story, defend it in an inquiry, and feign innocence, persuasive innocence, fighting innocence, in the face of rather incriminating artifacts.

To us, Combatants, this was all second nature. If you caught me standing over a body with a smoking gun, I could persuade you that the butler did it. That's why I was a "mouth." But Alex, well, let's just say that if Alex were the body that I was standing over, the police would probably arrest him before they arrested me.

Preparation Is a Prelude to Action. It Is Not Action

Preparation is an essential element in success. But it is not success itself. Regardless of preparation, you cannot win if you do not compete. No matter how practiced, you cannot prevail if you do not perform. So prepare as much as you can, as long as you can, and as thoroughly as you can. And then act. But make sure you act.

Preparation requires information. In a business negotiation, information is power. Do not allow the need to prepare and the desire for preparation to eclipse the reality that at some point, often sooner than you think, the time for preparation is over and the time for action begins. Do not escape into your preparations. Do not use preparation as an excuse for inaction. Do not let the making of the tool dictate the time for the job.

You should cease your preparations when one of several things occurs. First, when the predetermined time for action has arrived, act. When the starter gun goes off, your preparation is over. With the firing of that gun, further preparation will not, cannot, do anything to increase the likelihood of success. The only thing that can is a swift departure from the starting blocks. When the day and time for a meeting arrives, don't bother to re-review the price analysis of your commodities. That will be of little significance if you don't show up for the meeting.

You should also cease your preparations when the amount of time devoted to preparation is related inversely to the benefit realized. The first time you read a competitor's business plan, you learn a great deal in a relatively brief amount of time. The second time you read it you may actually learn more because the information you review the second time has the beginnings of an intellectual framework within which to assemble it. The third time may provide you with less information on an absolute scale but will probably provide you with mastery of previously overlooked detail. Thereafter, on average, the preparatory return on investment begins to decline sharply.

When you are spending more and more time to acquire less and less information, move on. Cease your preparations.

What to do when you are investing time yet receiving no return? Cut your losses. Not everyone is cut out for every task. No amount of preparation can turn the slave into a free man. Recognize that and change strategy. If the slave generation could not make it as free men and women, the next generation would. Preparation shifted from the futile point A to the productive point B. What remained constant was the objective and its attainment.

Alex was a soil compaction engineer. His particular field of inquiry was runways, as in military runways. He was reputed to be an expert. That is why he was chosen. It was our job to transform Alex from a rather lumbering, analytical, methodical, and slow-talking aviation engineer into a fast-thinking, intuitive, fast-talking Combatant. It was not looking good.

The challenge we faced was the extrication of a Combatant gone "native."

Misha, one of the Office's older Combatants, a veteran of Stalin's Red Army, had been sent years hence into Kurdistan to try and lend some coordination to the haphazard and unfocused efforts of the Kurdish popular

forces. He had been in Kurdistan for over five years, and like the mythical Kurtz in Conrad's *Heart of Darkness,* had slowly but surely ceased his contacts with Samson. It was rumored in the Office that Misha, whose cover story was that he was a KGB agent supporting the Kurds against the imperialist, hegemonist, Western forces of the shah and those of Iraq, actually began to believe that his cover story was true.

For several months now, Misha had ignored the Office's communications and failed to respond to the Office's agenda. Someone would have to go in to Iraqi Kurdistan and bring Misha out.

Kurdistan was the ancient homeland of the Kurdish nation, a distinct people with its own religion, language, ethnicity, and cultural heritage that had been ruled as much by the absence of rule as by its presence by three countries: Turkey from the north, Iraq from the west, and Iran from the east. With the ebb and flow of each land-lord's historical prospects, the Kurds lost more and more autonomy. Israel had a vested interest in the plight of the Kurds for several very good reasons.

First, a large minority of Jews were part of the Kur-dish nation. These Jews, who had lived with and among the Kurds for generations, had their lives intertwined with the prospects of the Kurds themselves. So although not suffering discrimination at the hands of the Kurds, when the Kurds suffered, so did the Jewish Kurds. Israel owed an obligation to those Jews to better their plight and help those among them who wanted to come to Israel. Israel also owed an obligation to those Kurds already in Israel to help unite them with the remnants of their families still stranded in Kurdistan.

Second, on the "real-politic" level, Israel had a strategic interest in what transpired in Kurdistan.

Israel had forged clandestine ties with the newly coronated shah of Iran, Reza Pahlavi, who saw himself as a link in the chain of great Persian shahs and not as a link in the chain of Arab and Islamic dictators or military strongmen common to the region. (Beauty, as they say, is in the eye of the beholder.) What could Israel offer this strategically situated king? Assistance in his control of the rebellious Kurdish minority in his county's northwest.

Israel also had an interest in stability in Turkey. Turkey was, after all, the model that Israeli optimists hoped would one day envelope the entire Middle East: a secular nation where religion was a component of life, not its determinant. If Turkey were to fail, what hope could there be for places like Iraq?

And, speaking of Iraq, although not a "frontline" country (that is, it did not share a border with Israel), it traditionally financed terrorist organizations that kept Israel in their crosshairs. It also always sent troops, weapons, and money to the frontline states during any of their wars and border skirmishes with Israel.

Here was a plan Metternich would have been proud of: Israel would assist Iran, stabilize Turkey, and trouble Iraq, by focusing the Kurds' ire and activity on Iraq. And it would do so by tasking the Office with that mission.

The Office accomplished the mission through a series of measures, one of which was the dispatch of Misha, a seasoned Combatant and toughened war veteran, under the cover of being a KGB agent to assist and train the Kurdish fighters. In support, Misha was equipped with Russian armaments (booty from Israel's wars with Egypt and Syria). And if Misha's assistance and that of his colleagues came at the price to the Kurds of a "temporary" shutoff of anti-Persian and anti-Turkish operations to focus first and foremost on Iraq, well, who would complain?

Problem was, Misha wasn't following orders. Encouraged by his anti-Iraq operations, he was now turning his sights, in the service of an independent Kurdistan, on Iran. And that could not be allowed to happen.

Misha would have to be brought back home. Yet doing so would not be easy.

Northern Iraq was outside the range of Israeli helicopters because the only way in was over the airspace of either Iraq, Turkey, the Soviet republic of Azerbaijan, or Iran, all of which were out of the question for a slow-flying chopper. So any air-rescue attempt would require a real jet, not a helicopter. But an American- or French-built fighter plane, which was all Israel had, would not only set "friend or foe" alarms ringing all over Iraq and the Soviet Union but would also, quite likely, deter Misha from boarding. So whatever was flown into Iraq would have to be a Russian aircraft. And the only way one could safely land a Russian aircraft on an unpaved runway was to have a soil compaction engineer certify the runway ahead of time.

Since Israeli air force officers (who know something about qualifying a dirt strip for military aircraft) are not exactly welcome in Iraq, we were tasked with transforming Alex into a "temporary" Combatant so that he could enter Iraq and certify the landing field. That, in turn, would allow an IAF pilot to fly a Russian plane into Iraq and bring Misha back from Kurdistani Iraq.

All this assuming, of course, that Misha would even agree to leave his beloved Kurds behind.

So in comparison to the overall challenges at hand, preparing Alex to be a Combatant seemed a small task indeed.

We began innocently enough with self-confidence exercises. We allowed Alex all day to study his cover story. We then gave him a written true/false exam based entirely upon his cover story. A monkey would have received a 50 percent score. Alex didn't even come close. We then told him his own story over and over again, the way one might tell a favorite story to a three-year-old until the child can finish the story's sentences. To no avail.

The problem to me was quite clear. Alex had no imagination whatsoever. Therefore, he couldn't lie. He couldn't even say his Combatant name, Sasha (as close as we could get him to Alexander without being too obvious about it), without a pained look of anguish crossing his face. Alex couldn't learn his cover because he would rather fail than depart his reality. He knew how to function in his world and he did so quite well, thank you very much. Alex was not about to take a fling on another life after having mastered this one so well.

Given the enormity of the Kurdish problem, its international ramifications, and Misha's plight, no one would pay much heed to some defeatist Combatants arguing that the star pupil wasn't going to graduate. But we knew that further preparation would be useless. We would never transform the aviation engineer into an agent.

Furthermore, we were reaching diminishing returns. Not only was Alex not progressing, he was regressing. The more we pressed, the worse he got. This was no time to intensify preparation. This was time to hang it up. We took Alex to a heart-to-heart.

"You're not going to make it," I told Alex. "You're pretty much useless as a spy, you know that, don't you?"

"Yep. That's what I told Mossad when they proposed me for the job in the first place. I could never act and I never wanted to. So what now?" Alex asked, always the good and dutiful student.

"Now, my friend." I paused. "Now you become luggage."

"Excuse me?"

"Now, Alex, you become what we call luggage. That means, sir, that you will travel with me into Iraq as though you are my carry-on. If spoken to, you shall not speak. If questioned, you shall not answer. Rather, I shall answer all questions or comments made to you. You, sir, shall not make a move or a gesture if there is anyone within ten feet who might possibly, even casually, misinterpret it as a sign of intelligent life. You, my friend, are Helen Keller with a plane ticket. You are the reverse invisible man—seen but not heard. You will trust me to make up for the guile you lack. And that is really all there is to it because there is no other way. Preparation, my dear Alex, is over. The performance begins."

19
Making Beira
HOW TO SUCCEED AGAINST THE ODDS

■ SUCCESS AGAINST THE ODDS

> *"VeYedei Moshe Kvedim . . . VeAharon VeHur Iamkhu*
> *BeYadav . . . Ad Ba HaShemesh."*
> "And Moses' Hands Were Heavy and Aaron and Hur
> Supported His Arms Until Sunrise."

VeYedei Moshe . . . Amalek, Israel's biblical nemesis, attacks the fledgling nation. Moses climbs to the mountaintop to demonstrate the Lord's tenacity and resolve by holding up the "rod" of God.

So long as Moses holds his arms (and the rod) in the air, Israel prevailed in battle. But whenever he dropped his arms, Israel's forces fell behind. Moses' arms tired. Yet he would not cease. Even when he can no longer hold his arms up himself he does not cease. Rather, he enlists two of his trusted aides to hold his arms aloft with him. And then too he will not stop. Not until Amalek is smitten will Moses rest. Then and only then does he drop his arms.

I was in darkest Africa, on crutches, in a car that would not start, in a guerrilla war zone, with a guide who could not speak English. Things were not going as planned.

Against the Odds

To attempt success in face of the odds is to act irrationally. To persist in the face of a daunting challenge is irrational. But rationality is merely a term to define the majority's sensibilities. It is not an objective measurement of sanity or probability of success. For if it were, there would be no discovery. Columbus and Magellan would be dockside drunks, the Wright brothers, wrong, and Intel, Out-tel.

It should not be surprising, therefore, that rationality is the kiss of death to persistence. It is the enemy of individual, iconoclastic success. Rational behavior condemns the heroic effort, ridicules the dogged performer, and destroys the lone dreamer. Rationality is the antithesis of emotional effort and, as such, will always halt that which must be brought about through belief and determination and not resources and capabilities.

It is rare the instance in which persistence is a rational exercise and allocation of resources. It is always "rational" to stop an unsuccessful effort. It is always "rational" to conserve resources. It is always rational to assess the situation to determine that "rationally" one cannot succeed.

Individual, entrepreneurial success is rarely rational. If it were, middle management would be wealthy and entrepreneurs, poor. If it were, David would have fled from Goliath and the Philistines would have conquered Israel; Churchill would have surrendered at Dunkirk and Germany would rule England. But that is not what happened. David acted irrationally and became king. Churchill behaved irrationally and beat the Reich.

Individual, entrepreneurial success is dependent on persistent effort to a far greater degree than it is on rationality. And, if you remember that fact, you will prevail against the odds, which is simply another way of saying that persistence beats rationality every time.

It was just several days since I had completed Combatant training. One, however, was not "graduated," so to speak, until the Combatant Corps' ritualistic "Test by Fire."
Since Combatant training was an individualized affair, TBF was tailor-made to fit each Combatant or what was

perceived to be the particular weakness of each Combatant. Only upon a satisfactory performance in TBF did one move on to bigger and greater things.

TBF was designed to be a challenging exercise in an unfriendly environment. It was not designed to place a Combatant, however, in harm's way. Rather, it was planned so that in the event of disaster, there would be some way, whether diplomatic or clandestine, to extract the Combatant without risking the loss of the Combatant's life and without having to deploy troops to the rescue.

TBF could be a Combatant's kiss of death.

Until TBF, the Combatant candidate ("Cc") trains in the Office's shadows; no one knows who the candidates are, where they are training, and how they are performing. But once the Combatant Corps decides that a particular Cc is ripe for TBF, that Cc's dossier is delivered to Samson and to Pinnacle along with the TBF assignment. Success or failure is now determined by Samson and Pinnacle, and failure means the Cc is out.

Second chances are a luxury the Office can ill afford.

The canard on my candidacy was that the training had been too easy for me. Having sweated the details over many long days and nights, I am not sure that I agreed, but the decision was not mine to make. Since the perception was that I waltzed through training, there was a real question regarding my tenacity: Could I be counted on to persist against the odds?

My TBF would test that tenacity.

Entrepreneurship

The entrepreneur is the ultimate Lone Ranger. You must take it upon yourself to be all things and to do all things. You have no one to turn to. You have no staff to call upon. You are, in a sense, beyond sensibility, for any sensible person would not undertake to do what you have undertaken to do.

To succeed, make yourself deaf to your surroundings. Do not listen to the naysayers and the detractors. Filter out the noise and follow your instinct. Know what you wish to do, determine what you must do, then do it. Do not wait for someone else to solve your problems. Do not wait for someone else to find the answers. Do not be deterred by the problems. Find the solution.

The Republic of Mozambique was a Marxist dictatorship in the throes of a nasty civil war. Ever since the early seventies, both before and after the Portuguese upped and left their former colony, Mozambique was embroiled in a bloody civil war with South African– and CIA-funded antigovernment rebels, known as Renamo.

Renamo held parts of the countryside while the government held the cities. The problem was that Mozambique's important cities—its capital, Maputo, and its industrial base, Beira—were coastal cities with ports in complete disrepair from years of war and neglect. Therefore, they were easily surrounded by the rebels. Since Maputo was the capital, the government's forces focused their efforts on keeping it open. Beira, which was a transportation lifeline connecting Rhodesia (Zimbabwe) through the "Beira corridor" to the port of Beira, was less fortunate.

The port city of Beira, although only three or four hundred miles north of Maputo, was virtually inaccessible. The city was surrounded, and had been for some years now, by Renamo. Beira's port was closed, and the city itself was under constant siege. The only way into the city was through a narrow government-patrolled corridor that led from the Zimbabwe border town of Matola southeast to the Indian Ocean and Beira. If anything came into Beira it came through the Beira corridor. And if anything came through the Beira corridor, it was fair game for Renamo.

The Beira corridor, which was the modern-day equivalent of the Wild West, complete with guerrillas,

bandits, and ambushes, was to be the site of my TBF. At the time, there were no flights between Maputo and Beira because of the guerrillas' antiaircraft rockets. To reach Beira, one had to brave the Beira corridor. My challenge would be to make it from Matola to Beira and back in twenty-four hours. It didn't seem like that big of a challenge. But what you don't know can hurt you.

I had to build my cover story and overall TBF plan. Once approved, I would be on my own. Through my research on Mozambique and considering that I did not want to tag myself as an arms merchant, I proposed to be the European representative to Africa of an international food company seeking to acquire and invest in the country's cashew plantations and processing plants. The Mozambique cashew industry, once a world leader, had fallen into disrepair. Its center, not surprisingly, was Beira. The international food company had so many different offices that even if someone were so inclined it would be hard to check my cover story in twenty-four hours. Offering investment in a war-torn country is always an easy sell.

The Rules of Success

To succeed as an entrepreneur you must become the smartest, the most nimble, and the most resilient. You must never waiver, for if you do, there is no backup. You must never stumble, for if you do, there is no second line. You must do on your own what your competitors do with a staff of hundreds. You must be willing to do all that it takes whenever needed without complaint or self-pity. You must face the odds and know that you will beat them. Then you must persuade the "odds" of that as well.

But you can follow the trail blazed by the scores of entrepreneurs who preceded you. They have left a pattern of conduct that is as applicable to you as it was to them. Learn from it and adopt it.

Choose the Best Associates and Advisors and Use Their Halo

Seek out the best "brand" names in each profession and engage them. While the price for such services is steep and often out of the realm of most start-ups, the credibility you acquire by relying upon your advisors' network will provide you with instant credibility and access to "blue chip" investors, customers, and strategic partners.

This is a simple rule to follow and one which will provide you with more mileage than perhaps any other. If you can engage a reputable firm, few questions will be asked of you and many positive assumptions regarding your bona fides shall be made. It was no accident that the notorious founders of the Bank of Credit and Commerce International (BCCI) retained Clark Clifford as their "face" to Washington. After all, if Clifford—advisor to presidents and potentates—will associate with BCCI (or its wholly owned subsidiary), then BCCI must be legitimate.

Do not seek to cut corners on this item. It is expensive to engage Mr. Clifford. But if you do, finances shall not pose a problem. In the long run, it is far more expensive not to engage Mr. Clifford.

My plan approved, I departed for Paris, where I would get my visa and flight to Harare. I had persuaded the Office that to stay in character, my cover required that I travel first class. So I was feeling rather chipper about things the night before my scheduled departure, and I invited the Mozambican ambassador to France to a wonderful Left Bank restaurant.

Dinner was delightful, and the ambassador was very happy to be entertained by one who would soon be an investor in his country. He was already seeking out ways to be my partner, and I would not disabuse him of the possibilities ahead of us. After dinner, and after we had shared several bottles of wine and a cognac or two, we left the restaurant. The ambassador had his car waiting outside and he offered me a ride. I preferred, however, that he not know where I was staying, and so I respectfully declined. He wished me bon voyage and drove off. I

turned to cross the Odéon intersection where I was standing and promptly and efficiently was struck by a car.

The car had driven over my foot, managing to break just about every one of the multitude of bones in it. The driver of the car, a kind and thoughtful young man, offered to take me to the police station to file a report. But that, of course, wouldn't do. Instead, he drove me to my hotel, where I hobbled up to my room. Perhaps because of the amount of alcohol I had consumed that evening, I was not immediately in that much pain. But by the time I made it to the room, my foot was the size of a basketball and I had sixteen hours to my flight.

I telephoned my Operator and explained the situation.

"Do you think we might postpone the TBF?"

"Why?"

"Because I broke my foot. Because I was run over."

"We know. We've been watching you. Not going to the police and not going to the hospital were the right decisions. But you can walk, can't you? There are crutches in Paris, aren't there? Are you suggesting to quit?"

"No. Never mind. I was only kidding. Sorry I woke you."

"Anytime."

Be Persistent

Some say that 90 percent of life is just showing up. Well, 90 percent of success is just showing up again. And again and again. Never give up. Never. Never accept no for an answer. Never. And always, always, follow up. After all, the harsh rules governing start-up companies make Murphy's Law ("Anything that can go wrong will") seem like a banal description of an average day at the office.

The most uniform comment made about successful entrepreneurs is that they never give up. Observers will comment on how, in a manner that defied all logic, the entrepreneur continued in his quest toward the goal. Well, of course. After all, the observers define logic as a majoritarian construct; that is, if a course of action or a set of choices does not make sense to the majority, it is illogical. But, of course, the majority has job security. The majority has a regular day job, draws a paycheck, and has no real likelihood of attaining economic independence. Of course, the determined, hardheaded acts of an entrepreneur would seem illogical to them.

Their observation on entrepreneurs' dogged persistence, however, is true. There are no shortcuts. The successful entrepreneur must get up every day and be prepared to roll that rock back up the mountain. Failing to do that is to condemn the enterprise and the entrepreneur to failure.

> **Early next morning, gritting my teeth, I bought a pair of crutches and a box of painkillers and headed to the airport for the long flight to Harare, the capital of Zimbabwe. Eleven hours later, I hobbled out of the airplane, onto the hot tarmac, and into the dark and dingy Harare International Airport. My good leg was numb from the flight and my bad leg was throbbing with pain.**
>
> **I had made reservations for a decent-sized rental car, but when I arrived at the Hertz counter the only car available was a small Ford Fiesta. I had no choice. I took the car.**
>
> **Equipped with a local map, I covered the distance to Matola in good time and made it to the Zimbabwe border crossing by 11:30 that morning. I was to be met on the other side of the border by a representative of the Mozambican Ministry of Agriculture, who was to make the drive with me to Beira. The Office would know when my twenty-four hours began and ended by the stamps in my passport. They would know when I had arrived in Beira by my activating a small twelve-watt transmitter that somehow made it via satellite to Tel Aviv.**
>
> **The border crossing was comprised of some barbed wire and two huts—one Zimbabwean, the other Mozambican. I parked the car. I looked across the border's**

fence for someone resembling a government official but saw none. I did spot a very young twenty-year-old, walking to and fro on the Mozambican side of the fence.

"Hey, you. Hey," I shouted at the youth.

"Hallo, hallo," he responded, walking over to the fence.

Unfortunately "hallo" was pretty much the extent of this fellow's English vocabulary. Like most Mozambicans, Daniel—as I understood his name to be—spoke only Portuguese. And the little English he knew, he spoke in a Portuguese accent so that whatever he said wound up sounding like The Girl from Ipanema. He was a most unlikely government official, but government official he was.

Choose a Compatible Partner

At some point in time, in order to advance your project and business, you are likely to select a partner. In a start-up and in the entrepreneurial court, this act will make or break you. You must be compatible. You must have a clear division of labor. You must have a clear demarcation of authority. You must have clear agreement as to who gets what. For if you don't, you will come apart. And no start-up can survive an internal war.

Matching a partner is the prince's quest for Cinderella: Either the glass slipper is a perfect fit or the glass slipper breaks. There can be no compromises on this point. Authority cannot be shared, for if it is, then no one has it. Responsibility cannot be shared, for if it is, then no one has it. And in a start-up, where decisions, critical company-threatening decisions, are made every moment of every hour of every day, there must be one decision maker imbued with all company authority. And that decision maker should be you.

Who is the entrepreneur's partner? Well, it certainly should not be a fellow entrepreneur. Therein lies a conflict. It certainly can be and should be someone with an entrepreneurial spirit, but it should not be one who shares the same skill set as you. First, because if he does, then you shall have conflict between you as you both want to perform the same tasks. Second, if you have selected a clone of yourself, you are effectively signaling to the world that you lack confidence in your skill set to get the job done, so you have brought in someone who has the same skill set as you but performs those skills better than you. People tend to notice those wearing a belt and suspenders.

Your partner should be one who complements you but does not duplicate you. A scientist for a businessman. A computer geek for a financial type. An inventor for a negotiator. Consider the old joke about why the GSS cops (Israel's General Security Services, its FBI equivalent) walk around in pairs: One reads, one writes. They are compatible.

> **After a tortured conversation in which I used everything from classical Arabic, broken French, and outlawed Spanish, he understood that I was indeed Jack Green and I understood that he did not have a car. This was not good news because rental cars from Zimbabwe were strictly prohibited from crossing the border and because the car I had was not one I would choose for an extended trip. A mere rule against cars wouldn't stop me from crossing the border, but making the trip in this Ford Fiesta might.**
>
> **I was greeted on the other side of the border fence by the young Daniel.**
>
> **"Oh. Mr. Green, good you are here. Time to go. Much late," Daniel said. Or at least that is what I thought he said. Since he was mixing Portuguese with the few English words he knew he was very hard to understand.**
>
> **"OK, Daniel. Let's go, then," I said, revving up the pitifully small engine.**
>
> **"Mr. Green, have to take cousin with me. OK?"**
>
> **Cousin? What cousin? I was losing precious time as it was. I certainly was not feeling hospitable. But then again I would need Daniel to get me down the corridor safely.**
>
> **"OK, OK, sure, bring your cousin."**

"Cousins," Daniel corrected me.

Lumbering toward the car were what looked to me like a team of African sumo wrestlers. I was hard-pressed to believe that the car would somehow carry the weight. But when families are awaiting loved ones through enemy lines, how was I to refuse? Moreover, I couldn't object if I had wanted to. After all, knowing neither the terrain nor how to ask for directions, I was completely dependent upon Daniel, and I suppose Daniel knew it.

Plan Your "Exit" from Day One

Your investors are *in* the company only because they hope to get *out* of the company (albeit at a higher valuation). Therefore, you should have a plan to get them (and yourself) out. Start each day by reviewing and updating a list of potential buyers for your company. Scour the financial, business, and trade publications, learning who is in your market and who is seeking to enter your market. Learn all about those companies. Find contacts at each one of those companies. Learn all you can about your contacts: Who is on the way up? Who is on the way out? By the time you are ready to sell your company, you should already know which company to turn to, whom to turn to at that company, and how much that company has in its coffers.

Sof Ma'ase Be Mahshava Tekhila (The end of a task is in its aforethought), said the Sages. There is no better rule to follow than that. If you cannot envision the end of your journey, your success is in the hands of fate. If you cannot envision how to make money from an idea, even a great idea, you will very probably not make any money. If you cannot imagine who will acquire your company, it is rather likely that no one will.

You should note that this rule does not mean that your exit should ultimately be the one envisioned and planned for. This rule does not mean that you should ignore opportunities and wear blinders to good fortune. This rule does not mean that strategies never get old, grow stale, or die. Rather, this rule simply means that you should begin each task with a plan for its completion. Because if opportunities do not arise and good fortune does not shine, you have direction that will eventually get you toward your goal.

As we set out on our way, the wheels of the car were under so much stress from Daniel and his cousins' weight that they appeared to be buckled inward. At thirty-five miles an hour the car's steering column began to emit deep and threatening noises. The road was pockmarked by mortar and artillery fire. Every now and then I could see an unexploded ordnance burrowed into the warm asphalt.

I drove this way for a little over an hour. Daniel sat next to me scouting out the mortar holes and unexploded shells, shouting "left, right, left" as the occasion called for. Unexpectedly, just when I felt that I was getting the hang of things, I hit a major hole. I felt the car drop into an abyss and die.

The cousins and I climbed out of the car to survey the damage. It was not an encouraging sight. The car was holding together, barely, in a pool of oil. The wheels seemed totally out of joint and the axle hung sadly to the ground. I wasn't going anywhere and it would take more than twenty-four hours to get there.

This was my Test by Fire. And this was the Fire.

My choices were rather limited. Going back to Zimbabwe would hardly be in keeping with the spirit of tenacity that I was supposed to demonstrate here. It was Beira or Bust.

"Daniel, push. Push the car."

"No, no. Walking. Walking to Zimbabwe."

"No, Daniel, no. Not walking to Zimbabwe, we pushing car. Push." I made the universally recognized "push" motions, but Daniel and company were not persuaded.

"No, no village. Walking to Zimbabwe, more good."

"No. No Zimbabwe. Beira. Push," I said as forcefully as I could.

Don't Give Away Your Stock

You should decide early on to believe—and to act upon your belief—that your equity is more valuable than your money. In following this belief, never volunteer to pay your service providers (or your employees) in stock. Rather, wherever possible pay cash and only cash. In so doing, you shall create the perception that your company's stock is valuable. After all, if you treat your equity as valuable, it must be valuable. Instead of foisting your stock on your service providers, ration it out to them. Do so, whenever you can, in exchange for the elimination of your company's debts to them. You shall then be able to use those favorable debt/equity swaps to increase your company's valuation to third parties.

This advice, which admittedly runs counter to the prevailing wisdom of paying for everything with your own currency, the company's common stock, simply reflects what we all know to be true about human nature: Something is considered to have value only if its owner treats it with value. To whom do you pay attention? To that expert who volunteers his advice or to that expert you hired and paid for? Which currency do you want? The one that is freely handed out or the one that is carefully rationed out?

You have two sources of currency: your own, of which you can print a limitless supply; and the government's, of which you have a limited amount. Which of these would you rather see have a higher value? The one whose quantity you control or the one you do not? Use cash.

I dug into my pocket and grabbed a wad of Zimbabwe dollars. I held them up and waved them as a pennant. Daniel and his cousins looked at one another and got into a heated discussion in Portuguese, of which I understood not a word. After a few minutes they apparently reached some agreement and the debate ceased. Daniel took the money, and after the family circled the car one more time, they were ready to push.

As the burly men pushed, a little Peugeot "tender," a smaller European version of an American pickup truck, appeared on the horizon, making its way from the Zim-

babwe border toward Beira. Daniel and company waved the fellow down.

They must have known the driver because Daniel and his cousins and the driver of the tender kissed and hugged like long-lost brothers. Then the driver hugged and kissed me. Then we all kissed one another. Only then did Machel, the tender's driver, walk over to my car, bend down to look at the undercarriage, and mumble toward me, with a sad shake of his hand, "Bad, bad."

Not an inspiring revelation.

After a consultation among Machel, Daniel, and me, we agreed that the car was going nowhere on its own power. Towing was the preferred solution. Machel went to the back of his truck, where he stored a large maritime rope, the kind that oil supertankers use. It was the thickness of an elephant's trunk. I tied our vehicles together with a nautical knot and yanked it once or twice for strength.

Machel opened the rear of his truck to let us in. The truck was packed to the brim with frozen chickens, ripe tomatoes, and a host of other unidentifiable, edible objects. In fact, as soon as Machel opened the door, the chickens and the vegetables cascaded out of the truck. We stood there in the African heat trying to stuff frozen chickens back into the truck before they defrosted.

After a sweaty interval, we had the car tied to the truck, the chickens stuffed into the rear, and Daniel and his three cousins perched on top of the chickens. We set off toward Beira. I was steering the rental car asserting "White Man's Burden" and in doing so avoiding the company of the birds. Daniel and friends could not completely sit up because their heads would bump up against the truck's top if they did, and they could not lie down because there simply wasn't room enough. So they half slouched, half sat, compressed against one another as our entourage all meandered along at what had to be no more than twenty miles an hour.

It was 5:00 P.M. and our shadows were growing longer. This was cause of some concern because the TBF rules required that I be in and out of Beira in twenty-four hours. Moreover, my visa was good for only twenty-four hours. So missing one schedule would become a personal failure that I would be able to muse upon in jail for having missed the other. But there was also the question of the car. I could, in theory, get to Beira, touch the water, turn around, and somehow hitch back to the border. Screw the car. But there were two problems with that approach: First, the Office would view the abandonment of a vehicle as the abandonment of operational equipment; namely, not favorably. It would count against me as much as an untimely performance would. Second, the Mozambican border guards would expect me to be leaving their country along with the vehicle in which I entered. To do otherwise would suggest that I sold the vehicle in Mozambique, which itself was a criminal offense.

So not only did I have to get to Beira and back, but I would have to repair—somehow repair—the car.

Unfortunately, going faster was out of the question. Even at slow speed, even in daylight, negotiating the holes in the road while being towed in my disabled car was difficult. With darkness it became impossible. Each hole I successfully maneuvered inevitably took me into another one that sunk me. And with every blow to the car's undercarriage I wondered what essential part was rolling away, forever lost to the bush.

We arrived in Beira just this side of midnight. It was much like Alice's Wonderland: a city of nearly two million inhabitants, once a glorious colonial provincial capital, living a zombielike existence in war-limbo. Surrounded by rebels, the city had no electricity, no running water, and a haphazard food supply.

As we drove along the city streets, the truck's headlights eerily flashed on some of the city's sights: here a throng of people so dark that only the whites of their eyes revealed their presence, there a skyscraper left in disrepair from the Portuguese's better days. Other drivers, the few that there were, drove without headlights, flashing them on only momentarily to avoid head-on collisions. I was told that the apartment towers were the ultimate manifestation of this surreal world because where once the wealthy inhabited the penthouses, today, in the absence of electricity and running water, only the poorest of the poor did so.

Machel pulled the truck over in front of a restaurant. Machel got out of the truck's cabin and we all followed suit while stretching our tired and cramped bodies. Machel and Daniel exchanged words and before I knew it, all of our passengers—and by now we numbered nearly a dozen—began to unload the truck, fire-bucket style, into the restaurant's kitchen.

Now this was not in my plans. I wanted to get my car to a mechanic, assuming that the town had one, as soon as possible. I tried to argue the point with Daniel and then with Machel himself, but it was useless. Machel had to unload the truck immediately; otherwise, the produce would turn bad. Anyway, Machel said, we had to have dinner.

"No, no dinner. Mechanic," I insisted.

"Yes, yes. Dinner, then mechanic," Machel replied.

Arguing with Machel was useless. A pudgy teddy bear of a man, he had a permanently affixed smile and was terminally good-natured. If he said dinner, he meant dinner. I turned instead to Daniel and tried to reason with him. I explained to Daniel that I had to be back in Zimbabwe the next day with the car. The only way that that might be even remotely possible would be to find a mechanic tonight. Dinner was fine, I promised, but only after the mechanic.

Daniel and Machel held a brief powwow. We finally agreed that Daniel would drive me in Machel's car to a mechanic, after which he would return me to Machel's restaurant for dinner. I wondered why dinner was necessary at midnight and how it would even be possible in a restaurant with no electricity, no gas, no running water, and no refrigeration, but I didn't think that this was the time to find out.

Daniel got behind the wheel of the truck and I resumed my position as "towee" in the car. We drove through the pitch black streets of the city for what seemed to me to be a very long time. Eventually, Daniel's headlights turned into a vacant lot. As I was being towed into the lot I could see that strewn around the lot like so many dinosaur fossils were the remains of cars. Rusted cars, parts of cars, tires, hoods open, parts asunder. It looked less the mechanic's lot than the wrecker's.

Stay Virtual

Don't buy anything unless it increases shareholder value. Fancy offices? Not for you. Share whatever office space you need. High-tech equipment? Forget it. Rent what you must and use copy stores and the post office for everything else. High-priced executives? Not for you. Everyone should earn less than they ever earned before. And everyone should make coffee.

In a start-up, your idea is your value. The entire cost of your operations should be measured by one feature only: Does that cost item substantially add to the value of your idea? If it doesn't, it's a luxury you can ill afford.

In a start-up—and you are a start-up until your debt is not a burden and the company is in the black and can reasonably expect to remain in the black for the foreseeable future—luxury is a negative; it is a flashing red light that you have your priorities wrong. It is an early warning sign—the best early warning sign—that disaster is on its way. A start-up with fancy offices and business amenities not found at more established companies is akin to the proverbial brother-in-law who borrows money to go on vacation, not to go get a job. Your family is watching. Be a skinflint with your investors' money. If it does not generate income, if it does not enhance the value of your core technology, you don't need it.

If this was the garage, the mechanic must be really good. It took only one look to tell that no money went into overhead or business promotion. As my car made the turn into the yard, I could see that scattered throughout the yard were beer cans into which a piece of kerosene-dipped burlap had been placed. It looked sort of like a Halloween party. This was about as low rent as anyone could get. Daniel stopped the truck in front of a shed, and our mechanic, the man upon which my intelligence career hinged, stepped wobbly forth.

The mechanic was a slight man with the bloodshot eyes of a heavy drinker. Of course, it was almost 1:00 A.M. and we had probably awakened him from a deep slumber. Then again, he had a beer can in one hand and a bottle of vodka in the other. He offered his beer to me but I took the vodka.

Daniel gave our mechanic, whose name I later learned was Franco, a summary of the events so far. Franco shook his head in sympathy. He then crawled under the car with one of the kerosene torches and made some intelligent-sounding moans. After what seemed like an interminable amount of time he pulled himself out, walked over to me, and put his arm around my shoulder. He pulled me closer to him and gave me a big two-armed hug and kiss on my lips.

"Nao problem," he said.

My heart sank to my stomach and beyond. It wasn't just the alcohol on his breath that did it. He truly did not seem to think that this car, this wretched relic of a car with broken axle, snapped wheels, and Lord knows what else, was a challenge to his pitiful garage. Daniel must have read my expression because, trying to comfort me, he said, "Don't worry. Him start early in morning."

That's when I really lost my cool.

"No, Franco start now. Not tomorrow. Now."

"But him no see now. Night. Him tired."

"Now," I said resolutely. "Now. We will make more beer cans for him. Come with me."

I grabbed Daniel by the arm and went to look for more cans, boxes, you name it, from which to fashion additional night-lights. Franco realized that I was serious and pitched in. By 1:30 A.M. we had fashioned a serious battery of lights for Franco to work with, and he was quite pleased with our efforts.

He said something to Daniel, they both laughed, and Daniel gestured toward the truck.

"What did he say, Daniel?" I asked. I was now rather suspicious of these conversations.

"He say, no problem. We come in morning."

"No, Daniel, you tell him now is morning. We come back now. Two hours, now."

Daniel looked at me, incredulous. By now, however, he no doubt realized that I was borderline insane. He therefore reasonably concluded that dealing with Franco would be better than dealing with me. He went back to Franco for another exchange. At first Franco shook his head violently, saying nao, nao, nao. Daniel persisted in his and Franco's head movements slowed down. Momentarily, they shared a hearty laugh, which of course worried me, and then Daniel came back beaming.

"Two hour, no problem," Daniel said.

There was little more I could do. Daniel started the truck and we were off to dinner. Two hours later we were back.

Upon entering Franco's yard, I saw my entire Combatant training flash before me. I was certain that I was witnessing the death knell to my career. There, in the battery of kerosene beer-can lights, Franco was sprawled out in his glory, like a "snow angel" without snow, surrounded by every part of the Ford that was not itself part of the chassis. Franco was sound asleep. The sound of his snores reverberated in the Beira night. In his right hand he held pliers and in his left he held a newly opened bottle of vodka. The car's hood was open, yet I feared to look inside. I knew full well that there could not be so many car parts on the ground and a working engine under the hood.

"Wake up," I shouted. Franco didn't move.

Court Those upon Whom You (Shall) Depend

As a start-up, your existence will at some point become dependent upon others. There is, after all, only so much one person, or even several, can do. There comes a point where you shall need an outside advisor. There shall come a time when you require an investment banker. Do not wait until you need one to find one. Rather, from your early beginnings introduce your company to these potential advisors. Tell them who you are and what you are doing. Keep them apprised of your progress. Flatter them with your interest. So that when the time for their engagement and assistance comes—and come it will—you shall have created enough goodwill to encourage them to move quickly in your support.

"Wake up, you lazy bastard," I shouted again. I kicked Franco's feet a few times and then bent over to shake his corpse. Franco slowly stirred. I dragged him up. He rubbed his eyes lazily and looked at us in disbelief. He excitedly and angrily said something to Daniel. Something about my mother, I believe. No matter.

"Work," I shouted at him. "Work."

I told Daniel to find coffee in Franco's shed and make a pot. Daniel found coffee but no kettle. No matter. I forced Franco to drink cold water mixed with the coffee grounds. He didn't like it. Then I forced the poor bugger to get back down on his back and get under the car. He did so but he continued to curse and talk about my family. By then I was in deep despair. I had no more energy, no more ideas, I just wanted sleep. But I wouldn't rest for fear that as soon as I did, my future would go down Franco's drain.

I stood over Franco, hitting him with my crutches every now and then to make sure that he had not fallen asleep. I had Daniel kick me every ten or fifteen minutes when I nodded off, and I exchanged the favor with him. At some point in time, and I am not sure when, I nodded off and the entire chain of command broke down. I awoke with a start. It was 6:00 A.M.

Franco was in his shed boiling water in a kettle that he produced out of some cabinet we overlooked. He was whistling and seemed chipper, energetic, and happy. I quickly turned to the car. It was a sight worthy of Lourdes: The car was intact, the hood was down, there were no parts or pieces on the ground. Franco walked toward me and the car, surveying it as he did like a proud father.

"No problem," he shouted when he saw us.

I jumped to my feet, crutches in hand, and circled the car. I touched the hood in disbelief. I couldn't believe my eyes. This was truly a miracle.

"Key," I said. "Give me the key." I wanted to drive this baby into the sunrise before I woke up from this hallucination.

Franco looked at me, at Daniel, and then back at me.

"Problem," he said.

I straightened out and opened the hood of the car. I figured that if Franco was reluctant to give me the key, there must be something wrong with the engine. There was. It was one giant block of soldering zinc. There were no pistons, there were no spark plugs, there was nothing that even remotely resembled an engine part. It was all one big glob of zinc.

After the initial shock wore off, Franco explained that last night, what with the poor lighting, his fatigue, and the alcohol content of the local beer, he could not quite get all the pieces to fit into the car. So rather than waste time on conventional mechanics, he went for a functional approach: "Let's just get all those pieces in anyway we can." He must have thought that so long as all of the pieces were in the engine or at least nearby the engine, they themselves would somehow figure out how to make the car go. Franco just soldered the engine and its pieces into place.

There was nothing to be done. Either the car worked or it didn't. I decided to try. Franco handed me the ignition key. My hands were shaking. I slid into the car and adjusted the driver's seat. I was skeptical that I was going anywhere but comfort is always a good thing. I put the key in the ignition and slowly turned it. The car sprang to life. The engine roared to the touch of the gas pedal, and even the radio was blaring. I couldn't believe my eyes. Machel, Franco, and Daniel broke into cheers and began an improvised dance, no doubt overjoyed by the thought that they would finally be rid of me.

I got out of the car and joined their jig. I was weeping—no, sobbing—for joy. I hugged and kissed them all and they hugged back. It was 11:30 A.M. I had to haul ass. I still had two hundred long miles to go on a bad road in a weird car in four hours' time.

I got back into the still-running car, closed the door, put the car in gear, released the clutch, and began to move. And move I did, but like a crab, sideways. There was a very strange phenomenon at work here: Even though I pulled the steering wheel all the way to the left, the car went straight ahead. And when I centered the steering wheel, the car went all the way to the right.

A quick look at the car's undercarriage explained it all: more solder. Apparently, with no spare parts to repair the broken axle, Franco did some improvising: He cut a few slices off the axle and solved any shortcomings with more solder.

At this stage of the game, I had come too far to fail. I'd learn how to steer the damn thing as it was. A lesser man would have cashed his chips. It was irrational to believe

**that I could get this thing to the border. In four hours.
TBF. Persistence. I would. In fact, I'd learn how to carry it
on my back if that's what it took to get me out of there. So
to the cheers and waving of my dear friends, I set out on
my way back up the Beira corridor to Zimbabwe.**

**Fortunately, I had the presence of mind to set off my
transmitter before I left. Hello/good-bye . . .**

**This is what happened next: Because I had to pull
hard left on the steering wheel to go straight ahead, the
tires were under constant strain. Because I was driving
like a bat out of Beira, the strain was exaggerated tenfold. Because I didn't care, the tires blew out. Not all at
once, mind you, but one at a time.**

Don't Get Caught Short

A start-up should always have ten months of its "burn rate" in
the bank. Follow this rule religiously. After all, it takes nine months
to have a baby. One should allow at least one month more to fund
it. Break this rule and you will learn the meaning of that colorful
venture capital phrase "cram round."

You must treat as gospel, as the received word of the Lord from
Mount Sinai, that everything will cost twice as much as you've bud-
geted for; that everything will take twice as long as the engineers
promise; that everything will take twice as long to be delivered; and
that everything will perform only half as well as advertised. And
that's if you're lucky.

But don't despair. There is a "one-dose-cures-all" remedy for
these ills. It's called money.

Build your war chest vigorously. Do not rely on others' projections and estimates of cost. Assume that everything you need will
cost several times more when it's available, and it is usually not available. Money raised in advance of disaster is a grain of sand in the
desert compared to the cost of money raised in the midst of disaster.

**The car had a functioning jack but no spare. I flagged
down the first oncoming vehicle. It, of course, didn't have**

a spare, but no matter. I bought the tires off the car itself and stuffed two in the trunk and two in the backseat. From there on in, I was changing tires at the rate of one every fifteen or twenty miles. When I ran out of the ones I had, I just peeled a few more hundreds off my wad of dollar bills and bought more tires off the next car on the road. Sure, those guys were stranded without their tires, but they had just earned more in a day than Mozambique earned in a year. And I was developing one hell of a tire-changing technique.

Before too long, I could see the border crossing ahead. It was a race against the clock and fortune. If the tires held up I'd make it before 3:20 P.M. If I had another blowout—well, it would have all been for naught.

Be Lucky

Like it or not, luck *will* play a substantial role in your success. Even if you do everything perfectly right, and you won't, you will still need a healthy measure of luck. So, at some point in your adventure, after you have done everything you possibly can do to succeed, lighten up and enjoy the ride. After all, there are some things that *are* out of your control.

At 3:18, with two minutes to spare, I crossed the border. I pulled the car over to the parking area and turned off the ignition. I waited for the border patrol car and hitched a ride into town with the border guards. I asked them to deposit me at the best hotel the city had to offer. And at 5:00 P.M. I was luxuriating in a bathtub at the Matola Hilton Hotel.

TBF.

GLOSSARY

AMAN: The Hebrew acronym for Military Intelligence. In contrast to Mossad, which gathers intelligence and carries out special operations, AMAN has the primary responsibility of analyzing all intelligence gathered.

BAYONET: Mossad's assassination team.

COMBATANT: An undercover Mossad agent who lives under deep cover in an enemy country.

FLARE: To be caught. A Combatant "flares," i.e., burns up, upon capture.

FLAT FEET: The Mossad surveillance team.

GRAY CELL: The Planning Committee for Mossad Special Operations.

GUTENBERG: The Mossad division that provided documents to Combatants.

HOLE: Israel's Military Command and Control Center.

IDF: Israel Defense Forces.

IAF: Israeli air force.

ILLUSIONS: The department responsible for camouflaging Combatant equipment.

KISS: A Bayonet assassination.

MARIONETTE: A Mossad case officer who "runs" a Combatant.

OFFICE: Combatants' euphemism for the Mossad.

PHONAC: A miniature walkie-talkie, the hearing part of which is placed in the ear while the microphone is clipped to a lapel.

PINNACLE: Mossad's acronym for the Mossad Directorate, its governing body.

POD: A team of Combatants.

RETAILER:　Individuals who were willing to spy against their own country on behalf of Israel. So called because of their tendency to "mark up" intelligence.

SAMSON:　Mossad's director of Combatants.

SIREN: Semiautonomous Mossad agency that tracks terrorists around the world.

STUDIO: Mossad's mission planning division.

UNTOUCHABLE:　Mossad field officer, one of the career intelligence officers who live in European countries friendly to Israel under diplomatic immunity, from where they recruit and operate Arab "agents" or "Retailers."

INDEX